AMERICA'S NEW ALLIES

America's New Allies

POLAND,

HUNGARY,

and the

CZECH REPUBLIC

in NATO

Edited by ANDREW A. MICHTA

UNIVERSITY OF WASHINGTON PRESS

Seattle and London

This publication was supported in part by the Donald R. Ellegood
International Publications Endowment.

Library of Congress Cataloging-in-Publication Data
America's new allies : Poland, Hungary, and the Czech Republic in NATO
    / edited by Andrew A. Michta.
        p.   cm.
    Includes bibliographical references and index.
    ISBN 0-295-97906-2 (alk. paper)
        1. National security—Europe, Central. 2. Europe, Central-
    -Foreign relations. 3. Europe, Central—Military policy. 4. North
    Atlantic Treaty Organization—Poland. 5. North Atlantic Treaty
    Organization—Hungary. 6. North Atlantic Treaty Organization—
    Czech Republic. 7. North Atlantic Treaty Organization—Membership.
    8. Poland—Foreign relations—1989- 9. Hungary—Foreign
    relations—1989- 10. Czech Republic—Foreign relations. 11. United
    States—Foreign relations—Europe. 12. Europe—Foreign relations—
    United States.   I. Michta, Andrew A.
    DAW1051.A47   1999
    355'.031091821—dc21   99-35704
                                                            CIP

CONTENTS

ACKNOWLEDGMENTS

I wish to thank the contributors to this volume for their hard work and their commitment to the project. Without their cooperation, this book would not have been completed.

I am greatly indebted to Dr. John Raisian, Dr. Thomas Henriksen, and Ms. Deborah Ventura of the Hoover Institution on War, Revolution, and Peace at Stanford University for their hospitality and support during the preparation of this manuscript. I also wish to thank the U.S. Department of State for its support under the Title VIII program. Among my colleagues in central Europe, I am especially grateful to Lieutenant Colonel Leszek Soczewica of the Military Protocol Division of the Polish Ministry of Defense for his friendship and assistance in my research. Special thanks go to the Buckman family of Memphis for their generous commitment to the International Studies program at Rhodes College.

Most importantly, I want to thank my wife, Cristina, and my daughter, Chelsea, for their continued encouragement and good humor throughout this undertaking.

Andrew A. Michta

AMERICA'S NEW ALLIES

Introduction

ANDREW A. MICHTA

Since the early 1990s, the efficacy of enlarging the North Atlantic Treaty Organization (NATO) has been vigorously and exhaustively debated in a number of academic and policy publications. This volume is not intended to revisit the argument over NATO enlargement into central Europe or the 1997 Madrid invitation to Poland, Hungary, and the Czech Republic to join the alliance. Today, NATO enlargement is a political reality. This fact sets the baseline for our analysis.

The contributors to this volume, though they differ on specific issues, share the view that the focus of discussion has now shifted to the long-term integration process itself. The success or failure of the 1999 NATO enlargement will have lasting consequences for the future of the alliance and for European security. As the dust of political and academic jousting over the enlargement decision settles, it is critical to review the assets and liabilities that Poland, Hungary, and the Czech Republic are likely to bring to NATO as its full members in the years to come. The inclusion of the central Europeans should be viewed in the broader context of the ongoing restructuring of the alliance. The key issue for the 1999 enlargement and the focus of this book is how the entry of Poland, Hungary, and the Czech Republic will ultimately fit into the continuum of NATO's evolutionary process, or, to put it simply, what the new entrants get from it and what they bring to the table.

Though a detailed discussion of NATO reforms falls outside our scope, this book treats enlargement not as a self-contained development but as an aspect of the transformation of NATO, under which a number of reforms in its structure and mission have been implemented since the early 1990s. The heated arguments over whether to bring the central

3

Europeans into NATO often overshadowed changes that had already taken place within the alliance.[1] Prior to the 1997 Madrid enlargement decision, the key landmarks of NATO's evolution were the June 1992 ministerial decision to engage in peace support operations, the growing recognition of the need for member nations to deploy forces outside their own immediate subregion, the proposal to reorganize NATO's integrated command structure, and the 1994 approval of the Combined Joint Task Force concept.

The process of internal reform of NATO in the 1990s has progressively transformed it away from the collective defense organization it was during the Cold War era and toward a future trans-Atlantic security community. This transformation is incomplete, and there are few parallels in history to guide it. It is marred by the inevitable tension between the traditional role of the alliance and its new tasks. The successful integration of the three new members is even more important if one considers the strain accompanying reform that by 1998 had begun to show within NATO. For example, disagreement over the issue of AFSOUTH (European Command of Allied Forces South) halted the reintegration of France into the NATO military command structure. Similarly, friction between Spain and the United Kingdom over Gibraltar, and between Spain and Portugal over the Canary Islands, underscored the obstacles to sustaining consensus within the alliance. The selection of the three new entrants also sparked contention, as a majority of European NATO members pushed for the inclusion of Romania and Slovenia in the first trench alongside the central Europeans. Most importantly, the ongoing dispute over the projected long-term costs of absorbing the three new members into NATO, and whether the European or the American side ought to shoulder the lion's share of the cost, goes to the core of intra-alliance strain associated with the enlargement issue. As defense budgets in Europe decline, the question must be asked, What can the three new entrants expect in terms of actual NATO assistance, and consequently, will the new NATO periphery be properly provided for or overextended? This is even more significant as Europe continues to fall behind the United States in terms of defense technology, leaving the United States in the position of principal provider of security to the new member states.

Another issue is whether, after 1999, the process of NATO enlargement can be kept open through the Partnership for Peace program, and whether the process will ultimately succeed in stabilizing the transitional postcommunist states. Notwithstanding official pronouncements about the "open process" and the movement from collective defense to cooperative security, it is unclear what the long-term consequences of enlargement will be. The impact of the new entrants on the alliance should serve as an indicator of how this evolution will proceed. If NATO successfully completes its transformation, it will become an institution for coordinating security-projecting military operations extending beyond the territory of its members. In other words, if NATO completes the transition to a democratic security community, it will not need a permanent threat in order to endure, and it will thrive in the current low-threat environment in Europe. It was this assumption that initially pushed NATO to negotiate and formalize a new relationship with Russia, and it seems to underlie the preference to rely on interoperability, integration, and reinforcement in place of the traditional stationing of troops to provide for the security of the new entrants. It remains to be seen, however, whether the Poles, Hungarians, and Czechs fully appreciate the implications of this NATO strategy and the security environment in the region it is likely to create for them.

The position of Russia vis-à-vis the alliance is critical in this regard. It is unclear to the new entrants, or to NATO itself, what the limits of the new partnership with Russia might be. That is, what would constitute grounds for NATO to rethink or terminate its "special relationship" with Russia?[2] The core of the alliance has retained the characteristics of the traditional collective defense organization, while at the same time NATO has moved to assert the "democratic security community" aspect of enlargement. The NATO reform process now in place is increasingly driven by considerations other than the single overriding geopolitical imperative that defined the cycles of enlargement during the Cold War era. The three new members join NATO at a time when the alliance continues to work through the central dilemmas of its structure and mission.

Poland, Hungary, and the Czech Republic expect to receive real security guarantees from NATO, on a par with those extended to members in the Cold War era. In that sense, their view of the alliance is closer to the traditional concept of collective defense. They have made considerable progress in reforming their economies and political systems, and they have begun working on military reform. Among the questions that will be answered in the first decade of the twenty-first century are what the ultimate impact of the new allies' membership in NATO will be on Russia and Ukraine, what the long-term enlargement costs will be, and whether the first round of enlargement will also turn out to be the final one. Answers to these questions depend on what kind of allies Poland, Hungary, and the Czech Republic prove to be. Their relative influence within the alliance and the value the alliance guarantees to them will ultimately depend on their ability to contribute to the alliance missions. Whether or not they will be treated as full members in the alliance will rest on the qualitative value of their contribution, in both the military and the political arenas. As long as they are not perceived as meaningful contributors, they will continue to have inferior status. The important question that this book seeks to address is whether the appropriate yardstick to measure their contribution ought to be found on the military or the political side of the equation.

The long-term success or failure of NATO enlargement has an important dimension in American foreign policy. Although the end of the Cold War has led to an increase in isolationist sentiments in the United States, the recent experience of the Balkan wars has demonstrated to all but the most skeptical how important NATO and American leadership of the alliance remain to the future security of Europe. That in Europe today no imminent threat confronts the core continental powers is in large part a testimony to America's success in stabilizing and transforming this formerly explosive region of the world. As NATO takes its first step into the area that during the Cold War was "enemy territory," and as Washington works to reshape the trans-Atlantic core of NATO, it is imperative that we consider the implications of the enlargement decision on NATO and the U.S. security position in Europe.

For the United States, the success of absorbing the new entrants into NATO is important from a very practical perspective. Since the end of the Cold War, the United States has radically cut its forces in Europe, from

320,000 to approximately 100,000 in 1999. In addition, there has been a shift of nuclear weapons out of Europe. In short, while the United States continues to provide the bulk of logistics and support, the European military contribution to the alliance is now more important than ever to sustaining NATO's missions and commitments in the region. It has become apparent in the aftermath of NATO's 1999 air campaign against Serbia that the United States will increasingly look to its European allies to contribute ground forces for out-of-area operations. If the NATO objective of promoting transparent defense planning and multilateral information sharing is to result in a genuine European-American cooperative security arrangement, the absorption of the three new members into the alliance must be successfully completed. Their military potential matters to NATO—especially in the case of Poland, the largest of the three new members. In this book, we hope to identify aspects of the process that are likely to facilitate the successful integration of the three countries' armed forces with NATO, as well as those that are likely to hinder it.

Several broadly shared assumptions served as guides for all the contributors. First, the current round of expansion is occurring in a generally benign security environment in central Europe, notwithstanding the turmoil in the neighboring Balkan peninsula. Hence, security considerations for the three entrants run parallel with, and are often overshadowed by, their broader objective of rejoining the affluent West. In that context, for the central Europeans NATO membership is part and parcel of the ongoing postcommunist modernization; as such, it is tied to their aspirations to join the European Union early in the twenty-first century. (Poland, Hungary, and the Czech Republic anticipate that they will join the EU around 2003–2006). Second, historical memory remains a potent factor shaping the policies of the three new NATO members. They often view NATO as an insurance policy to prevent a repetition of the trauma that marked most of their national existence in the twentieth century. Third, all three are in dire need of military modernization if they are to become meaningful contributors to the alliance. Although they have been making efforts to streamline and upgrade their militaries, they expect that NATO membership will provide them with infrastructure funds to complete their military reform, as well as access to Western armaments industries. They also expect an overall increase in foreign investment in their economies due to increased investor confidence in their stability and security. In that sense, Poland, Hungary, and the Czech Republic see NATO membership as a step in the direction of the EU, as well as a benefit in and of itself.

Another common thread that runs through this volume is the persistence of residual problems inherited from the communist era. Poland, Hungary, and the Czech Republic share a relative weakness of civilian expertise on national security matters. Also, though the three have established the institutional framework for effective civilian control over the military, they need to consolidate it and to build a military ethos compatible with that of other NATO militaries. One test of the long-term success of the enlargement process is how effectively the the new allies' inclusion in NATO contributes to the consolidation of their democratic institutions and the emergence of a Western military ethos. The contributors to this book address this question by reviewing the new entrants individually and then framing the debate in the broader context of NATO's evolution.

Although the 1999 inclusion of Poland, Hungary, and the Czech Republic is generally considered to be the first round of NATO enlargement after the Cold War, in reality NATO had already expanded into the territory of the former Warsaw Pact in 1990, when it took in the five new Länder of former East Germany. The book opens with a review of the East German case in order to draw lessons that might be pertinent for the current entrants from Germany's eight years of experience since the incorporation of the East German military into the Bundeswehr, the West German army. This is not to suggest that the East German case can be applied directly to the three new allies; indeed, it is different in many respects from those of the 1999 NATO entrants. In the German case, the National People's Army was directly taken over by the Bundeswehr. The East German experience also differs from that of the central Europeans in terms of institutional design and specific policy decisions. Nevertheless, the East German case does provide a rare "ground-floor" insight into the process of democratizing the postcommunist army and the cost of the wholesale transformation of a Warsaw Pact military ethos to make it compatible with NATO's. The trauma at the "micro level"—that is, the problem the former communist military encounters as it attempts to build a Western-style democratic army—is shared across central Europe. As a social laboratory, East Germany provides fascinating insights for making projections about the new members.

Four issues of the East German case are particularly relevant to the 1999 NATO entrants. First, there is the task of ensuring loyalty to NATO through reindoctrination of the former East German military. This is a central question for the Poles, the Hungarians, and the Czechs as well. Second, there is the task of changing the command structure and adapting equipment to fit the NATO model. "Interoperability" is the fundamental goal for all new entrants, and we can learn much about this problem from the German experience. Third, there is the task of preparing former East German personnel to deal with parliamentary oversight, something that is equally at issue in the Polish, Hungarian, and Czech cases. Finally, there is the task of coping with a perceived decline in professional status in society, along with some economic hardship, that is common to all former Warsaw Pact militaries.

The three chapters focusing on Poland, Hungary, and the Czech Republic, respectively, address three crucial "post-enlargement" questions: What are the new entrants likely to get from NATO? What will NATO get from them? And what will the enlargement mean for the alliance as a whole as it continues to adjust to the post–Cold War environment? Each chapter seeks to answer these questions at several levels of analysis. First, it reviews the political dimension of enlargement as seen from Warsaw, Budapest, or Prague, in the belief that the expectations the three bring to the table will have lasting effects on the long-term success of enlargement. Each chapter looks at the way in which NATO enlargement fits in the context of its country's historical experience and the geostrategic transformation of central Europe in the aftermath of the Cold War. It reviews the level of popular support for NATO membership among Poles, Hungarians, or Czechs, as well as the rationale for such support. Each case study discusses the state of the armed forces and the military reform programs of the new members, including their level of modernization and interoperability with NATO, their defense budgets, and their readiness to participate in NATO operations. The contributors also consider the issue of civil-military relations, as well as the domestic prestige of central European militaries.

The three country studies are followed by a chapter on the practical policy considerations that went into the NATO enlargement decision and that are likely to remain significant for years to come. The goal of this summation is to identify the extent to which the initial objectives of NATO enlargement have become transformed by the inevitable political compromises attendant on the expansion process. The key question here is whether the implications of enlargement for NATO as an international organization are what all its advocates in the West and in central Europe initially hoped to achieve. This task is far more complicated than it might appear at first glance. Many aspects of the enlargement process remain unknown. Since the initial round was only part of a larger process of changing NATO's mission, the decision remains controversial. This continued debate after the 1999 enlargement is tied to different core assumptions about the role of the United States in Europe and the world. It is unlikely to end any time soon because it is a function of ongoing policy deliberations about further enlargement and the evolution of the alliance.

The book's concluding chapter offers projections about the possible contribution the new allies can make in the context of the ongoing restructuring of NATO, as it adjusts to its new role in the Balkans after the 1999 air campaign against Serbia. It also speaks to the implications of NATO enlargement for regional security in central Europe. For Poland, Hungary, and the Czech Republic—with their recent memories of Soviet domination—national security and military power are still, at the core, first and foremost *national* matters. However, NATO is committed to "de-nationalizing" the security policies of member states and providing an institutional framework for thinking about security in cooperative terms. NATO membership makes it difficult for states to "re-nationalize" their military, and helps weaker countries to build relations with their more powerful neighbors without a heavy element of insecurity. Thus, NATO provides a mechanism to transcend the vagaries of power politics in Europe—something that is especially important for the smaller European states, and, considering their experience in the twentieth century, for the central Europeans most of all.

Historically, in addition to its primary mission of containing the Soviet Union, NATO has deflected the pressures on member states to compete for regional influence in Europe. Today, an ancillary objective to this fundamental goal is to create a mechanism for managing regional conflicts in Europe and along its periphery, with NATO's intervention in Kosovo providing an important test case. If the 1999 enlargement serves to alter the "national" pattern of the new members' thinking about security, it will be at least a partial success, notwithstanding the shortcomings of the process or the present weakness of their military establishments. The test of 1999 Nato enlargement may ultimately be found in the political rather than the military arena.

Notes

1. See Thomas-Durell Young, *Reforming NATO's Military Structures: The Long-Term Study and Its Implications for Land Forces* (Carlisle Barracks, Pennsylvania: Strategic Studies Institute, US Army War College, 1998).

2. See *1998 Strategic Assessment* (Washington, D.C.: National Defense University, 1998).

1 From the NVA to the Bundeswehr

BRINGING THE EAST GERMANS INTO NATO

DALE R. HERSPRING

The case of the East German military is different from those of all other members of the former Warsaw Pact.[1] The NVA (Nationale Volksarmee, or National People's Army) was the only armed force disbanded in the aftermath of the collapse of communism. In every other instance, the old army remained in place and underwent a process of democratization and reform. In East Germany, however, several thousand former NVA officers and enlisted personnel were offered the option of joining the Bundeswehr, the West German military, while the vast majority were given their walking papers.

Because the East German experience was so different from the experiences of the other eastern European militaries, it is both important and instructive. It is important because it provides a unique opportunity to look at the process of integrating former NVA officers into the Bundeswehr and at the kind of individual produced by one of the most rigidly controlled and ideologically committed of all of the Warsaw Pact militaries. It is instructive because in the process of integrating these former members of the NVA into the Bundeswehr, the Germans have had an unparalleled opportunity to deal with the kind of professional produced by a communist political system. Some adjusted to the new democratic environment and some did not, but all came to the Bundeswehr heavily influenced by their past in the East German army. A close look at the NVA professionals and the many problems they encountered while being integrated into the Bundeswehr speaks volumes about the difficulties all of the former communist polities have encountered in attempting to resocialize members of their armed forces. I doubt that any former communist military has not encountered similar problems to varying degrees.

The Problem

On October 3, 1990, the Bundeswehr faced a task unprecedented in recent European military history: dealing with members of a formerly hostile army that neither had been defeated on the battlefield (as had been the case with the Wehrmacht) nor had collapsed as a result of internal strife (as occurred in a number of other countries during the twentieth century). Not only did the Bundeswehr have to figure out what to do with some sixty thousand former members of the NVA, along with their formidable stocks of equipment and munitions, but Bonn was also forced to find a way to integrate many of its former opponents into its own armed forces at a time when Germany was reducing its military—a result of an agreement reached by Helmut Kohl and Mikhail Gorbachev in July 1990 on Russian preconditions for the unification of Germany.

When it came to the NVA, West German Defense Minister Gerhard Stoltenberg wanted as little as possible to do with those who had served the East German communist party (the SED). How could they be expected to be loyal now to a democratic polity? In time, however, it became clear to the military leadership that at least some former members of the NVA would be taken into the Bundeswehr as part of Kohl's overall attempt to show East Germans that they were welcome in this new, united Germany. The task then became one of organizing the practical details of the transition. Although it was clear that political officers, officers over fifty-five, and those who had worked with the Stasi would be excluded, a large pool of potential candidates remained.

Kommando-Ost Is Created

On August 14, 1990, Stoltenberg informed Lieutenant General Jörg Schönbohm that he, Schönbohm, would be taking over as commander of Kommando-Ost, as the new East German structure was to be called. From Stoltenberg's standpoint, assigning the highly capable and politically sensitive Schönbohm to the former German Democratic Republic

(GDR), where there was a serious danger that the NVA could completely disintegrate, took precedence over the command he had been scheduled for.[2]

It was at this point, after considerable discussion, that Stoltenberg laid out the basic rules that were to guide the transition process. On October 3, former NVA members would become part of the Bundeswehr, subject to the Federal Republic of Germany's constitution and expected to follow the provisions of the Bundeswehr's policy of "innere Führung." On that date the Bundeswehr would take over command responsibility for all personnel and equipment that formerly belonged to the NVA.[3] Each unit would be reconstituted with both Bundeswehr and NVA personnel. Furthermore, beginning on September 1, all NVA conscripts undergoing basic training would be trained by Bundeswehr personnel in accordance with its precepts. Finally, starting on October 15, all forces in the former GDR would come under Kommando-Ost, which would administer two military district commands (Leipzig and Neubrandenburg). Kommando-Ost was placed directly under the command of the Ministry of Defense in the person of the general inspector of the Bundeswehr.[4] Kommando-Ost would exist for a six-month transition period—from October to April, 1991, though in fact it lasted until June 31, 1991, when it was succeeded by the Korps and Territorial Kommando-Ost.

To implement this plan, the military decided that all key positions in the former GDR would be taken over by Bundeswehr officers.[5] There would be no doubt about who was in charge. To quote one senior West German officer who was directly involved in the transition process: "We want complete responsibility; we are not here as advisors but as leaders. That goes not only for commanders but for staff officers as well."[6]

Bundeswehr personnel arrived in the GDR on September 17 to begin their work. The task was urgent. With the end of the GDR on October 3, the size of the Bundeswehr rose to about 590,000 soldiers. In order for the West Germans to meet the criteria outlined in the agreement Kohl had concluded with Gorbachev, the Bundeswehr had to be reduced to 370,000 soldiers by December 31, 1994.[7]

Schönbohm laid out in his memoirs what he saw as his major tasks at that time:

In short, [they] consisted of taking over the NVA, guaranteeing its security and control, dissolving troop units platoon by platoon, releasing the overwhelming majority of soldiers, concentrating the mass of material, weapons, and munitions, building new units of the Bundeswehr, and working together with Soviet troops in order to facilitate their withdrawal.

In the meantime, Schönbohm's greatest problem was to prevent chaos—the NVA had almost collapsed, and the West Germans were worried that unless the East German military had a better "sense of clarity for its future, . . . Kommando-Ost would face very serious problems."[8] In addition, the Bundeswehr was concerned not only that some of the soldiers themselves might do something stupid but also that some of the radical left-wing groups in the former GDR might move to seize NVA weapons.

Kommando-Ost would have a combined staff of 240 commissioned and noncommissioned officers from the west and 360 officers and NCOs from the former NVA. By the time he reported at Strausberg in October, Schönbohm was overseeing some 93,000 former members of the NVA as well as 1,300 Bundeswehr soldiers who were involved in the transition process,[9] including training the 15,000 conscripts who had been called to the colors on September 1 and retraining NCOs and company or platoon commanders (estimated at between 15,000 and 17,000 for the following year). It is hard to overstate just how difficult the task facing Kommando-Ost was. Not only did it have to come up with a new infrastructure to replace the NVA's, but also painful personnel reductions had to be carried out, facilities had to be rebuilt according to much higher West German standards, environmental damage at many NVA facilities (not to mention former Soviet bases) had to be overcome, and a massive amount of equipment and munitions had to be guarded as well as disposed of. At the same time, Schönbohm and his colleagues had to find a way to reach out to the former NVA professionals—the vast majority of whom felt they had been betrayed and were initially very suspicious of the "Wessis."[10]

Another problem was uniforms. What kind of uniforms should the former NVA soldiers wear? Obviously, they could not expect to become part of the Bundeswehr while still wearing their old NVA uniforms.

Acutely sensitive to the psychological aspects of the unification process, Schönbohm persuaded Stoltenberg to use the NATO olive-green uniform. These uniforms were available in the necessary numbers and sizes and would be sufficient to outfit both officers from the west and former members of the NVA. Indeed, Schönbohm underlined the importance of this decision when he noted, "It was of decisive psychological importance that soldiers in a *single* German army should wear the same uniform."[11]

How to Handle Former NVA Personnel?

Militaries the world over have certain characteristics in common. One of the most important is a willingness to carry out orders—once a political decision has been made. And make no mistake, the decision to incorporate former members of the NVA into the Bundeswehr was not a military decision. From a military standpoint it made no sense—the Bundeswehr was being reduced, and many career officers and NCOs were being forced to leave. If anything, taking former NVA personnel into the Bundeswehr would hurt morale.

In spite of their personal feelings, however, once the federal government made a decision to include former NVA personnel in the Bundeswehr, the country's military leaders quickly fell into line. For example, despite his earlier opposition, Stoltenberg worked to facilitate the process. On October 3 he issued an order to Bundeswehr personnel that stated, "We want to give as many of them [NVA soldiers] as fair a chance as possible, to test their suitability for the soldierly profession or as a civilian employee".[12] All together, approximately fifty thousand members of the NVA would join the Bundeswehr, including twenty-five thousand short-term regular and professional soldiers. All former NVA soldiers over fifty would leave the armed forces by December 31.

To bring some order into the process of incorporating former NVA professionals into the Bundeswehr, Bonn divided them into two main categories. The first was the conscripts. They immediately became full-fledged members of the Bundeswehr and received the same pay as their western counterparts. The second category was the short-term regular and professional soldiers, who were further divided into four subcategories. The first included those who would serve for an additional period (the *Weiterverwender*). They would remain in their current positions, receive a temporary rank, and be paid at a rate to be decided by the Bundeswehr. The second subcategory consisted of those who were in "reserve" (*Wartestand*)—individuals for whom no position was currently available. They would receive 70 percent of their former pay on a temporary basis and would be released at the end of six months, if not before. The third subgroup consisted of short-term regular soldiers (*Soldaten auf Zeit*) who would serve on contract for two years, with a rank in accordance with Bundeswehr regulations. The fourth subgroup consisted of short-term regular soldiers and professional soldiers who would serve for more than two years. Such assignments would be made on the basis of the needs of the service as well as the capabilities of the individuals concerned. When it came to officers, decisions would be made only after they had passed an examination by an independent committee concerning their suitability (a process very much like that used to determine the suitability of former Wehrmacht officers for service in the West German military when the Bundeswehr was first set up).[13]

According to a Bundeswehr officer who was directly involved in the absorption process, for practical purposes Bonn divided former NVA personnel into three additional categories. First, there were those whom the West Germans wanted to see leave the military within three months (that is, by December 31, 1990). They were promised a lump sum gratuity of between five thousand and seven thousand deutsche marks, based on their rank and service. The second category included officers whose services the Bundeswehr needed until most of the units to be disbanded had been dissolved. Finally, there were those who would be offered the chance to stay for a longer period.[14] Any from the last group who wanted to serve for an additional two years and then become a professional soldier had from October 1 to December 15 to apply. Original plans called for accepting up to twenty thousand professional and short-term regular soldiers, who would be offered a two-year contract. During that time they would go through a "testing period":

On the one hand, it gives the NVA soldier the possibility to consider thoroughly the finality of his decision (further service or a release

from duty), and on the other hand, it gives superiors and the personnel leadership, who are running this test, time for evaluating a soldier
who was socialized in another system and in another army.[15]

Once the evaluation was complete, individuals could be accepted for
conversion to regular Bundeswehr officers at any time. The rank a former
NVA officer would be assigned in the Bundeswehr would be decided by
the West Germans. As the relevant document noted: "The Federal Minister of Defense determines which rank [officers] may temporarily hold.
He will take into account their conduct, training, length of service, career
path, and function within the NVA and will place them in an appropriate
rank in the Bundeswehr." Furthermore, it was made clear that professional or short-term regular soldiers would be released for a number of
reasons: if they requested it, when their term of service ended, if they had
violated human rights or the law, or if they had worked for the Stasi. Such
individuals could also be released under other circumstances: if a professional soldier had served the minimal required time, if a soldier lacked
technical qualifications or personal aptitude, if he was not needed, or if
his position was eliminated.[16]

Schönbohm and his colleagues faced a difficult situation. On one
hand, they needed former NVA soldiers—the number of Bundeswehr
troops allocated to Kommando-Ost was insufficient to man the units
they were taking over. One Bundeswehr officer who was sent to the east to
reorganize an artillery division wrote:

> My main problem was manpower, or rather the lack of it. In all, I had
> more than 120 officers, 100 NCOs, 400 soldiers, and 100 civilians.
> My mission—to reorganize and transition the ex-NVA artillery
> organization into a Bundeswehr division artillery—could not be
> accomplished by myself. In addition to the ex-NVA manpower
> already mentioned, I had a team of West German officers: three lieu-
> tenant colonels, all of whom had already been artillery battalion
> commanders; one major; three captains; and one lieutenant. I also
> had two teams, each consisting of a captain and two warrant officers,
> who were responsible for basic training.[17]

In November, Stoltenberg stated that just to guard the munitions and weapons depots in East Germany, he would need more than the fifty-thousand-man limit imposed by the Bundestag's Budgetary Committee on October 24.[18]

In spite of the Bundeswehr's need for the services of these men, no one could promise them that if they stayed, their future would be guaranteed. Only a few would eventually be taken into the Bundeswehr permanently. Indeed, although an individual could apply to become a temporary soldier for two years, he had to be accepted by the Bundeswehr. Further service also would be decided by West German authorities. Schönbohm was in a quandary. As he himself said, "We needed the help of officers and NCOs from the NVA, but we couldn't deny that over the long haul we could take only a limited number of them into the Bundeswehr."[19]

Former NVA Members Respond

As October 3 approached, Admiral Theodor Hoffmann, the last commander of the NVA, was embittered by the whole process. Bonn had spoken about equality, but it was far from evident. "There was no longer even a hint of equal partnership, [and] also no reference to the right of former NVA members or institutions to have a say. All decisions were in the hands of the Minister of Defense and his deputies."[20] While one can understand Hoffmann's bitterness—which was shared by many other NVA officers—the fact was that the East Germans and their political system had lost. Why should the Bundeswehr permit former NVA personnel or the now nonexistent Ministry of Disarmament and Defense to have a say on such a touchy subject? Considering their former loyal service to the hated SED state, they were lucky that they were being given a chance to serve in the Bundeswehr at all.

Within the NVA morale continued to sink. On September 13, for example, Defense Minister Ranier Eppelmann went out of his way to deny reports that up to 60–80 percent of professional soldiers had resigned. At the same time, he admitted that if the current wave of resignations were to continue, that percentage could be reached by the end of the month.[21] The reasons for this low morale were not hard to find. Despite reports that the West Germans would take a number of NVA officers into the Bundeswehr, the average officer and NCO knew only too well that this was problematical.

Former NVA soldiers faced a crisis. The prospect of being thrown out on the street with little or nothing to do at a time of high unemployment was especially sobering. A former NVA naval officer serving in the Bundeswehr toward the end of November captured the precariousness of the situation when he observed, "Soldiers may not stand on the streets because they know where the weapons and munitions are currently stored. I have a stomachache releasing soldiers and officers here in Rostock with an unemployment rate of 30 percent. They have to be employed, regardless of where."[22]

Schönbohm was fully aware of the problem and was earnest in his efforts to resolve it. He wrote: "Those soldiers who were forced to leave the armed forces should, to the degree possible, be given the opportunity to improve their transition to civilian life through career training programs.[23]

The Bundeswehr's approach to this problem was twofold. On one hand, Bonn continued to make it clear that it would not countenance any attempt on the part of its personnel to treat former NVA officers as second-class citizens. On September 24 the general inspector issued an order that stated:

> In accordance with the principles of the Unity Law, from the day of unification we are all soldiers of the Bundeswehr. I expect the duty of comradeship to be taken seriously. Our different backgrounds [werdegänge] and differences of opinion cannot be permitted to endanger the unification process. There may not be any sweeping judgements or prejudices. Radical forms of speech and behavior by individuals cannot be justified.... We can only bring about reorganization and change together.[24]

Defense Minister Stoltenberg reiterated this point in a speech he gave in early October, when he promised that there would be no Bundeswehr soldiers of "first and second class." Concerning differences in pay—Bundeswehr personnel from the west received higher pay than those from the east—he assured his listeners that this would only exist during the transition period.[25]

Schönbohm would repeat this message over and over throughout his tenure at Kommando-Ost. He called for patience and "above all, understanding for the former soldiers of the NVA, who are under tremendous psychological pressure."[26] He never tired pointing out that former NVA soldiers—many of whom had lived for forty years under a communist dictatorship—"have the right to make a mistake."[27]

Operationalizing this lofty sentiment would not be easy. It required important concessions on the part of both sets of officers. It would also necessitate considerable understanding and patience as the East Germans became members of a democratic armed forces—at a time when they still harbored deep suspicions of their new colleagues. They would have to perform their duties in an exemplary fashion while learning to live in a new and confusing environment.

From the standpoint of the former NVA officers, no better person could have been chosen to carry out this difficult task than Jörg Schönbohm. Despite his earlier expressions of dislike, if not disdain, for what the NVA represented, once he had been given the task of incorporating former members of the NVA into the Bundeswehr, he devoted all of his efforts to ensuring that they were given a fair chance. He worked hard to make certain that their living conditions (which were abysmal) improved, while taking on those in Bonn who wanted little or nothing to do with former NVA personnel. Indeed, had it not been for Schönbohm, the world these officers and NCOs entered on October 3 would have looked and developed quite differently.

One of the first things Schönbohm did was to visit as much of the GDR as possible. He was determined to change the public attitude toward the military—fostered by many years of life with the NVA and the Soviet armed forces. Both militaries were closed to civilians. Military personnel kept to themselves, and there was minimal contact between the two groups. Schönbohm was out to change all of this. He and his fellow officers visited every town and spoke to every civic leader they could find. He wanted to convince the East German populace that the Bundeswehr was different from the NVA they had known—and he had some successes. For example, on October 19, 1990, Schönbohm arranged for the oath taken by new recruits to take place in the center of a small town called Bad Salzungen. A few thousand people attended, and Schönbohm noted later that he had spoken with an Evangelical pastor who declined his invitation to be present on the platform while the ceremony took place. The pastor said he did not want to be part of a military "spectacular." After the ceremony, the pastor approached Schönbohm to say that the ceremony had been conducted much differently than he had expected. He remarked that perhaps everyone should be more flexible in dealing with each other. According to Schönbohm, "for me that was an encouraging experience."[28]

The Spoils: Equipment and Munitions

Few westerners, including many specialists, realized just how much equipment and what a large supply of munitions the GDR possessed prior to unification. Indeed, the liaison teams sent to the GDR soon discovered that the NVA had more firepower—including almost 300,000 tons of munitions—than the entire Bundeswehr, even though the latter was four times as large. The Bundeswehr also inherited 2,272 tanks, 7,831 armored vehicles, and 2,460 artillery pieces. In addition, the air force had about 400 planes and the navy around 60 ships. Finally, the Bundeswehr was now the proud owner of an additional 1.2 million hand weapons and around 100,000 motor vehicles.[29]

Even more impressive was the way in which this equipment was maintained: it received far better care than the military personnel who serviced it. For example, although there were problems with the heating systems in barracks, the equipment was kept in heated halls. As one article put it, "in the NVA technology and weapons were taken care of in a first-class manner; however, people played no role."[30] Schönbohm's most immediate task was to find a way to guard this massive acquisition.

The problems it would face in trying to guard NVA equipment should not have come as a complete surprise to the Bundeswehr. NVA officers had warned several weeks earlier that in view of disciplinary problems, they could not guarantee that weapons dumps were being guarded. Indeed, they spoke of increased thefts of weapons.[31] Bundeswehr officers assigned to the former GDR reported that "often munitions were not only in bunkers, but since they were filled to capacity, munitions were stored in the open." In addition, electricity was often turned off to the high-tension wires surrounding the bunkers—a situation that required the assignment of greater numbers of soldiers as guards. The guardroom itself was in horrible condition.[32] It was soon discovered that just to secure the munitions would take far more men than anyone had expected. One source reported that the Bundeswehr had stated that eleven thousand soldiers were needed just to guard munitions.[33] In terms of morale, this made conditions worse. Conscripts were spending 40 percent of their time on guard duty—in contrast with the situation in the west, where a conscript spent only 5 percent of his time that way. The situation was so bad, according to Schönbohm, that not only were officers through the rank of captain being assigned to watch duty, but even staff officers found their names on watch lists.[34]

Things would get worse. Schönbohm's deputy, General Werner von Schewen, told of news he received at Christmas to the effect that all the qualified officers who were guarding munition and fuel dumps in the former GDR would leave the Bundeswehr by the end of the year.[35] There was a mad scramble to find enough Bundeswehr officers in the west to fill the gap.

The problems facing the Bundeswehr were made more difficult because the munitions were unstable and were not in the FRG's inventory. Thus there was a certain irony in Schönbohm's comment that "for the first time in my life as a soldier, I have too much ammunition."[36] Not only could he not use the ammunition, but given the limits placed on Germany by the Conventional Force Agreement, Bonn also had to find a way to eliminate munitions.

The East Germans had recognized the problem early on and had tried to give some of their weapons and munitions back to the Russians. The latter, however, were faced with their own problems and refused to accept them. The NVA made an effort to cut back the size of its inventory by donating some equipment to Third World countries. On September 1, for example, the Ministry of Disarmament and Defense reported that the GDR had given 65 heavy trucks, trailers, smaller trucks, and water-tank trucks, as well as camp kitchens and mobile homes, to Ethiopia, Angola, and Mozambique.[37] In view of the amount of equipment on hand, however, such actions represented a drop in the bucket.

Bonn got rid of some of the NVA's equipment by passing it on to the United States for use during the Gulf War. Most of it consisted of trucks, water tanks, generators, engineering equipment, and chemical and biological warfare protective equipment. Altogether it was worth some $1.2 billion.[38]

One of the few weapons systems that the Bundeswehr decided to put into its inventory—on a temporary basis—was a squadron of 24 MIG-29s. The planes used more fuel than their western equivalents, but the opportunity to obtain world-class aircraft, together with the pilots and technicians to fly them and keep them in the air, was too good to pass up.

Bonn then decided to sell, give away, or destroy the thousands of tanks, helicopters, ships, and other items of equipment from the NVA. Transportation and armored personnel vehicles were sold to Sweden. Berlin gave armored personnel carriers to Pakistani peacekeepers in the former Yugoslavia, and other combat vehicles to Kazakhstan, Kyrgyzstan, and Mongolia. Bonn also supplied a considerable amount of equipment to relief agencies. According to one report, "in reply to 13,000 requests, some 7,000 well-mounted vehicles of all kinds, 3,000 trailers, a considerable amount of fire-fighting and disaster equipment, and 19 million pieces of clothing" were given to relief agencies.[39] Meantime, civilian contractors were employed to destroy the bulk of the equipment. By 1995, the process of getting rid of East German military equipment was nearly complete.

The NVA Professionals' Background

NVA officers came from a very different world from that of their West German colleagues. To begin with, it is worth emphasizing that the former NVA officers had been the sworn enemies of the Bundeswehr. As one former NVA air force officer put it, "Only a year and a half ago, I had Bundeswehr personnel in my radar sights. Now they're inviting us over."[40] In this sense, both former NVA officers and their Bundeswehr colleagues had been taught to view each other as potential enemies. There was an important difference, however. Former NVA professionals were being asked not only to join but actively to support a system they had sworn to oppose for their entire service lives. Many Bundeswehr officers were fully aware that this placed the NVA professionals in a difficult situation. As one West German NCO observed, "How lucky I am to be standing on the right side."[41]

Most of the NVA officers claimed that although the party leadership had not succeeded "in creating a genuine hatred [*Feindbild*] toward the soldiers of the Bundeswehr," they would have been prepared to do their duty if they had been called upon. "I did not know whence the enemy would come, but if he were to cross our border, he would then be my enemy. That concept was clear."[42] At the same time, if there was one feeling toward the FRG that was prevalent among NVA professionals, it was jealousy—the "Wessis" had everything while the NVA officer had lived in a world of need for many years.

It is important to keep in mind that NVA personnel were far more isolated from everyday life than were their Bundeswehr colleagues. Not only was hatred of the West—and the FRG in particular—pounded into their heads almost daily, but they also were barred from watching Western television or listening to Western radios, from having contact with individuals from the West, and even from possessing Western currency. This does not mean that no one listened secretly to forbidden sources of information or that a soldier ran out of his apartment when a relative from the FRG came to visit. But a career military officer had much to lose. "The risk that one accepted in order to be better informed was not worth it to the officers." Everything in his life was directed toward the Soviet Union—his advanced education, his tactics, his strategy, and his force structure. In short, little information was available that would permit an officer to develop ideas in opposition to those advocated by the party leadership. Indeed, one source claimed that NVA officers were more poorly informed politically than the civilian population and on many occasions were "even less aware of what was going on in the outside world than those who lived in the same apartment house." Even trying to learn English could lead to unpleasant questions. Why does the officer want to go that route? Is he planning to defect?[43]

Another reason for the isolation of the NVA officer was the severe military obligations that were placed on him. Combat readiness was much higher in the NVA than it was in any Western military, including the Bundeswehr. To gain some idea of just how prepared the NVA was for combat, consider the following. The NVA had eleven motorized divisions —six active and five in reserve. All could be in the field and ready to go within two to three days.[44] Or, as a former East German officer put it with regard to the active divisions, "each unit had to be ready to have 85 percent of its personnel and material fully combat ready and to be able to leave its base in 45 minutes, regardless of whether it was a weekday or a weekend or over Christmas or over Easter."[45] By contrast, the most the Bundeswehr ever had on alert (in the 1960s) was 30 percent of its troops.[46] On average, this meant that NVA officers put in more than sixty hours a week, and in some cases more than seventy-two.[47]

The NVA's high level of combat readiness began to slip in 1986 because of the increasing use of NVA troops in the civilian economy. Nevertheless, the important point is that the vast majority of officers (certainly those at the level of army captain or above) had spent most of their lives under these extreme conditions. Indeed, some would find it difficult to adjust to the much more lax life of a soldier in the Bundeswehr.

Another sign of how prepared the NVA was for the next war was the existence of medals already struck and ready to be awarded for a campaign in the west. The East Germans had even created shoulder boards for a "Marshall of the GDR"—a rank to be awarded to Erich Honecker, Interior Minister Erich Mielke, and Defense Minister Heinz Kessler.[48] In addition, East Berlin had created "doomsday" complexes to protect the country's political and military leadership.[49] Senior party officials also carried reserve commissions in the NVA, ready to assume their duties in a crisis.[50]

The crippling hours worked by NVA officers meant that time with their families was limited. The normal work day lasted at least ten to eleven hours and often was longer. For most, the idea of a Sunday afternoon free after two o'clock was the most that could be expected.[51] For the average soldier, the situation was even worse. "He had permission to leave the base once per week. A third of the air defense forces were in a constant state of combat readiness. The units of the air force had to be ready to leave their base with completely loaded weapons systems and support equipment within two hours."[52]

Perhaps one of the most telling contrasts between the East German and West German military systems was the different way each handled duty at Christmas. During the holidays, 85 percent of Bundeswehr soldiers were at home on leave, while 85 percent of NVA personnel were at their barracks. Hans-Peter von Kirchbach, who commanded a former NVA division after October 3, wrote that the division he took over could be under way in less than sixty minutes. He also noted the presence of a Soviet alarm system right in the East German unit, which placed this unit under the direct control of the Kremlin in the event of a crisis.[53]

In short, the NVA was an "Army for war—a war machine. While in the Bundeswehr the individual occupied center stage, in the NVA everything was sacrificed for combat readiness."[54] From a political standpoint this meant, as a former NVA officer put it, that "all of our thoughts and actions were measured by combat readiness and combat capability." There was no time to worry about political issues, except at higher levels of rank or on a military staff. The same was true of ethical questions. "We had no time to think about things such as a soldier's truth or career ethics."[55] Duty came first.

There were at least two reasons behind this high level of combat readiness. First, from a political standpoint, it helped convince the Russians that the NVA was an indispensable ally in the event of war—after all, no other eastern European military force could have reacted so fast with such a formidable military force during a crisis. The GDR's military prowess, combined with its economic strength (when measured against other eastern European states) was aimed at convincing the Russians not to make a deal with Bonn at the expense of East Berlin. The second reason was that it kept officers from having time to think about political questions, while convincing the rank and file of the danger presented by the imperialistic West. After all, the NVA would not be in such a high state of alert if it were not being threatened by NATO and the FRG. Unfortunately, from the party's position, "these arguments stood on weak feet and on occasion were really primitive."[56]

In addition to imposing a very busy work schedule, the NVA was one of the most heavily indoctrinated militaries in the entire Warsaw Pact. But it would oversimplify matters to assume that the average NVA officer was only "a loyal instrument of the communist dictatorship."[57] While some joined for ideological reasons, many young men became members of the NVA because they were enamored of the technology, the chance for adventure, or the opportunity to improve their standard of living. The party was always present, but it was not the all-consuming organization that many in the West believed it to be. There was a tendency to assume that the party was right, however, probably because that was the only view of reality these overworked officers encountered.

At the same time, the SED's ideology did not impregnate every aspect of an NVA officer's life. What the average NVA officer seems to have taken away was a belief in the rightness of socialism, and a commitment to a system that he believed was actively working for peace in Europe. According to one NVA officer, "to be a good soldier, one had to be a good socialist." Certainly there was the occasional "hundred-percenter"—the "SED Party Functionary in Uniform"—but as one West German observer put it, "I never encountered conviction in the sense of the 'real existing socialism,' [but] rather the belief that socialism was better than capitalism and that the NVA had contributed to peace through its contribution to the balance of forces."[58] For practical purposes this meant that the NVA officer was trained to go along with the general goals outlined by the party. He was a party soldier in the sense that he accepted the party's general guidelines, not because he was a fanatic communist. The longer he served, the more he accepted the party's presence as a fact of life—as something that was as much a part of military life as cleaning a rifle.

Regardless of how much an individual might have resisted fully accepting communist ideology, he was subject to party discipline. One East German officer who participated in a number of the events of 1989–1990 at a very high level hit the nail on the head when he observed that the reason NVA officers did not react creatively when the situation began to change prior to unification was "found in the policy of the SED, which, when it did not suppress independent thinking, still channelized it and offensively fought critical thinking."[59]

Anything that might create a sense of ideological pluralism—a situation in which a soldier might owe psychological allegiance to anything

outside this narrow party-military environment—was strongly discour-
aged. I have already spoken of the SED's efforts to isolate NVA officers
from external influences. The situation was the same when it came to
what the party considered "unhealthy" internal factors. Religion serves
as a good example. The party leadership made it clear that such ideas
"stopped at the door of a military facility."[60] Fewer than 10 percent of NVA
officers were baptized. The party apparatus carried out an aggressive
campaign against religious membership of any kind. No NVA officer
could openly proclaim his allegiance to a religious community; if he did,
he risked having his military career cut short. Indeed, the civilian population often viewed the military as a hotbed of anti-religious feeling. This
strong sense of public mistrust of the NVA created serious problems for
Schönbohm and Kommando-Ost. When the Bundeswehr first arrived in
the east, many of the clergy and believers in the former GDR saw little
difference between the NVA and the Bundeswehr when it came to hostility toward religion.

Another factor that served to isolate NVA personnel from their surrounding environment was the all-pervasive sense of secrecy. Everything
that went on within the NVA was a secret—civilians often knew very little
of what was happening in the military. As one former East German officer
put it: "Every NVA facility was more or less viewed as secretive."[61] Contacts with the civilian world were also limited. A Bundeswehr officer
wrote: "One lived mostly in residential areas built especially for NVA
members. Contacts with the civilian populace were limited; one discovers
in many places a state within a state. The press and public relations limited themselves to nice official statements."[62]

Life within the military was strictly regulated by the "need to know"
philosophy. If a soldier did not require information to do his job, it would
be withheld from him. Indeed, information was highly compartmental-
ized. Naval officers knew nothing about ground force capabilities, and
even officers who were part of the ground forces had limited knowledge
about a unit's operational plans. NVA officers were not trained to ask
questions. After all, asking for information you might not be authorized
to see could get you into serious trouble. Better to keep your mouth shut
and mind your own business.

The result of this situation was that discussions—especially political discussions—were more limited than they were in other communist militaries. NVA personnel were so atomized that the idea of discussing politics with fellow officers almost never arose. This was part of the reason, according to one study conducted in the GDR, why—in contrast to Poland and Hungary—military reform did not really take hold in the NVA. "Forces from the SED willing to consider reform were neither conceptually nor organizationally able to negotiate, to formulate the further development in the GDR of a politically relevant reform wing."[63] It seemed as if the majority of NVA officers were locked in a state of political unconsciousness. They were used to having others do their thinking for them.

Leadership Style

Another major difference between the NVA and the Bundeswehr was the relationship between superiors and subordinates. In the NVA, superiors were not approachable. When it came to dealing with senior officers— or officers at all if one were enlisted—"discussions ... were a one-sided affair. Personal opinion was not a matter for debate."[64] Schönbohm ran into this sense of isolation in speaking to a number of former NVA officers. His open, easy-going, approachable style was new to them. As he described the situation: "And then one of the officers said to me, 'I have been an officer for eighteen years. The fact that I can talk so freely with a general is for me completely new.'"[65] This sense of isolation on the part of senior officers may have contributed to their different approach for dealing with subordinates.

Not only were NVA officers less approachable than their West German counterparts, they were also more numerous and carried out different functions. In the NVA, the ratio of officers to enlisted personnel was one to eight; in the Bundeswehr, it was one to forty.[66] As von Kirchbach put it: "In a division staff of the NVA, which controlled about 10,000 men, there were more officers than in a corps staff of the Bundeswehr, which was in charge of 70,000 men."[67] When it came to NCOs, the ratio in the NVA was one to one; in the Bundeswehr it was one to three. One observer estimated that 50 percent of the NVA officers were doing what NCOs did in the Bundeswehr.[68] Where the Bundeswehr delegated authority, the NVA did not. In terms of an NCO corps, the NVA had nothing approaching the situation within the Bundeswehr. To quote another observer: "With the exception of warrant officers and senior NCOs, who had served for a long time, both in their own eyes as well as in the eyes of the officers they were a special kind of 'senior soldier'—they took on command and leadership positions only in exceptional circumstances."[69] By contrast, NCOs in the Bundeswehr were well known for their independence and self-confidence, something that was severely lacking in the NVA.

This top-heavy officer corps led to a much faster promotion rate in the NVA than in the Bundeswehr. Both factors made it necessary for the Bundeswehr to take two special steps: one to create an NCO corps and the other to equalize the officer rank structure between the two military forces.

Another area of considerable difference between the NVA and the Bundeswehr was discipline. In the NVA, the catchword was "blind obedience"; in fact it was part of the oath taken by every NVA soldier. As General Ulrich de Maiziere, the former inspector general of the Bundeswehr, put it, "The oath left no room for a conscience"—a situation which contrasted sharply with that in the Bundeswehr, where "conscience stood above an order."[70]

Indeed, life in the NVA was considerably more brutal than it was in the Bundeswehr. Von Kirchbach told the story of a man who came into his office after he had taken over in Eggesin. The man told of shoveling snow when two NVA officers approached. Because he was wearing an NVA jacket, he was mistaken for an NVA soldier. The two officers beat him so badly that he was hospitalized with serious injuries. Von Kirchbach said that he investigated the matter, and much to his surprise, he discovered that the man was telling the truth. The NVA officers thought the man was a soldier intentionally missing from a returning formation.[71] A Bundeswehr officer caught hitting a soldier in such a manner would have been dismissed from the service.

Life in the NVA was also characterized by a dual sense of morality. There was an officially accepted morality, and there was an individual's private morality. Applying the rules of private conscience to aspects of public life could be dangerous to one's career. For example, everyone recognized that the five-year plan was a joke. Statistics were notoriously inaccurate, and no one seriously believed them. Nevertheless, officers had little choice but to parrot the official party line. If the party lecture, which soldiers had to attend, said that the GDR was ahead of the FRG in a particular area, the fact that the claim was inaccurate was irrelevant. After all, the idea of a free press was completely unknown. "In this climate, opportunistic personalities were created, which made it very difficult to build genuine comradely relationships."[72] Besides, if an individual did not play the game correctly, he had to deal with the possibility that his "incorrect" ideas would be reported to the so-called Abteilung 2000, populated by Stasi officers. Over the long run, those officers who were best at deception were often the most successful in their careers.

Another result of the aloof leadership style in the NVA was the harassment of junior conscripts by more senior ones. Called *dedovshchina* in the Russian military, this was a way of helping officers maintain discipline. More senior conscripts kept more junior ones in line by threats, promises, and intimidation. This permitted officers to remain above the fray—after all, the junior conscripts could always take comfort in the fact that they would eventually be senior conscripts, and then they could inflict their wrath on their own juniors. To quote one former East German officer: "In units filled with conscripts of varying service years, there was always discrimination and repression of the more junior ones. Neither discussions nor punishment helped. We were never able to deal correctly with this problem."[73] Indeed, the whole idea of law as it was understood in the West was something the NVA could never come to grips with. Law was for maintaining order and ensuring that the party's or government's wishes were carried out. "There were no legal principles that gave the member of the military any . . . political, social, cultural, or juridical rights vis-à-vis the state."[74]

From a military standpoint, the NVA's leadership style, in addition to the way it treated subordinates, was harmful because it stifled initiative. Since the leadership did not trust the rank and file, everything that was done was determined from above. This created a hopeless situation, as a former NVA officer noted: "The real absurdity came about because the same command authorities who drew up the littlest detail constantly demanded that all tasks be carried out creatively and with initiative."[75]

The NVA leadership—like their Soviet colleagues—never understood that overmanagement destroys initiative. Criticism was tolerated, but only to the degree that the facts and opinions were in agreement with the prevailing point of view.[76]

Creature Comforts

Another area in which the NVA and the Bundeswehr differed significantly was that of living conditions. Considering the incredible hours that NVA personnel put in, one might have expected NVA officers to go to great lengths to ensure that their people were treated properly. This certainly has been the approach taken in most Western militaries. In fact, the living conditions afforded enlisted NVA personnel were horrible. These were conscripts (as opposed to professional soldiers) about whom no one seemed to care. According to one report, a barracks had eight showers for more than 2,000 men![77] As another put it, "the bathrooms and the toilets were at the level of 1936."[78] And Schönbohm noted, "We had to close all of the 141 kitchens"—they were all far below Western standards.[79] Von Kirchbach's description of the NVA's barracks was especially graphic. "The rooms, washrooms, toilets are almost all completely in disrepair. They stink horribly. In spite of sometimes recognizable efforts to improve the situation with the means at hand, in general total structural and technical neglect is visible."[80] Other observers came to the same conclusions: "The living standards for soldiers were even worse. They had to be content with extremely old furniture, filthy washrooms and toilets and showers. There was a central shower building in the barracks, but it was closed for hygienic reasons and because the building was unsafe."[81]

Conclusion

Whether for good or ill, former members of the NVA were now part of the Bundeswehr. For some, the relationship would be short: they would be leaving for lives in the civilian world at the earliest opportunity. The seven thousand deutsche marks collected by those who left looked good to a lot of men, who saw the money as a way to start a new life.

Others, however, would opt to stay on in the Bundeswehr, to try to continue their military careers. It would be no easy undertaking. Not only

would they have to convince the West Germans of their military expertise, but they also would be required to prove that in spite of their very
different background they could and would adapt to the world of the
Bundeswehr. Making this transformation would be difficult and at times
even humiliating. These were competent officers who had proved they
could function in one of the world's most demanding military environ-
ments. Now they had not only to admit that much of what they had
learned was wrong but also to learn to do things in a very different fashion. What was once right was now wrong—and vice-versa.

Not surprisingly, the post-1991 period was hard for the West Germans,
too. At a time when the Bundeswehr itself was being downsized, they
had to work with East Germans who had been their sworn enemies only
months before. In spite of their years of learning to hate everything the
NVA, as a party army, had stood for, these West Germans had to be prepared to defend their new colleagues against continued attacks from those
in the Bundesrepublik who found the presence of former NVA personnel
in the Bundeswehr an abomination. Indeed, there would be occasions
when Schönbohm was locked in what seemed to an outsider to be mortal
combat with the defense ministry in Bonn over how these newcomers
were treated.

Patience would also be at a premium on the part of Bundeswehr officers serving in the east. When it came to bringing about the transition, it
was these men who were on the front lines. They were the ones who
would spend countless hours trying to reshape the remnants of the NVA
into Bundeswehr soldiers. They did this knowing full well that many of
their new colleagues would be forced to leave the unified German military regardless of how well they performed.

By 1998 there were only 4,797 former members of the NVA serving in
the Bundeswehr.[82] Of this total, 1,343 were officers, the rest NCOs. Two
officers were serving in senior command positions. And although there
were few reports of conflict between Bundeswehr officers and those who
had served in the NVA, a new problem had arisen that put former NVA
professionals at a serious disadvantage. One of the keys to a good assignment was having friends and colleagues in the personnel department,
but here were no former NVA professionals in such positions. There were

also signs that former NVA officers were being excluded from certain positions—such as teaching at Bundeswehr educational institutions—because of their background. Finally, senior officers such as Schönbohm and von Schewen, who had worked hard to help former members of the NVA adapt to the Bundeswehr, had left the military. Only von Kirchbach remained, but it was questionable how much assistance he could provide to these men.

If nothing else, a close look at the East German experience shows clearly the kinds of problems one can expect to encounter in "democratizing" former members of a communist military: a lack of initiative, an unwillingness to ask questions, a failure to understand Western ideas of leadership and discipline, an inclination toward brutality in handling subordinates, a tendency to leave politics to the politicians, a penchant for secrecy, a failure to treat enlisted personnel the way officers do in the West, and a tendency to accept the idea of a dual morality. Not all former communist militaries have encountered these problems to the same degree as the NVA, but it would be surprising indeed if a large number of them did not.

Notes

1. This chapter draws on my more detailed study of the last days of the NVA and the transition to the Bundeswehr. See Dale R. Herspring, *Requiem for an Army: The Demise of the East German Military* (Lanham, Maryland: Rowman and Littlefield, 1998).

2. See "Schönbohm befehligt zentrales Kommando," *Frankfurter Allgemeine Zeitung,* 28 August 1990.

3. Based on Edgar Trost, "Probleme der Personalauswahl," in Dieter Farwick, *Ein Staat—Eine Armee* (Bonn: Report Verlag, 1992), 170–205.

4. Jörg Schönbohm, *Zwei Armeen und ein Vaterland* (Berlin: Siedler, 1992), 31–32.

5. Trost, "Probleme der Personalauswahl," 176.

6. Hans Peter von Kirchbach, Manfred Meyers, and Victor Vogt, *Abenteuer Einheit* (Frankfurt am Main: Report Verlag, 1992), 48.

7. Friedrich Steinseifer, "Zusammenfügen und verkleinern," *Truppenpraxis* 1 (1991): 19.

8. Schönbohm, *Zwei Armeen und ein Vaterland,* 47.

9. *Ibid.,* 33.

10. *Wessi* was a somewhat unflattering term used by East Germans to describe West Germans.

11. Schönbohm, *Zwei Armeen und ein Vaterland*, 33. Emphasis in the original.

12. Cited in Trost, "Probleme der Personalauswahl," 184.

13. For the legal document setting up these categories as well as noting the responsibilities of former NVA personnel in the Bundeswehr, see "Die NVA im Einigungsvertrag," *Europäische Wehrkunde* 10 (1990): 572–573. See also Hermann Hagena, "NVA-Soldaten in der Bundeswehr: Integration—Nicht Resteverwertung," *Europäische Wehrkunde* 10 (1990): 568.

14. Hisso von Selle, "Going from East to West: The Ninth Panzer Division Artillery," *Field Artillery* (June 1993): 29.

15. Herbert König, "Bericht aus einer anderen Welt," *Truppenpraxis* 3 (1992): 234.

16. "Das Dienstverhältnis der Soldaten der Volksarmee soll ruhen," *Frankfurter Allgemeine Zeitung*, 29 August 1990.

17. Von Selle, "Going from East to West," 28.

18. "Soldaten dürfen nicht auf der Strasse stehen," *Frankfurter Allgemeine Zeitung*, 30 November 1990.

19. Schönbohm, *Zwei Armeen und ein Vatrland*, 33.

20. Theodore Hoffmann, *Das Letzte Kommando* (Berlin: Verlag E. S. Mittler & Sohn, 1993), 301.

21. "Soldiers Still Leaving NVA," *British Broadcasting Corporation*, 13 September 1990.

22. "Soldaten dürfen nicht auf der Strasse stehen."

23. Jörg Schönbohm, "Deutsche kommen zu Deutschen," in Farwick, *Ein Staat—Eine Armee*, 43.

24. Schönbohm, *Zwei Armeen und ein Vaterland*, 39–40.

25. "Die Bundeswehr im beigetretenen Teil Deutschlands," *Soldat und Technik* 11 (1990): 780.

26. Schönbohm, *Zwei Armeen und ein Vaterland*, 51.

27. "Die Einheit auch in der Bundeswehr gestalten," *Soldat und Technik* 11 (1990): 776.

28. Schönbohm, *Zwei Armeen und ein Vaterland*, 92.

29. Wolfgang Gülich, "Der Prozess der deutsch–deutschen militärischen Vereinigung aus der Sicht eines Brigadekommandeurs in den neuen Bundesländern: Versuch einer ersten Bewertung," in Paul Klein and Rolf Zimmermann, eds., *Beispielhaft?* (Baden-Baden: Nomos Verlagsgesellschaft, 1993), 24–25.

30. "Schönbohm klagt: Uns fehlen Unteroffiziere," *Die Welt*, 24 December 1990.

31. "Bonn: NVA-Bestände als Golfhilfe für die USA," *Die Welt*, 22–23 September 1990.

32. See von Kirchbach's discussion in "Die Kasernen," in von Kirchbach, Meyers, and Vogt, *Abenteuer Einheit*, 99–98.

33. "Noch 88 000 NVA: Soldaten im Dienst," *Süddeutsche Zeitung*, 8 November 1990.

34. Schönbohm, *Zwei Armeen und ein Vaterland*, 84.

35. Von Schewen, Tape 27 in Jürgen Eike, "Interwiews zum Film 'Die verschwundene Armee'" (taped interview made for a television program).

36. "East German Army Full of Surprises," *San Francisco Chronicle*, 14 December 1990.

37. "GDR Defense Ministry Donates Army Trucks, Equipment to Third World," *Inter Press Service*, 1 September 1990.

38. "Bonn: NVA-Bestände als Golfhilfe für die USA."

39. "Germany Disposes East's Assets; UN Gets Chunk of Communist Regime's Military Goods," *Defense News*, 13 March 1995.

40. "Bonn Braces for Absorption of East Germany's Army," *Los Angeles Times*, 30 September 1990.

41. Günter Holzweissig, "Auflösen: Ohne Rest?" *Deutschland Archiv* 10 (1990).

42. Frithjof Knabe, *Unter der Flagge des Gegners* (Opladen: Westdeutscher Verlag, 1994), 103–104. The first comment was from a former NVA colonel, the second from a commander.

43. Günther Gillessen, "Die Armee die dabeistand," *Frankfurter Allgemeine Zeitung*, 10 November 1990.

44. "Wir müßen unsere Feldwebel neu backen," *Die Welt*, 1 December 1990.

45. Ruediger Volk and Torsten Squarr, "Die innere Zustand der NVA," in Farwick, *Ein Staat—Eine Armee*, 257. Another source claims that a unit had to be able to leave its base combat-ready within one hour. See Herbert König, "Bericht aus einer anderen Welt," *Truppenpraxis* 3 (1992): 236. Regardless of which source is more accurate, the fact is that no Western army could have matched this reaction time. It could be attained only as NVA officers have suggested—if everything was subordinated to combat readiness. According to the former head of East Germany's ground forces, the Soviet military was at a 100-percent level of combat readiness. Since the NVA was closely integrated with Soviet forces, East Berlin was forced to maintain a high level of readiness as well. While this is probably true, the political benefits from such a highly prepared military within the Warsaw Pact and in East German–Russian relations is also significant. See Horst Stechbart, Tape 35 in Eike, "Interviews zum Film 'Die verschwundene Armee.'"

46. Von Schewen, Tape 27, in Eike, "Interviews zum Film 'Die verschwundene Armee.'"

47. Frau Dr. Pietsch, Tape 14 in Eike, "Interviews zum Film 'Die verschwundene Armee.'"

48. "Kein DDR-Marshall Honecker," in Volker Koop, *Erbe NVA: Eindrücke aus ihrer Geschichte und den Tagen der Wende*. 2d ed. (Waldbröl: Akademie der Bundeswehr für Information und Kommunikation, 1993), 126.

49. "Doomsday-Wandlitz lag bei Prenden," in Koop, *Erbe NVA*, 215–216.

50. In "Schnelldurchgang zum Offizier," in Koop, *Erbe NVA*, 138–140. Given the high level of professionalism within the NVA, such a practice could not help but create resentment on the part of regular officers. How could an individual who had attended only a three-month course expect to serve at the same level of

competency as an officer who spent ten to eleven hours every day carrying out his duties?

51. See Karl-Heinz Marschner, "Dienen bis zum Ende," in Farwick, *Ein Staat—Eine Armee*, 208.

52. Schönbohm, "Deutsche kommen zu Deutschen," 37.

53. Von Kirchbach, Meyers, and Vogt, *Abenteuer Einheit*, 85, 93–94, 97.

54. Dieter Farwick, "Einige Antworten," in Farwick, *Ein Staat—Eine Armee*, 305.

55. Lothar W. Breene-Wegener, "Kameraden oder Bösewichte?" *Truppenpraxis* 5 (1990): 440.

56. König, "Bericht aus einer anderen Welt," 236.

57. Brenne-Wegener, "Kameraden oder Bösewichte?" 442.

58. "Zur Einleitung," in M. Backerra, ed., *NVA: Ein Rueckblick fuer die Zukunft* (Koeln: Marksu Verlag, 1992), 14.

59. Hans-Werner Weber, "Gläubigkeit, Opportunismus und späte Zweifel: Anmerkungen zu den Veränderungen im politisch-moralischen Bewußtsein des Offizierskorps der NVA," in Backerra, *NVA*, 58.

60. Horst Prayon, "Die 'Feinde' von einst sollen Kameraden werden," *Europäische Wehrkunde* 11 (1990): 637.

61. Marschner, "Dienen bis zum Ende," 216.

62. Prayon, "Die 'Feinde' von einst sollen Kameraden werden," 637.

63. Hans-Joachim Reeb, "Wandel durch Annäherung," *Truppenpraxis* 2 (1991): 181.

64. Paul Klein, Ekerhard Lippert, and Georg-Maria Meyer, "Zur sozialen Befindlichkeit von Offizieren und Unterofizieren aus der ehemaligen Nationalen Volksarmee," in Klein and Zimmermann, *Beispielhaft* 56.

65. "Wir dienen demselben Vaterland," *Truppenpraxis* 4 (1991): 337.

66. Gillessen, "Die Armee die dabeistand."

67. "Personalfragen," *Abenteuer Einheit*, 79.

68. Von Selle, "Going from East to West," 30.

69. Klein, Lippert, and Meyer, "Zur sozialen," 54.

70. "Wert militärischer Tugenden entscheidet sich am Wofür," *Die Welt*, 12 October 1990.

71. "Schatten der Vergangenheit," in von Kirchbach, Meyers, and Vogt, *Abenteuer Einheit*, 132.

72. Hans-Joachim Reeb, "Eingliederung ehemaliger NVA-Berufssoldaten in die Bundeswehr," *Europaeische Wehrkunde* 8 (1990): 848.

73. König, "Bericht aus einer anderen Welt," 238.

74. Kurt Held, Heinz Friedrich, and Dagmar Pietsch, "Politische Bildung und Erziehung in der NVA," in Backerra, *NVA*, 227.

75. Marschner, "Dienen bis zum Ende," 210.

76. Klaus-Jürgen Engelien and Hans-Joachim Reeb, "Wer bist du—Kamerad?" *Truppenpraxis* 6 (1990): 652.

77. *Economist*, 22 August 92, 37.

78. Bernhard Ickenroth, "Der einstige 'Klassenfeind' in der Kaderschmiede für Politoffiziere der NVA," *Europäische Sichterheit* 5 (1991): 283.

79. "Schönbohm klagt: Uns fehlen Unteroffiziere," *Die Welt*, 24 December 1990.

80. Von Kirchbach, Meyers, and Vogt, *Abenteuer Einheit,* 36

81. Von Selle, "Going from East to West," 30–31.

82. Figures provided to this author by a former NVA officer.

2 Poland

A LINCHPIN OF REGIONAL SECURITY

ANDREW A. MICHTA

In 1997 in Madrid, NATO invited Poland to join its ranks, partly in recognition of the progress the country had made since 1989 in transforming its political and economic institutions. Less than a decade after the collapse of communism, Poland was arguably the most successful new democracy in central Europe. It had established an effective presidential-parliamentary system, introduced a new constitution, consolidated its political parties, and gone through orderly transfers of political power following three parliamentary and two presidential elections. Saddled under communism with a crushing foreign debt, hyperinflation, and pervasive shortages, Poland by 1998 had become Europe's fastest-growing economy, with a stable currency and a sustained growth rate in gross domestic product (GDP) of approximately 5 percent per year.[1] In 1997 the European Union began negotiating with Poland the systemic adjustments necessary to transform its associate EU membership into full-member status early in the subsequent decade.

Because of its size and its geostrategic location at the heart of central Europe, Poland is the most important of the three new entrants into NATO. It has the potential to become a meaningful political and military contributor to the alliance. At the same time, the dual tasks of modernizing its armed forces and transforming its foreign policy into an effective tool of NATO's relations with the East, especially with Russia, dwarf those of the other two members of NATO's 1999 "incoming class."

In order to evaluate the potential for the successful incorporation of Poland into the alliance, I consider in this chapter three areas that will determine its value to NATO: (1) the record of Poland's response to the changed geopolitical environment following the unification of Germany and the disintegration of the Soviet Union, with a focus on Polish-German relations, (2) the record and current priorities of Poland's Eastern policy, especially its relationship with Russia, and (3) the current state of Polish military reform in preparation for NATO membership, including organizational changes, equipment modernization, and the defense budget. The discussion concludes with an assessment of the assets and liabilities Poland is likely to bring to the alliance, and the impact of its NATO membership on the regional security environment in central Europe.

A New Central Europe

The current security environment in central Europe has been defined by two watershed events: the unification of Germany and the dissolution of the USSR. A historic change in Poland's security situation came in 1990, a year prior to the disintegration of the Soviet Union, when the Federal Republic of Germany and the German Democratic Republic moved to become one state. From Warsaw's vantage point, the defining moment of that transition was Bonn's commitment to remain within the trans-Atlantic security system, despite earlier Soviet pressure for a neutral Germany. From Bonn's vantage point in 1990, the emergence of a stable, democratic, and secure Poland became a vital national interest of the newly unified German state. In the critical early years of the postcommunist transition, the preservation of NATO set the stage for the most dramatic shift in the geostrategic environment in central Europe.[2] The preservation of NATO as the linchpin of the trans-Atlantic security system made it possible for Germany and Poland to reach out to each other in the context of continued American commitment to Europe.

The post-1990 redefinition of Polish-German relations was a sea change in that the rapprochement would modify the legacy of the previous two hundred years. Notwithstanding the alliance-wide implications of the 1990 German unification formula, from Warsaw's perspective the unification presented Poland with a dramatically new geopolitical reality: for the first time the country bordered a NATO member—a democratic German state committed to cooperation with its eastern neighbor.

Historically, beginning with the disappearance of the multinational Commonwealth of Poland-Lithuania in the eighteenth century, the dilemma of Polish geopolitics was that of a medium-size, relatively weak country caught between the competing interests of Russia and Germany. The resurrected Polish state of the interwar period ultimately fell victim to this power dynamic. Between 1918 and 1939, the Second Republic (Druga Rzeczpospolita) sought in vain to square the geopolitical circle by trying to balance itself between Germany and the Soviet Union while it looked to France and Great Britain for security guarantees.[3] The fate of interwar Poland was sealed in 1939 when Berlin and Moscow concluded the Ribbentrop-Molotov agreement, a treaty providing for the fourth partition of the Polish state. Even though Germany was subsequently defeated in the war, the consequences of the Ribbentrop-Molotov pact, including the loss of Poland's eastern territories (*kresy*) and its dependence on the Soviet Union, continued for nearly half a century. During the Cold War the regional security architecture in central Europe was defined not only by the Soviet strategic objectives embedded in the "coalition warfare" doctrine of the Warsaw Pact, but also by the continued hostile relationship between Poland and the Federal Republic of Germany.

The strain in Polish-German relations was caused in part by the memory of the wartime atrocities the Germans had committed in Poland, and also by the fact that after the war Poland was compensated with German territory for the land Stalin took from it in the east. The 1945 border adjustment literally shifted the Polish state farther west. In the process, it deepened Poland's dependence on the Soviet Union, for in the absence of an explicit German acquiescence to the loss of its territory to Poland, only Moscow could effectively guarantee Poland's postwar western borders.[4] Therefore, although Bonn and Warsaw took limited steps to improve their relations (beginning in the late 1960s with German Chancellor Willie Brandt's *Ostpolitik,* followed by the Conference on Security and Cooperation in Europe in 1975), the full settlement of the border issue would not be achieved until after the collapse of communism and the merger of the two German states.[5]

Although most of the debate preceding the 1997 NATO summit in Madrid focused on Polish-Russian relations, in fact it was the Polish-German reconciliation that had laid the foundation for NATO enlargement into central Europe. In 1990, Poland and Germany seized the historic opportunity to redefine their relationship. At the time, Poland's foreign minister, Krzysztof Skubiszewski, spoke of a unique chance to remake Polish-German relations in the image of those of France and Germany, whereby centuries of hostility could be overcome through economic, political, and security cooperation. The signal that Germany was intent on following a similar course vis-à-vis Poland was Bonn's readiness to negotiate a treaty confirming the post–World War II Polish-German border.

In 1991, Poland and Germany concluded two historic agreements that confirmed the permanence of their existing borders and affirmed the two countries' mutual commitment to good neighborly relations. The treaties were critical to Poland's aspirations to join NATO, because they changed the power dynamic in central Europe. They marked the first step in overcoming the historical burden of the Polish security dilemma, for they were accompanied by Bonn's clear commitment to work for the inclusion of Poland in the existing European institutions, as well as NATO. Without Polish-German reconciliation, Poland's goal of "returning to the West" would have been unattainable.

The treaties were also vital to the future of regional security in central Europe as a whole. Poland's opening to Germany and the desire for eventual reconciliation between the two nations were the first steps toward improved Polish-Russian relations. If any future partnership between Poland and Russia were to develop, and, similarly, if Russia and Germany were to build a stable cooperative relationship, Poland had to feel secure in the region. Without the 1991 treaties, and without Germany's vocal support for Poland's membership in NATO, Poland would have continued to fear that any future collaboration between Bonn and Moscow might ultimately prove detrimental to its security.[6]

The Polish-German treaties of 1991, and Bonn's support of Poland's membership in NATO, reflected a consensus among the foreign policy elites in both countries. For the two societies, however, the treaties marked only the beginning of the process of reconciliation. Both societies recognized that it would take at least a generation to change Polish and German perceptions of each other. In addition to the burden of Nazi atrocities during the Second World War, the Poles would have to come to terms with their residual fear of Germany, which for forty-five years had allowed the Polish communist regime to justify the country's dependence

on the Soviet Union.[7] Similarly, the Germans would need to look beyond
the economic disparity between the two countries and start treating the
Poles as their partners in the east.

As the 1990s neared an end, for the first time in fifty years Poles and
Germans were engaged in open dialogue about their intimate and often
torturous common past. The historical record and the rights of the
remaining Polish minority in Germany, and of the German minority in
Poland, were often argued with an intensity and openness that would
have been impossible only a decade earlier. The more conservative segment of the Polish media on occasion raised demands for additional
German compensation for wartime destruction.[8] On the German side,
organizations of German expellees charged that the postwar eviction of
Germans from the territories given to Poland was a violation of international law and hence required compensation to the affected families.[9]
Still, no matter how intense the rhetoric, Poles and Germans remained in
agreement on the basic premise that a strong working relationship
between their two countries was essential to the creation of an effective
security architecture in central Europe.

After 1991, Germany took the lead in Europe in lobbying for the inclusion of Poland in NATO. The improvement in Polish-German relations
led to a dramatic increase in Polish-German military cooperation, which
by 1998 was second only to that between Poland and the United States.
The Polish-German-Danish cooperation, including transfer of the headquarters of the tri-national corps to Szczecin in northwestern Poland
(planned for 1999), was indicative of the new spirit of Polish-German
relations, as well as of Poland's acceptance by the Danes as a future partner in NATO.

As Polish security in the West began to improve because of the changed
Polish-German relationship, it generated a renewed interest in Poland's
becoming a "bridge" between East and West.[10] Since 1991, Warsaw has
repeatedly affirmed its determination to distance itself from the idea that
Poland wanted to join NATO in order to become again a "frontier state"
—an alleged outpost of the West against resurgent Russian pressure. Notwithstanding the argument (heard often in the West during the NATO
enlargement debate) that by joining NATO Poland would only aggravate

its relations with Russia, in fact the signing of the 1997 Russia Charter and the Madrid invitation to Poland, Hungary, and the Czech Republic to begin formal membership talks would in the long run contribute to a better Polish-Russian relationship. Though the Russians had been opposed to the enlargement, in 1998 they demonstrated that they were ready to adapt to the new geostrategic environment in central Europe. Regardless of its often harsh rhetoric, Moscow appeared prepared to live with Poland in NATO. And since NATO provided the Poles with a new sense of security vis-à-vis Russia, it became possible for Warsaw to reach out to Moscow without fear of renewed Russian domination.

Poland's "return to the West" by way of Germany and NATO solved the country's strategic dilemma by changing its relationship with Germany and ending its historical dependency on Russia. The 1991 breakthrough in Polish-German relations altered the geostrategic environment in the region and made Poland's aspirations to join NATO realizable. This in turn set the stage for a new chapter in Polish-Russian relations. Only with Poland outside the "gray zone" of European security—that is, anchored in the Western security system—could Polish-Russian relations eventually evolve away from their historical pattern of hostility toward a partnership in which Poland might serve as a "bridge" across central Europe.

Eastern Policy: In Search of a Paradigm

In contrast to Poland's dramatically changed relations with Germany, for most of the 1990s its relations with Russia remained cold, at times bordering on hostile. In the early years of the postcommunist transition, the issue of Soviet troop withdrawal, as well as the mutual indebtedness of the communist regimes, put a severe strain on the relationship. Tension was aggravated by residual Polish insecurity vis-à-vis Russia and by Russia's sense of humiliation over the loss of its superpower status and its influence with the former satellite. For the Poles, overall uncertainty about the outcome of the revolutionary transformation in the Soviet Union compounded the problem, generating confusion in Warsaw and leading at times to contradictory policy choices. Poland's nervous reaction to the failed 1991 coup against Gorbachev, its equally ambiguous response to the bloodshed in Lithuania in the same year, and tension in relations with Russia in 1991 over the future of the Kaliningrad District are cases in point.

Until the formal disintegration of the USSR, Warsaw tried to hedge against a possible reversal of the decomposition of its former hegemon. The Poles pursued a "two-track" policy, on one hand dealing with Moscow on such critical bilateral issues as trade or the status of the Soviet military in Poland while on the other attempting to initiate a dialogue with the rising national independence movements of the non-Russian republics. In the end, the policy satisfied no one and alienated both the Russians and the non-Russian nationalists. From Moscow's point of view, the "two-track" formula amounted to de facto interference in Soviet internal affairs; to the leaders of emerging independence movements in the non-Russian republics, Poland could be faulted for timidity in supporting their cause against Moscow.[11] In either case, the "two-track" policy was hardly a recipe for improving Polish-Russian relations or preparing for future relations with Poland's non-Russian neighbors in the east.

Although the policy was effectively nullified by the dissolution of the Soviet Union in December 1991, by then the damage had already been done. On the Polish side, mistrust was amplified by fresh memories of the country's recent humiliating subjugation by Russia. Taking into account the record of the Second World War, the Cold War legacy, and the early post–Cold War missteps by both Warsaw and Moscow, it should not be surprising that an early improvement in Polish-Russian relations after 1991 was highly unlikely, if possible at all. Rather than moving forward with new initiatives (as was the case in Poland's relations with Germany), Warsaw first had to revisit its past relations with Moscow—something the Russians were clearly reluctant to do. A succession of Polish governments (representing both the right and the left of the country's political spectrum) dealt with Moscow on the premise that a working Polish-Russian relationship could be built only after Poland's continued insecurity vis-à-vis its former hegemon had been taken out of the equation. Likewise, Russia was not yet prepared to accept the reality of an independent Poland tied to the West.

As the design of the European security architecture after the Cold War began to shift away from the early vision of a pan-European system centered on the Conference on Security and Cooperation in Europe (a solution that Russia had supported) and toward a formula based on the existing trans-Atlantic institutions—including NATO enlargement—Moscow's attitude toward Warsaw hardened. To the very end, Russia attempted to halt the enlargement process. As late as 1997 it issued ominous warnings about the consequences of enlargement for its relations with the West and for the arms control regime in particular. Furthermore, since the Polish foreign policy elite across the political spectrum remained unified in the view that Poland's membership in NATO was of vital national interest, until the 1997 NATO summit in Madrid there was precious little room for improving Polish-Russian relations. This was underscored in 1993 when, despite the reemergence of the Polish post-communist left as a powerful factor in the country's politics, Warsaw continued to insist on its right to aspire to NATO membership, denouncing Moscow's objections as an encroachment on Polish sovereignty.[12] President Lech Wałęsa, with his power base in the Solidarity camp, as well as Aleksander Kwaśniewski, his successor and the leader of the postcommunist Union of the Democratic Left (SLD), remained unanimous in their pro-NATO policy. Moscow's response was predictably hostile, as both sides awaited resolution of the NATO enlargement issue. Though during that period the Poles did not see Russia as a threat, they insisted on entering NATO in part because of the residual fear that a resurgent Russia might pose a renewed threat to Polish sovereignty and security.

Between 1991 and 1997, Poland's Eastern policy was built around a series of limited bilateral treaty initiatives intent on stabilizing the country's eastern periphery. These eventually led to improved Polish-Lithuanian and Polish-Ukrainian relations, with Ukraine progressively looking to Poland as its gateway to the West. Polish attempts to enter into a constructive dialogue with Belarus failed once Belarus's President Lukashenka embarked on his quest to restore authoritarian state controls in Minsk. Most importantly, until the 1997 NATO enlargement decision, Russia remained aloof, preferring to deal directly with the United States and NATO in general while still treating Poland as a pawn in a great-power diplomatic game.

In 1998 the Russian attitude toward Poland began to show signs of change. NATO's decision to invite Poland into the alliance, and the offer to Moscow of a special NATO-Russia relationship, ended the enlargement debate and laid the groundwork for a Warsaw-Moscow rapprochement. In this perspective, NATO's 1997 decision to expand into central Europe can be seen as the beginning of a new chapter in Polish-Russian relations, because it brought about a closure to the early post-1991 transition.

In 1998 there was evidence that Poland was ready to seek a new relationship with Russia and that Russia might be willing to respond in kind. This manifested itself in a series of initiatives from Warsaw to reignite the dialogue with Moscow, including a "private visit" to Moscow by Poland's President Aleksander Kwaśniewski in the summer of 1998. Kwaśniewski went to Moscow allegedly to attend the Tchaikovsky competition, but the real goal of the visit was to meet unofficially with Boris Yeltsin. With the NATO enlargement issue finally behind, there were indications that Moscow might be prepared to explore a new relationship with Poland. Reportedly, during their meeting Yeltsin welcomed Kwaśniewski's visit and suggested that in their bilateral discussions the issue of Poland's NATO membership ought to be set aside.[13] Kwaśniewski's greatest coup was getting Yeltsin's public commitment to visit Warsaw—a veritable breakthrough in Polish-Russian relations when considered against the record of the previous several years.

In 1998 the Poles also tried to improve relations with the Russian defense establishment, even issuing a standing invitation from Poland's defense minister, Janusz Onyszkiewicz, to the Russian defense minister to come to Poland. Onyszkiewicz's determination to reopen the Polish-Russian dialogue on military and security issues was underscored by his offer to "clear his calendar of any and all appointments to accommodate the Russian defense minister's schedule."[14] These Polish overtures to Russia, especially the unofficial "Tchaikovsky summit" and Yeltsin's declared readiness to move beyond the issue of NATO enlargement and to explore bilateral Polish-Russian relations in other areas, marked the first step in improving Polish-Russian relations after the bruising enlargement argument.

The new assertiveness in Poland's Eastern policy in 1998 stemmed from its new sense of security after the Madrid invitation to join NATO, as well as from the growing conviction among the Polish political elite that with each passing year, the collapse of the Soviet empire and the rise of the newly independent states became ever more permanent.[15] By 1998 Warsaw had apparently concluded that even if some form of pan-Slavic empire in the east could still be reconstituted, the process would take years. Furthermore, any pressure for a renewed Russian imperial drive in the former Soviet Union would now have to contend with the existence of parliamentary institutions, which should blunt any putative Russian expansionism. Most importantly from Warsaw's vantage point, by the time Russia could again threaten the security of central Europe, Poland would be firmly anchored in both NATO and the European Union.

Although in 1999 it may be difficult to look beyond the most contentious aspects of the 1991–97 Polish-Russian argument over NATO enlargement, one should allow that Poland's membership in NATO may ultimately prove to be the beginning of a future Polish-Russian reconciliation. So long as Poland had remained outside the Western security system, relations between Warsaw and Moscow had focused predominantly on the settling of accounts from the past. Though in the early post-1991 years Polish-Russian relations had been strained, Poland's aspirations to join NATO were reaffirmed by Warsaw and grudgingly recognized by Moscow. Compared with the historical record, this appeared to be a better platform for a serious engagement between the Poles and the Russians on the security and economic interests shared by both.

Russia's apparent willingness in 1998 to reengage with Poland augured well for the future of the dialogue. It was also a vindication of the view that Moscow would eventually reconcile itself to the reality of Poland in NATO, notwithstanding the harsh rhetoric of the early enlargement debate. The apparent thaw in Polish-Russian relations following the 1997 NATO summit in Madrid may also suggest that at the very least, foreign policy issues, including NATO enlargement, were not at the top of Moscow's priorities. For example, despite Moscow's opposition to NATO enlargement, Poland and Russia were able to resolve the Kaliningrad District controversy. The Polish-Russian agreement on cooperation between the northeastern Polish voivodships and the Kaliningrad District was signed on 22 May 1992; it became binding in October of that year and has been in effect ever since. The agreement successfully neutralized a potentially explosive issue of territorial access and bilateral relations along the only remaining stretch of the Polish-Russian border.[16]

Another important step that showed promise for the future of Polish-Russian relations was the resolution of the mutual indebtedness issue that both countries had inherited from the communist era. During a visit to Moscow in November 1996 by Polish Prime Minister Włodzimierz Cimoszewicz—when Russia's stated opposition to Poland's membership in NATO was at its peak—the Poles managed nevertheless to reach an agreement that allowed the Russian central bank to license Polish banks to operate in the Russian Federation. In fact, already in 1995–96 (at the height of the NATO enlargement controversy) one could discern an increase in the Polish-Russian dialogue on trade and other bilateral issues. Finally, one should not discount the importance of personalities: the 1995 election of Aleksander Kwaśniewski and the 1996 reelection of Boris Yeltsin as presidents of Poland and Russia, respectively, eased the personal animosity that had marked the earlier relationship between Lech Wałęsa and Yeltsin. Kwaśniewski, fluent in Russian and a former communist party functionary, could find common ground with Yeltsin much easier than Wałęsa, the founding father of Solidarity.

Military Reform

Since the collapse of the Warsaw Pact, the Polish armed forces have undergone a series of organizational and personnel changes. Like all postcommunist transitions, military reform in Poland was often contentious and painful; at times, it spilled into domestic politics, causing bitter infighting between the parliament and the president. In 1995 it even threatened a constitutional crisis over the issue of civilian control over the military. By 1996, however, the argument over the proper relationship between the military and the government in democratic Poland was settled in the new *Law on the Office of the Defense Minister,* which unequivocally reaffirmed civilian control over the military. The replacement of General Tadeusz Wilecki with General Henryk Szumski as chief of the General Staff marked an end of turmoil within the defense ministry.

The first phase of military reforms between 1991 and 1997 included substantial cuts in manpower, the decision to replace the three Soviet-era military districts (the Silesian District, the Pomeranian District, and the Warsaw District) with four (the Silesian, Pomeranian, and Warsaw Districts and the new Cracow District), the successful development of the foundations for a new NATO-compatible civil-military air traffic control system, and several efforts (largely failed) at equipment modernization. In addition, during that time Poland became an active participant in the Partnership for Peace program (it was the first partner to turn in the "Presentation Document" in Brussels), it continued to contribute to peacekeeping training and operations, and it participated actively in NATO's Bosnia operations.[17]

The current phase of military reform in Poland began with the passage on 9 September 1997 of the program *Army 2012: The Foundation of the Modernization Program for the Armed Forces 1998–2012*.[18] In mid-1998 the program was augmented by the additional "65 itemized objectives" to be achieved in preparation for Poland's formal inclusion in NATO in 1999.

Compared with the earlier reform program, the biggest changes introduced by Army 2012 fell in the areas of command structure and budgetary process. Also, Army 2012 began for the first time to address in earnest the urgent need for reforming the Polish defense industry, with an eye to preserving the residual research-and-development (R&D) potential of the Polish defense sector. Most importantly, the program was viewed from the outset as the key step in adapting the Polish armed forces and the country's entire defense system to NATO standards.[19] This was a radical departure from the earlier reform package, in which planners had attempted to hedge their decisions in order to retain the largest autonomous defense potential possible in case Poland failed in its effort to join NATO. The plan in the early 1990s to develop a new generation of the Polish main battle tank, Goryl, was indicative of that approach. In contrast, Army 2012, along with the "65 objectives" added to the program in 1998, fully reflected Poland's anticipation of impending membership in NATO. Army 2012 was a short-term plan and a long-term forecast in one package. It allowed fifteen years for its implementation, but by design it limited the specifics of the programs to between five and seven years, beyond which the plan outlined only long-term forecasts.

Army 2012 prioritized the phases of reform, beginning with the organizational structure and personnel levels of the armed forces, followed by
training and finally by equipment requirements. The program stipulated
that the armed forces would be reduced in size to 180,000 persons by
the year 2004—below the level called for in the Conventional Forces in
Europe treaty (234,500). By mid-1998, however, it became clear that even
that number might prove unsustainable in light of projected budgetary
constraints; instead, it seemed more realistic to plan for a force no larger
than 160,000 persons.[20] The planned personnel reductions would be
accomplished primarily by cutting the number of draftees serving in the
Polish army and by increasing the ranks of professional personnel. As
outlined in the program, the new emphasis on recruiting professional
NCOs, warrant officers, and soldiers was to be accompanied by a further
shortening of the compulsory military service to twelve months.

Although the program was being tailored to a predominantly draftee-
based military force, it also reflected the direction in which the Polish
army ultimately wanted to go. Army 2012 projected that in fifteen years
the professional component of the armed forces would stand at 61 percent of total personnel, including a reduction in the size of the officer
corps from 46 percent of total personnel in 1997 to a projected 30 percent
by the year 2004, and an increase of NCOs from 23 percent to 40 percent.
The reductions within the officer corps, especially among the most senior
personnel, would be accomplished through retirement and through
retraining and reassignment. This was an especially urgent issue for the
senior officer corps: in 1998 the Polish armed forces had approximately
3,500 colonels and 120 generals. A proposal mooted in mid-1998 suggested that for the Polish officer corps sufficiently to open up the career
advancement path for the younger, Western-trained, junior officers, cuts
in the senior officer corps would have to be as high as 2,000 colonels and
100 generals.[21]

After Madrid, Polish defense priorities were no longer driven by the
need for an "all around" defense, as they had been in the early 1990s.
Hence, the 1997 reorganization program did away with the recently
established four military districts, replacing them with two districts:
the Pomeranian District and the Silesian District, which corresponded

better to the restructured national air defense system. The cities of Byd-
goszcz and Wrocław were selected as headquarters for the two new districts. Also, in a departure from the previous model and in keeping with
the introduction of the Ground Forces Command structure, the new
districts were limited to providing administrative and logistical support
to the army; their command authority would be limited to the envisioned
Territorial Defense Forces (Siły Obrony Terytorialnej).

The two new districts, plus the Air-Mechanized Corps with its command headquarters in Cracow, were established as an interim solution. In
addition, by mid-1998 the Ministry of Defense began to work on a new
structure for local military administration, based on the proposed fifteen
or sixteen new administrative regions (*województwa*)—as envisioned in
the state administration reform debated by the Sejm (parliament)—to
serve as the logistical and support centers of the armed forces.[22] This
aspect of the restructuring betrayed a degree of confusion, especially in
light of the fact that the final shape of Poland's new administrative map
was still being debated in the parliament, with no clear indication at the
time as to how many of the new consolidated *województwa* would replace
the preexisting forty-nine administrative units.[23]

Army 2012 envisioned three phases of reform: 1998–2002, 2003–2007,
and 2008–2012, with most of the structural changes concentrated in the
first two phases. The single most important change in the structure of the
Polish armed forces, already introduced in 1997, was the establishment of
the Ground Forces Command, which would control all the existing military districts—close to two-thirds of the entire Polish army. The most
urgent objectives identified in the Army 2012 program were those articulated in anticipation of Poland's NATO membership and appended to the
plan after Madrid. To meet one of these additional "65 objectives" for
NATO integration, Poland committed itself to making approximately
thirty thousand soldiers from its operational forces available for NATO
missions. The Poles will contribute forces to both NATO's Main Defense
Forces and to its power projection missions within the ACE Rapid Reaction Corps (ARRC) or the Immediate Reaction Forces (IRF). The Twelfth
Mechanized Division in Szczecin and the Eleventh Armored Cavalry
Division are to be part of NATO's Main Defense Forces, with select units

assigned to ARRC duties. The Polish units assigned to NATO's projection missions are the Twenty-fifth Air Cavalry Brigade, the Tenth Armored Cavalry Brigade (part of the Eleventh Armored Cavalry Division), the Twelfth Mechanized Brigade (part of the Twelfth Mechanized Division), and the Sixth Air Assault Brigade, including the Eighteenth Air Assault Battalion and the Sixteenth Paratroopers Battalion (which had served within SFOR in Bosnia and was already fully interoperable with NATO forces).

Another short-term goal for NATO membership was Poland's preparation of two naval bases, one in Gdynia and one in Świnoujście, as well as airfields in Malbork and Poznań-Krzesiny (with three additional airfields to be selected at a later date), for use by NATO forces. In addition, storage depots in Przewóz-Potok and Cybowo would be made usable for NATO operations, including support for reinforcements and stock replenishment. In order to make these facilities suitable for NATO use, the Polish government promised to upgrade its air traffic control and communications equipment, as well as its refueling and docking systems.

Military training was another area in which the Polish armed forces needed to improve in their preparation for NATO membership. In 1997–98, the existing training programs (especially in the Polish Air Force) were below NATO requirements. Warsaw was aware that in order to bring its armed forces more in line with NATO's, it had to begin a vigorous effort to train more NCOs while limiting the commissioning of officers. The increase in the NCO corps, in addition to the retirement or reassignment of a large number of older senior officers, was critical to transforming the Polish army into a Western military force. In order to make the training and educational systems more responsive to NATO requirements, Army 2012 made three officer academies directly subordinated to the Ground Forces Command; these were the Tadeusz Kościuszko Officer School in Wrocław (Wyższa Szkoła Oficerska im. Tadeusza Kościuszki), the Stefan Czarniecki Officer School in Poznań (Wyższa Szkoła Oficerska im. Stefana Czarnieckiego), and the Józef Bem Officer School in Toruń (Wyższa Szkoła Oficerska im. gen. Józefa Bema).

The defense ministry also needed to limit its nonessential expenditures. In 1997 it became clear that it was no longer able to support the infrastructure inherited by the Polish armed forces from the Warsaw Pact era, nor was there any need for it in light of the new missions for the Polish army in NATO. Considering how critical some of the Polish army installations were to the economic survival of Poland's smaller, less-affluent communities, efforts to close them down between 1991 and 1997 had met with only limited success. In 1998, almost a decade after the collapse of communism, the defense ministry still maintained airfields, railroad ramps, barracks, storage depots, and medical facilities that could easily support an army of half a million.[24] Army 2012 finally targeted specific sharp cuts in the infrastructure, calling for a 35-percent reduction by 2012, with 20 percent of the cuts to fall before 2003.

In 1998 the equipment modernization program remained the most hotly debated issue within the Polish defense establishment. The argument centered on the question of "offset contracts" to be awarded to Polish defense manufacturers by Western suppliers as a condition of military contracts. In the Polish defense sector, where the Solidarity trade union was still a potent political force, the needs of the armed forces and the interests of the union often clashed. In 1997 the Polish government identified eleven weapons programs that it considered central to its planned equipment modernization program, including communication and command systems, air defense systems (including the Loara program), anti-tank systems, helicopters (the Huzar program), and armor (especially a wheeled personnel carrier).[25] Other programs, including naval ships, additional ground forces equipment, small arms, and support vehicles, were given lower priority. In fact, considering the budgetary constraints under which the defense ministry operated, most of the "second priority" items outlined in the modernization program constituted a wish list rather than realizable goals.

A glaring omission among the eleven weapons programs identified in the Army 2012 equipment modernization plan was the acquisition of a multipurpose fighter aircraft (F-16 type). Although Polish defense officials frequently declared the purchase of F-16s or F-18s as one of their highest priorities, the prohibitive cost required a separate budgetary authorization by the Sejm, which as of 1998 was not forthcoming.

Regardless of the ultimate size of the restructured Polish armed forces, it was clear that Army 2012 assumed the preservation of the existing three services: the ground forces, the air and air defense forces (consolidated after the dissolution of the Warsaw Pact), and the navy. The ground forces would include the operational forces and the territorial defense forces. Among the "65 objectives" for NATO integration appended to the program, the most important were improvements to communications, infrastructure, and quality of staff.[26] In 1998 the Poles focused their resources mainly on modernization of the communications systems and on training the personnel who would operate the equipment.

Defense Budget

No matter how sophisticated long-range plans for military reform may be, budgetary allocations ultimately determine their success. The Polish military modernization program in preparation for NATO membership is no exception. The ability to implement the proposed reforms even partially, and hence Poland's ability to contribute substantially to the military potential of NATO, hinges ultimately on the size of the defense budget.

The Army 2012 program stipulated Poland's ability to develop forces interoperable with NATO based on a projected increase in military spending equal to 3 percent of GDP annually. This was based on a commitment the government had made in 1994 and which had been confirmed by the Sejm on 16 February 1995. The government subsequently revised the 1995 projections, with the proviso that whereas between 2003 and 2012 defense expenditures would grow at the overall rate of increase of the state budget, between 1998 and 2012 they would average 3.2 percent of GDP.

In 1998, the key to the projected defense spending levels was an anticipated average GDP growth rate of 4.2 percent. In addition, the Ministry of Defense expected to net 120 million new Polish złotys (PLN) annually (approximately 35 million dollars) from the sale of assets no longer needed by the armed forces, to be spent directly on equipment modernization;[27] the total value of such assets was estimated at close to 2 billion PLN ($570 million). According to the defense ministry's 1997 projections, the structure of defense expenditures would shift from the currently dominant personnel costs (personnel, 51 percent; training and maintenance, 33 percent; equipment purchases and R&D, 16 percent) to a pattern in 2012 in which personnel and maintenance costs would be substantially curtailed while equipment purchases were increased (personnel, 34 percent; training and maintenance, 29 percent; equipment purchases and R&D, 37 percent). Notwithstanding these projections, the structure of the Polish defense budget for 1998 saw a further increase in personnel costs (to 63 percent) and a further decrease in equipment modernization spending (to 12 percent).[28]

The lower-than-expected budgets remained a serious constraint on Polish planners, putting in question the equipment modernization program, especially the ambitious plan to purchase modern Western aircraft and to develop the Polish attack helicopter Huzar and the indigenous mobile anti-aircraft platform Loara. As of 1998, the Poles had not reached the recommended 3 percent of GDP level; in 1997 the defense budget stood at 2.3 percent of GDP, and in 1998 it was projected at 2.26 percent (possibly as high as 2.29 percent).[29] In real terms, however, the budget for 1998 was 4.9 percent larger than that for 1997—an encouraging development in the first year of implementation of the Army 2012 program (tables 2.1 and 2.2).[30] More importantly, Poland's defense expenditures as a percentage of GDP (2.3 percent of the GDP averaged by Poland from 1995 through 1997, as well as the projected 2.26 percent of GDP for 1998) placed it at the higher end of the European average, among the major contributors to NATO (table 2.3). In effect, although the budget fell short of the promised 3 percent of GDP, it still allowed Poland sufficient resources to develop an effective—if carefully targeted—modernization program.

By the second half of 1998, as the date for Poland's formal inclusion in NATO approached, the reform had achieved significant progress in transforming the organizational structure of the country's defense establishment, especially by resolving the issue of civilian control over the military —an issue that had raised serious concerns in the West during the last years of the Wałęsa presidency. In addition, despite continuing delays in the area of equipment modernization and a budget that consistently fell

TABLE 2.1
Ministry of Defense (MOD) Budget Expenditures Relative to GDP and Total State
Budget, 1991–1998, in Millions of PLNs (Current Prices)

Year	GDP	State Budget Expenditures	Total MOD Budget	National Defense Budget
1991	80,882.9	24,185.8	1,821.2	1,807.1
1992	114,944.2	38,189.0	2,564.4	2,536.5
1993	155,780.0	50,242.8	3,846.5	3,309.2
1994	210,407.3	68,865.0	5,117.0	4,127.5
1995	286,000.0	91,169.7	6,594.4	5,249.4
1996	357,200.0	108,661.3	8,313.2	6,003.3
1997	437,300.0	127,919.8	10,076.7	7,275.0
Budget bill for 1998	511,100.0	143,440.8	11,550.3	8,263.9
1998	511,100.0	143,440.8	11,678.7[a]	8,345.1

Source: *Budget MoND 1998* (Warsaw: Budgetary Department Press and Information Office, Ministry of Defense, 1998), 14.

[a] Includes additional monies for pay raises for MOD employees (approximately 100 million PLN), costs related to NATO enlargement (15.8 million PLN), and the cost of the Polish contingent in Bosnia (12.6 million PLN).

short of the promised 3 percent of GDP, the Poles had made good progress in modernizing their communications and coupling their analog technology with NATO's digital systems. The complete reequipment of the Polish armed forces that would bring them up to NATO standards remained a task that by Warsaw's own admission would take at least fifteen years to complete and would cost an estimated US $7.76 billion.[31] This meant that the Poles would have to spend at least 20 percent of their defense budget on new equipment each year for the duration of the Army 2012 modernization program—a goal that in 1998 the defense ministry already recognized as unrealistic. In the final analysis, Warsaw and Brussels will have to reach a decision about the extent to which additional NATO resources might be necessary to complete the Polish equipment

TABLE 2.2
Ministry of Defense (MOD) Budget Expenditures as Percentage of GDP and Total State
Budget, 1991–1998

Year	Percentage of GDP		Percentage of State Budget	
	Total MOD Budget	National Defense	Total MOD Budget	National Defense
1991	2.25	2.23	7.53	7.47
1992	2.23	2.21	6.72	6.64
1993	2.47	2.12	7.66	6.59
1994	2.43	1.96	7.43	5.99
1995	2.31	1.84	7.23	5.76
1996	2.33	1.68	7.65	5.52
1997	2.30	1.66	7.88	5.69
Budget bill for 1998	2.26	1.62	8.05	5.76
1998	2.29	1.63	8.14	5.82

Source: *Budget MoND 1998* (Warsaw: Budgetary Department Press and Information Office, Ministry of Defense, 1998), 14.

modernization program, or whether a more suitable approach might be one that selectively targets areas in which NATO's mission and Polish needs converge.

Still, even within existing budgetary constraints, in 1998 Poland was capable of increasing its contribution to NATO by further streamlining its organizational structure and better managing its available resources. This point may be illustrated by looking at Warsaw's 1998 per-soldier expenditure compared with those of other states. Although Poland's expenditure—the equivalent of US $13,682—was nowhere near the expenditures of developed European NATO members or of other major European militaries (for example, Germany was spending $93,750, Denmark, $97,264, Holland, $126,783, and the United Kingdom, $146,903), the Poles were still outspending Turkey ($10,642) by more than $3,000 and were almost on a par with Switzerland ($13,759).[32] Taken in the

TABLE 2.3
Defense Expenditures of Poland and NATO Member States as Percentage of GDP,
1985–1997

Country	Average 1985–89	Average 1990–94	1995	1996	1997
Belgium	2.8	2.0	1.7	1.6	1.6
Denmark	2.1	2.0	1.8	1.8	1.7
France	3.8	3.5	3.1	3.0	3.0
Germany	3.0	2.2	1.7	1.7	1.6
Greece	5.1	4.5	4.4	4.5	4.6
Italy	2.3	2.1	1.8	1.9	1.9
Luxembourg	1.0	0.9	0.8	0.8	0.8
Netherlands	2.9	2.4	2.0	2.0	1.9
Norway	2.9	2.8	2.3	2.4	2.2
Portugal	2.8	2.7	2.7	2.5	2.6
Spain	2.2	1.7	1.5	1.5	1.4
Turkey	3.3	3.8	3.9	4.1	4.3
United Kingdom	4.5	3.8	3.1	3.0	2.8
NATO Europe	3.3	2.7	2.3	2.3	2.2
United States	6.0	4.7	3.8	3.6	3.4
Poland	3.1	2.4	2.3	2.3	2.3

Source: *Budget MoND 1998* (Warsaw: Budgetary Department Press and Information Office, Ministry of Defense, 1998), 16.

context of the country's overall GDP, the figure represented a considerable commitment of resources, especially in light of the relatively low pay scale in the Polish army.

In 1998 the statistical Polish soldier "cost less" than his NATO equivalent. This led some in the General Staff to argue that Poland would be able to achieve disproportionately higher qualitative results by further reducing the size of its armed forces and thereby increasing per capita spending.[33] The most radical proposal, mooted in mid-1998, was to consider reducing the size of the Polish armed forces to as few as eighty thousand personnel and simultaneously to begin the transition to a professional army. Under this plan, money would have been spent on the ground forces, the air force, and the support infrastructure necessary for cooperation with NATO; the navy would have been limited to coast guard functions. The proposal was based on the premise that the current size of the Polish armed forces made the available resources per soldier too low to train and retain quality professionals. Therefore, unless the army were reduced by at least 50 percent of its 1998 total, it would have no choice but to rely on the draft system for the foreseeable future, notwithstanding official assertions that it intended to increase its professional ranks down the line. For example, in 1998 the monthly pay for a private in the Polish army was 1,160 PLN (approximately $330). Even more poignant was the virtual absence of a real pay differential between privates and NCOs; a section commander, for example, made 1,320 PLN ($377) per month, and a company quartermaster sergeant, 1,511 PLN ($431). Even at officer rank, pay levels were low: in 1998 a company commander made 1,690 PLN ($482) per month, a battalion commander, 1,899 PLN ($542), and a regiment commander, 3,002 PLN ($857). In 1998 the highest paid officer in the Polish armed forces, the chief of the General Staff, earned 7,052 PLN ($2,014) per month.

Even if the 1998 military pay scale did not adequately reflect the military standard of living in Poland, because it did not allow for supplemental benefits, the numbers and their spread reflected a pattern that seemed to have persisted from the communist era, whereby rank rather than pay was used as a reward for service. The communist practice of relying on easy promotions had distorted the Polish army's structure, creating what some officers jokingly referred to as an "army of colonels"—a military force heavily weighted at the top, with weak junior officer and NCO corps. Those in the General Staff and the defense ministry who in 1998 called for a dramatic reduction in the size of the Polish armed forces pointed out that unless resources were freed to "invest in people," the Polish army would continue to fight a losing battle in trying to make the transition to a Western-style military. The logical conclusion of their argument was to eliminate the draft altogether and to create a professional Polish army at the earliest possible date.

The Balance Sheet: Political Contribution

The formation and realignment of alliances are historically significant
only insofar as they generate lasting shifts in the power equation.
Nowhere has this been truer in recent years than in the case of NATO's
enlargement into central Europe, especially the inclusion of Poland as a
full-fledged NATO member. Although one should not discount the real, if
initially modest, Polish military contribution, the core of Poland's value
to NATO will ultimately rest in the political arena.

The redefinition of Polish-German relations in the context of NATO,
and its encouraging implications for the future of Polish-Russian relations, may bring about a lasting change in the security environment of
central Europe. Poland's membership in NATO has the potential to dramatically change the regional security equation and, ultimately, to do away
with a fundamental historical tenet of European geopolitics: German-
Russian competition for regional domination.

When viewed from Warsaw, Poland's inclusion in NATO is not only
a matter of national security but also a powerful historical symbol. In
the eyes of the Poles, the 1997 allied decision to include their country in
the first batch of new entrants marks the final break with the legacy of the
half-century of Soviet control. It makes real Poland's historical aspirations
to reestablish its Western ties and to develop a Western political identity.
On yet another level, NATO membership solves the Polish historical
dilemma of being a medium-size power caught between two dominant
states vying for regional supremacy. It settles the issue of Polish-German
relations by locking it into the trans-Atlantic equation. Finally, NATO
membership addresses the remaining Polish security concern—Poland's
residual fear of Russian resurgence and renewed pressure from the east.

Among the more interesting aspects of Poland's adaptation to the
consecutive stages of the enlargement process is its growing appreciation
of NATO not just as a defensive alliance but also as the indispensable
skeleton of a larger Euro-Atlantic security system.[34] The Poles consider
NATO's close links to the European Union, the West European Union,
and the Council of Europe to be the essential elements of the emerging
Euro-Atlantic security architecture. In the context of NATO's evolving
structure and mission, the Poles have set out as their central national

security objective the achievement of full participation in the broadest range of European institutions possible.

The Poles have argued that their country—after Germany—will be the key military partner of the United States in central Europe. Although Germany and Poland will indeed provide the bulk of NATO forces in the east, this belief takes an excessively narrow and one-sided view of Poland's potential value to the alliance. The real significance of Poland in NATO rests in its ability to channel the relationship between the West and Russia. Considering the torturous history of Russian-Polish relations, at a minimum Poland in NATO cannot become a liability to the alliance; at a maximum it should become an asset. Since for NATO the relationship with Russia will for the foreseeable future remain its highest priority in the east, Poland's relative political value in NATO will be measured by its ability to engage Russia effectively.

One of the more promising ancillary effects of Poland's drive to join NATO has been Warsaw's renewed interest in its relations with the East. Admittedly, prospects for Polish-Russian reconciliation (along the lines of the rapidly progressing Polish-German relationship) are still remote; however, they ought not to be dismissed out of hand. As a NATO member Warsaw will find itself more securely tied to the West, and thus it will be more likely to reevaluate the burden of its three hundred years of relations with Moscow. In this way, rather than in terms of a purely military contribution, Poland may indeed become a "special ally" to the United States in central Europe on matters specific to the region.[35]

On a more practical level, it remains to be seen how successfully the Polish public will adapt to the realities of NATO membership and to the new role the Polish armed forces will play in NATO. Although there is broad public support in Poland for NATO membership, it is unclear whether Polish society understands the full implications of alliance obligations. There is also a historically determined sense of unease about changing the traditional concepts of national security. Though anti-NATO sentiments in Poland are rare, the country's historical experience in World War II mitigates against placing excessive confidence in external security guarantees in general. It was that historical determinant that in 1991–95 made the General Staff believe that Poland should preserve a large indigenous military force, regardless of budgetary constraints and the priority of establishing interoperability with NATO. One should remember that Polish nationalism had endured in the armed forces throughout the communist era. At the time, the Poles had identified military autonomy with patriotism, and only recently have they begun to come to terms with the idea of "de-nationalizing" the country's security policy within NATO.

Not surprisingly, to the majority of Poles today NATO's paramount value still rests in its deterrent function against another aggression from the east. This view argues that Poland must be prepared to resist an attack long enough to allow the allies to move; otherwise, it risks a repetition of 1939, when France and Britain did not act in Poland's defense in part because Poland had been defeated in a matter of weeks. In this view, Poland must give NATO sufficient time to activate Article 5—that is, it must have its own contingency plan to fight a delayed action against the aggressor.[36] It will take time before this view, defined by the experience of World War II and the Cold War, is fully reconciled with NATO's concept of security.

One such alternative conception for Poland was offered by Zbigniew Brzezinski at a conference in Cracow in July 1998. Brzezinski argued that Poland needed both a small professional army and a draft-based "home army"—a territorial defense force that would train to resist in the event of foreign occupation. The first would participate in NATO defense planning and contribute to the fulfillment of Poland's allied defense obligations; the second would plan to continue resisting the enemy on the home territory lost to the aggressor, harassing its forces and keeping the resistance alive.[37] In 1998 it was not yet clear whether the Poles would find a formula that successfully spoke to both their history and the present-day reality of NATO.

Another domestic policy issue that came into focus in 1998 concerned Polish society's support for the kind of allied missions that the new NATO would likely undertake. Support for Poland's membership in NATO has run consistently high, with close to 80 percent of the population in 1997 in favor of it. It is not clear, however, that the level of support would remain equally high in the event Poles were asked to send their conscripts out of the country not for peacekeeping duties (which have historically enjoyed a very high level of support in Poland) but to fight a war as part of Poland's allied obligations. Throughout the entire process of NATO enlargement, there was little discussion in Poland of the impact NATO membership might have on the country's military ethos. The Poles have a proud historical record of sacrifice and military prowess in defense of the motherland and in fighting abroad for the restoration of their country's independence. Still, the generally accepted concept of the Polish soldier is tied closely to the idea of defense of the national territory. Since in the foreseeable future Poland will have to rely on an army consisting largely of draftees, the procedures under which its army will be deployed outside the country have to be addressed in Sejm legislation.

The Balance Sheet: Military Contribution

Although second to the foreign policy dimension in overall importance, Poland's military contribution to NATO will be significant. In line with the changing concept of national security, the Polish armed forces have been sufficiently reformed to be a meaningful part of NATO, in terms of both territorial defense and alliance-wide missions.[38] In comparison with the political issues, especially the impact of Poland's inclusion in NATO on the region's security, the practical side of Polish military modernization is less important. A broad modernization program that would bring the entire Polish armed forces close to the NATO standard (as defined by the principle contributors) simply cannot be sustained under the present Polish budgetary reality.

The Poles need to invest first and foremost in the training and retention of their military personnel in order to complete the reform program. The administrative changes of the past decade, especially the institutional restructuring of the relationship between the Ministry of Defense and the General Staff, have effectively dealt with the organizational questions of civil-military relations in Poland. As of 1998 Poland had in place an organizational framework to make its military a full member of NATO. Now it needed to fill that institutional skeleton with personnel who would transform the Polish armed forces into a Western army. This transformation would include the dissemination of such basic skills as the requisite fluency in English. In the most practical sense, in 1998 the English language proficiency of the more senior officers was generally inferior to that of the junior officers, and senior officers also lacked the experience of being exposed to Western educational institutions. This could be addressed either through additional and time-consuming intensive language training for the senior officer corps or by rapidly promoting the younger officers.[39] Although, as Defense Minister Janusz Onyszkiewicz pointed out, more than 90 percent of the officers on active duty in 1998 had been promoted or commissioned after 1989,[40] this did not necessarily mean that the younger, Western-educated generation of Polish officers was moving to center stage.

Equipment modernization is another issue that will have to be approached with an eye to the long-term interests of the Polish army and NATO. So far, it has been hopelessly tied up in the politics of reform in the country's defense industry. By 1998, the early attempt to preserve the defense sector by creating a national military-industries consortium of twelve key plants was clearly failing. In early 1998, two-thirds of forty-five defense establishments in Poland were heavily in debt, owing more than 1 billion PLN (over $289 million at the exchange rate of early 1998). To address the problem, the government was considering declaring thirty of those enterprises "national strategic assets" and bringing them under the National Military Industries Fund. The plan would allow for the privatization of some factories, but it would retain a majority state ownership in the defense sector. According to Deputy Minister of the Economy Dariusz Klimek, the defense industry would begin the process of limited privatization in 2001, but with the stipulation that no major layoffs would result.[41]

In short, as of 1998 the power of the defense industry lobby (*zbrojeniówka*) was proving strong enough to derail a cost-benefit approach to the equipment modernization of the Polish armed forces. Some reductions in Poland's ambitious procurement program had taken place, notwithstanding the political fallout from these decisions. For example, in addition to abandoning the Iryda support aircraft project, the defense ministry also eliminated the Goryl tank program, which would have replaced the currently produced Polish version of the T-72; instead, in a compromise move intended to preserve employment at the Łabędy tank factory and to maintain a source of spare parts, the production of a modified T-72 version was approved. The decision was intended as a half-measure to facilitate the eventual conversion of the Łabędy tank line to civilian production. In 1998 the Loara program remained active, though like all other Polish R&D and procurement programs, it was virtually on hold pending budget decisions.

The most visible among the procurement issues that continued to polarize the military and the defense industry in 1998 was the Huzar program, which sought to adapt the Sokół civilian helicopter platform to military applications. From the start, the story of the Huzar had been fraught with intrigue and, more recently, with allegations of downright corruption in the choosing of two Israeli missile and electronics systems over comparable American or western European equipment. Arguments over alleged improprieties in the awarding of the Israeli contract obscured the basic weakness of the entire undertaking: the Huzar represented a 1970s technology that was only marginally suitable for use as a military attack helicopter.[42]

In August 1998, a report of an official inquiry into the Huzar program, conducted by the Highest Control Chamber (Najwyższa Izba Kontroli) of the parliament, revealed that the awarding of the contract for the missile and electronic equipment to Israeli firms had been procedurally flawed—the strongest indication to date that the program had been marred by corruption and influence peddling.[43] Still, in 1998 the defense ministry appeared committed to go ahead with the Huzar on the premise that the Sokół platform was viable; the government would concede only that the Israeli contract had become a political liability.[44] This position was also supported by the Bureau of National Security, a national security council to President Kwaśniewski.[45]

There is no question that a reform of the Polish defense sector is badly needed and that Poland needs to preserve its core capacity. However, some defense officials have suggested that instead of attempting to build entire weapon systems "in-house," the Polish defense sector would likely have benefited more by entering into subcontracting agreements with NATO weapons manufacturers. This would have allowed for the transfer of the necessary technological skills to Poland while also tying the Polish defense industry into the allied system.[46] As Poland assumes its place in NATO, this may ultimately prove to be a better approach to modernizing its defense sector.

Conclusion

Poland clearly has the political will, at the level of both the government and the society at large, to make a contribution to NATO. In the strictly military area, it has shown that it can create a force interoperable with NATO's. Despite the equipment modernization problems, NATO can reasonably expect—judging from the pace of reform and the amount of resources committed to it—that by the year 2003 Poland will have restructured its forces into three corps. In addition, the Ground Forces Command should be fully operational and capable of interacting with NATO commands. Likewise, the Polish navy should have completed its personnel reductions and restructuring and have the degree of integration with the Danish and German navies that will permit joint patrol duties in the Baltic Sea.

As the Polish army becomes part of NATO forces, the equipment modernization program will remain very much a work in progress. Still, this issue is less important than it might appear. The argument that the Polish army is not up to NATO standards and that the cost of its modernization would be an excessive burden on Poland and on NATO needs to be reexamined. Although it is certainly true that the Polish army as a whole is nowhere near the levels of readiness, training, and equipment of the United States armed forces or the forces of the United Kingdom or Germany, one should keep in mind that other members of the alliance (especially those comparable to Poland in size and economic potential) are not necessarily superior. If instead of the United States or the United Kingdom one takes as a point of reference the armed forces of Spain, Turkey, or Greece, the potential contribution of the Polish army looks quite different. In contrast to another case of NATO enlargement into central Europe—the inclusion of the Federal Republic of Germany—the inclusion of Poland does not require a substantial expansion of the allied infrastructure. Indeed, Poland can become a meaningfully contributing member of NATO with relatively moderate expenditures targeted at the infrastructure and communications to ensure compatibility.

After 1999 the Polish defense ministry and the General Staff will probably revisit the question of how deep the drawdown of the Polish forces should ultimately be. In 1998 only the most radical among the senior officer corps were calling for the transition to a small, fully professional army. Whatever the conclusion, the debate is bound to be a heated one, for it will tackle assumptions about the character of the Polish armed forces that have been in place for generations. Other aspects of the proposed future restructuring, such as the phased-in elimination of obsolete hardware (especially in the Polish air force), are unlikely to cause much dissent. Since the air force expects eventual reequipment with Western aircraft, it can quickly shed its MiG-21s while retaining its Su-22 and MiG 29 aircraft for the transition period. Likewise, the Polish armed forces clearly need to acquire a helicopter for their air cavalry brigade, though it is debatable whether the Huzar program is the best the country can do. A more productive way for the Poles to approach their equipment acquisition program might be to negotiate direct purchases from Western firms while entering into cooperative manufacturing arrangements as part of the contract. Considering the overall state of the Polish defense sector, the best route to its modernization appears to lead through joint-venture manufacturing agreements, even if that means giving up some of its engineering and design capacity inherited from the Warsaw Pact era. Similarly, concerning the need for a high-performance aircraft, the best interim solution might be a leasing arrangement in place of an outright purchase.

In the final analysis, Poland's membership in NATO will be tested first and foremost in its political dimension, especially its role in NATO's relations with Russia and other post-Soviet states. As Poland becomes America's key "new ally" in central Europe, the success or failure of its NATO membership will have far-reaching implications for the future of the alliance enlargement plans. If Poland's membership in NATO becomes ultimately a liability, it may lead to a political backlash in Washington and Brussels and effectively foreclose any prospects for further expansion. If it proves to be a success, the enlargement issue may be revisited early in the next century.

Notes

1. Polish economic reform began in January 1990 with a radical shock therapy program, the so-called Balcerowicz Plan. In 1998, the father of the Polish economic reform, Finance Minister Leszek Balcerowicz, called for replacing the Polish tax code with a flat tax.

2. It is important to note that the Soviet position in 1990 called initially for the simultaneous dissolution of both the WTO and NATO as the prerequisite for the unification of Germany.

3. This interwar Polish attempt to navigate between Germany and Russia was aptly described by the founding father of the Second Republic, Marshal Józef Piłsudski, when he spoke of his country's "sitting on two shaky stools, of which one would eventually have to collapse."

4. Although the Polish communist regime launched an elaborate propaganda campaign claiming that the forcible transfer of ethnic Poles from the areas taken by the Soviet Union in the east to the former German territories in the west was a "repatriation"—a return to the "prehistoric Polish lands"—the fact remained that one-third of the territory of the Polish state reconstituted after the war had previously belonged to Germany.

5. The extent of Poland's concern over the border issue is best seen in the fact that the Mazowiecki government, the first postcommunist government in Poland, was considering delaying negotiation on Soviet troop withdrawal from Poland until after the borders had been explicitly recognized by Germany.

6. Indeed, prior to the signing of the 1991 Polish-German agreements, Polish politicians often privately raised their fears of "another Rapallo"—a reference to the 1922 German-Soviet treaty leading to rapprochement between Berlin and Moscow, which dramatically degraded Poland's security position between the two wars. Source: the author's meeting with Polish parliamentarians, January 1991.

7. A good, concise discussion of the key aspects of Polish-German relations can be found in Hanna Suchocka, "Polsko-niemieckie stosunki dzisiaj," in Mirosław Piotrowski, ed., *Polityka integracyjna Niemcy-Polska* (Lublin: Wydawnictwo Towarzystwa Naukowego Katolickiego Universytetu Lubelskiego, 1997), 145–159.

8. "D-marki za zniszczenie Warszawy," *Życie Warszawy,* 9 July 1998.

9. The issue of former German property on Polish territory was joined on account of an exchange of letters between Warsaw and Bonn on 17 June 1991, indicating the German position that the 1991 bilateral treaty did not settle the property question—a position which the Polish side rejected. See Krzysztof Skubiszewski, "Niemcy, nie piszcie historii na nowo," *Gazeta Wyborcza,* 9 July 1998.

10. See Jan Karski, *Polska powinna stać się pomostem miedzy narodami Europy Zachodniej i jej wschodnimi sąsiadami* (Łódź: Wydawnictwo Universytetu Łódzkiego, 1997).

11. The leadership of Lithuania's Sajudis in particular appeared suspicious of

Poland's intentions, viewing Skubiszewski's "two-track" Eastern policy as an attempt by Warsaw to leverage the relationship as a means of gaining a stronger position with Moscow.

12. "Założenia polskiej polityki bezpieczeństwa" and "Polityka bezpieczeństwa i strategia obronna Rzeczpospolitej Polskiej" *Wojsko Polskie: Informator '95* (Warsaw: Wydawnictwo Bellona, 1995), 12–32.

13. Witold Laskowski, "Koncerty prezydenta," *Wprost,* 12 July 1998.

14. The author's conversation with Defense Minister Janusz Onyszkiewicz, Ministry of National Defense, Warsaw, Poland, 6 July 1998.

15. Stanisław Bieleń, "Kierunki polityki wschodniej III RP," *Patrząc na Wschód: Z problematyki polityki wschodniej III RP* (Warsaw: Centrum Badań Wschodnich Universytetu Warszawskiego, 1997), 15.

16. The status of the Kaliningrad District was an early stumbling block in Polish-Russian relations, as well as a factor in Russia's and Poland's relations with Germany. Early post-Soviet plans for the future of the rump territory, including a mooted German proposal to use Kaliningrad as the area of resettlement for the remaining Volga Germans, created considerable concern in Warsaw over the future of Polish-German relations. The Russians subsequently increased the tension by raising the issue of extraterritorial access to their military installations in Baltiysk.

17. For a discussion of Polish military reform, see Andrew A. Michta, *Soldier-Citizen: The Politics of the Polish Army after Communism* (New York: St. Martin's Press, 1997).

18. *Armia 2012: Założenia programu modernizacji Sił Zbrojnych w latach 1988–2012* (Warsaw: Ministry of National Defense, 1998).

19. Army 2012 was accepted by the Council of Ministers, but the government did not give the document the status of a decree. Therefore, although binding on all government agencies, the program was also left open to future modifications (some introduced in 1998) to accommodate additional NATO requirements that would arise in the process of NATO enlargement.

20. The author's interviews at the Ministry of Defense, Warsaw, July 1998.

21. The author's conversations with senior officers at the Ministry of Defense, Warsaw, July 1998.

22. The author's conversation with Minister of Defense Janusz Onyszkiewicz, Warsaw, 6 July 1998.

23. The question of the new administrative divisions was finally settled in late July 1998 with a compromise between the parliament and the president that established sixteen new administrative regions.

24. At peak strength in the 1980s, the Polish armed forces were 400,000 strong.

25. Despite constant discussion of the need for an F-16 type fighter aircraft, the Polish armed forces appear to have greater need for a wheeled armored personnel carrier. (The author's conversation with General Franciszek Gągor, director of the Department of Foreign Military Affairs, Ministry of Defense, Warsaw, 7 July 1998.)

26. The author's conversation with Ryszard Król, director of the NATO Department in the Ministry of National Defense, Warsaw, 8 July 1998.

27. In mid-1998, 1 US dollar equaled about 3.4 PLN. In all my calculations in this chapter I rounded the exchange rate off at the ratio of 1 dollar to 3.5 PLN to allow for the projected devaluation of the złoty in 1998.

28. *Basic Information on the MoND Budget for 1998* (Warsaw: Budgetary Department Press and Information Office, Ministry of National Defense, 1998), 10.

29. The Polish defense budget includes both appropriations that go directly to the armed forces and additional appropriations that go to health care, social welfare programs, state administration costs, and so forth. Therefore, in order to assess the actual contribution to the armed forces, in the tables in this chapter the figures actually allocated for national defense are separated from the total Ministry of Defense budget. The actual figures remain a subject of some controversy. Since the Polish defense budget contains items not normally found in the defense budgets of other NATO members (such as pre-1990-era retirement payments), it could be argued that in 1998 the Poles would spend about 2.0 percent of GDP, not 2.6 percent as itemized in the budget.

30. *Basic Information on the MoND Budget for 1998,* 7.

31. Data taken from *Estimated Cost of NATO Enlargement: A Contribution to the Debate* (Washington: Embassy of the Republic of Poland, 1998).

32. *Basic Information on the MoND Budget for 1998,* 18.

33. The author's interviews at the Ministry of Defense, Warsaw, July 1998.

34. See Julian Kaczmarek and Adam Skowroński, *Bezpieczeństwo: Świat Europa-Polska* (Wrocław: Atlas, 1998), 146–156.

35. The author's conversation with Minister Maciej Kozłowski, undersecretary of state in the Polish Ministry of Foreign Affairs, Warsaw, 8 July 1998.

36. Jan Nowak Jeziorański, "Słoń i jeż," *Wprost,* 19 July 1998.

37. Ibid.

38. Kaczmarek and Skowroński, *Bezpieczeństwo,* 170–171.

39. The problem of poor English language skills is one of the most difficult issues confronting the Polish armed forces. It goes beyond the planning phases and becomes critical to actual operation on the battlefield, where high levels of emotion and the "noise" of the battle make the ability to communicate effectively and quickly with other NATO units critical to accomplishing a mission.

40. The author's conversation with Defense Minister Janusz Onyszkiewicz, Warsaw, 6 July 1998.

41. "Polish Factories under Threat of Closure," *Jane's Defence Weekly,* 16 July 1998.

42. In conversations with the author in 1997 and 1998, people familiar with the Huzar project (both in Poland and in the US) suggested that the Sokół platform was poorly suited to carry the amount of equipment and armor required for the missions envisioned by the Polish army.

43. "NIK: nieprawidłowości w programie 'Huzar,'" *Rzeczpospolita,* 1 August 1998.

44. The author's conversation with Defense Minister Janusz Onyszkiewicz, Warsaw, 6 July 1998.

45. The author's conversation with Colonel Marek Dukaczewski, Warsaw, 8 July 1998.

46. Another example of defense industry politics prevailing over the needs of the Polish armed forces was the fiasco of the Iryda, a support aircraft the army was forced to accept because of pressure from the parliament and heavy lobbying by Solidarity unionists from the defense sector. Following several spectacular crashes (and the death of two test pilots), the Iryda program was finally abandoned. A subsequent investigation revealed that the funds for the Iryda had not even been properly appropriated in the first place.

3 Hungary

AN OUTPOST ON THE TROUBLED PERIPHERY

ZOLTAN BARANY

NATO membership has been the quintessential foreign policy goal of Hungarian governments since 1990. Seven years after Gyula Horn—then foreign minister of the last communist government—publicly speculated about the plausibility of his country's future membership in the alliance, NATO selected Hungary as one of its first new entrants. In Budapest, the invitation to join NATO has been widely considered a prize for Hungary's democratic consolidation, successful economic transformation, and political stability.

In this chapter I examine Hungary as a new NATO member from four perspectives: the country's regional security at the end of the Cold War, its campaign for accession to NATO, the successes and shortcomings of civil-military relations and especially civilian oversight of the armed forces, and the strengths and weaknesses of the Hungarian military establishment. The chapter is not a polemic concerning support for or objection to NATO expansion. Arguments for and against have been adumbrated by many policymakers and commentators.[1] My task is to examine Hungarian security and military affairs since the fall of communism. What we learn will help us determine what Hungary brings to the table in Brussels as a new member of the NATO alliance.

Hungarian Security after the Cold War

The collapse of European communism and the end of the Cold War brought dramatic changes to Hungarian security. Although Hungary had remained a member of the Warsaw Treaty Organization (WTO) until its official dissolution in July 1991, the possibility of Hungarian neutrality was first mentioned in February 1989 by an unlikely source, the Soviet academician Oleg Bogomolov, a close advisor to President Mikhail Gorbachev.[2] Bogomolov himself may have been surprised by the avalanche of discussion generated by his remarks. Scholars and military experts published hundreds of articles on the subject, debating the merits and demerits, the rationality and feasibility of Hungarian neutrality.

The reason for the intense debate over Hungarian security was the growing recognition by politicians, the military elite, national security experts, and the informed public that the country would find itself in a security limbo following the end of the WTO. They realized that from a low risk–high stability situation, Hungary was about to enter an era marked by new security challenges and potential instability. The withdrawal of the seventy-eight thousand Soviet occupation troops enjoyed unanimous popular endorsement, but few understood that once the troops were gone, Hungary would be left without such fundamental defensive capabilities as protection of its air space. The general population was unaware that the country's military doctrine was practically the same as that of the USSR, which fully disregarded Hungarian security imperatives, and that Hungary's preparation for its defense was woefully inadequate.[3] In short, the defensive potential the emerging democratic state inherited from the *ancien régime* was unsuitable for the security scenario taking shape in the region.

Challenges to Hungarian Security

Since 1990, defense officials and politicians have been quick to point out that Hungary has no specific enemy and is under no direct threat. Still, there are a number of potential challenges they must take seriously, particularly because of Hungary's unfavorable geostrategic position. It has no natural borders intimidating to land forces; it is relatively easy to overrun, as a number of armies have demonstrated throughout the past millennium; and its military establishment has weakened considerably since 1989.

In the 1990s, several neighboring countries (Czechoslovakia, Romania) found themselves facing security dilemmas similar to Hungary's, while others (republics of the former Yugoslavia) encountered explosive situations requiring drastic increases in defense budgets. Although in Hungary the 1990s were a period of substantial contraction in military expenditures, not all of the region's armed forces have experienced such reductions in their defensive potential (table 3.1).[4]

In spite of the losses incurred during the recent Yugoslav War and the destruction of some of its defense industry, rump-Yugoslavia (Serbia and Montenegro) still possesses a military potential that is impressive by the region's standards. Many industrial enterprises across the country are capable of producing small arms, and Russia continues to ship supplies to the Serbian military, particularly to its air force. In addition, Yugoslavia's airspace is well guarded. The Yugoslav National Army's (JNA's) personnel are well trained, and a significant proportion of them are battle-tried. Croatia's defense outlays have been considerable, its armed forces are highly motivated, and many current officers and NCOs participated in the Yugoslav War. Although MiG-21s constitute the backbone of Croatia's air force, Zagreb has already ordered for them an upgrade package developed by Israel, which will result in machines on a par with MiG-29s. On a per-capita basis, Slovenia's defense outlays are more than twice as large as Hungary's.

In the north, Slovakia's military represents a potential danger for Hungary, given the presence of an entire air force regiment equipped with MiG-29s in addition to the ten MiG-29s "inherited" from the Czechoslovak armed forces. Moreover, Slovakia's offensive capability is strengthened by Su-22 and Su-25 airplanes, dozens SS-22 ballistic missiles, and the S-300 air defense missile system.

In stark contrast to Slovakia, Romania's existing military arsenal and ongoing equipment acquisition programs are characterized by an unambiguous Western orientation. Romania recently acquired four Hercules transport planes from the United States, and most of its 110 MiG-21 fighters have already been upgraded with the Israeli package. On order are four AN/TPS-117 radar-locator systems from Lockheed-Martin, which satisfy top NATO standards. During his July 1998 visit to Washington, President Emil Constantinescu committed Romania to the purchase of additional US-made Bell helicopters, notwithstanding the dire economic situation at home and his finance minister's threat of resignation should the deal materialize.[5]

TABLE 3.1

Defense Spending by Hungary and Its Neighbors, 1997

Variable	Hungary	Austria	Croatia	Romania	Slovakia	Slovenia	Ukraine	Yugoslavia
Population (in millions)	10.16	8.04	4.70	22.77	5.37	2.01	50.85	11.35
Total personnel in armed forces (in thousands)	49.1	45.5	58.0	227.0	41.2	9.5	387.4	114.2
Defense budget (in billion $)	0.51	1.70	1.20	0.77	0.60	0.21	0.81	1.10
Defense expenditures per capita (in dollars)	50.3	211.4	255.3	33.8	111.7	106.3	15.9	96.9
Main battle tanks	797	174	285	1,255	487	109	4,063	1,270
Fighter aircraft	80	24	20	291	109	NA	790	170
Flying time (average annual hours per pilot)	50	130	NA	40	50	NA	NA	NA

Source: *The Military Balance, 1997–1998* (London: IISS, 1997), and the author's computations.

For the purposes of this discussion, I leave out the Ukraine, whose military strength is simply not in the same ballpark with that of Hungary and its neighbors, and Austria, a long-consolidated democracy that is unlikely to present any danger to Hungary.

Hungary and Its Neighbors: Democratization and the Minority Issue

Hungary is one of the four central European states (along with the Czech Republic, Poland, and Slovenia) in which democracy may be said to have been consolidated. Postcommunist Hungarian politics have been characterized by a level of stability uncommon in the region; indeed, it is the only central or eastern European state where, as of early 1999, each of two freely elected governments has served out its full term without a constitutional crisis. The same is expected of the governing coalition that was formed after the May 1998 elections by the Alliance of Young Democrats–Hungarian Civic Party, the Independent Smallholders' Party (ISP), and the Hungarian Democratic Forum.

According to political and military elites, Hungary's regional security is determined primarily by its neighbors' success in democratic consolidation and their treatment of ethnic Hungarian minorities. Of Hungary's seven neighbors, only Austria and Slovenia may be considered stable democracies. There are small ethnic Hungarian populations in both states, whose treatment has not been a cause for concern in Budapest. The other neighbors are also home to smaller or larger Hungarian minorities, and all of them have encountered difficulties in their democratization processes.

Although nearly four million ethnic Hungarians live in neighboring states, until 1989 Hungary could not pursue improvements in their condition, given its limited sovereignty and its sharing of membership in the WTO with its neighbors. The first postcommunist coalition government (1990–1994), led by József Antall and, following his death in 1993, Imre Boross, intended to change that. Although Antall was not a nationalist, some of his early statements (such as, "In spirit I am the prime minister of fifteen million Hungarians," referring not only to the ten million living in Hungary proper) could be and were taken out of context by the nationalist leaders of neighboring states (that is, Romania and Slovakia), who needed precisely such gaffes to whip up anti-Hungarian sentiment.

The early blunders of Hungarian foreign policy should be chalked up not to revanchism but to inexperience. A few months before taking office, Antall was a museum director, and his foreign minister, Géza Jeszenszky, a college professor with no political experience. More troubling was the presence of István Csurka, an unabashed nationalist, among the vice presidents of Antall's Hungarian Democratic Forum until 1993, when he was belatedly forced to resign.[6] Csurka and his supporters soon established the Hungarian Justice and Life Party (MIÉP), a right-wing nationalist organization that came in far below the threshold necessary for parliamentary representation in 1994 but did considerably better in 1998 by sending 14 deputies in the 386-seat national legislature.

Hungary's policies toward its neighbors became more conciliatory under the socialist-liberal coalition government (1994–1998) led by Prime Minister Gyula Horn. After long and contentious negotiations, Budapest signed basic treaties with Slovakia (1995) and Romania (1996). Hungary's relationship with Slovakia, among all its neighbors, has been the most acrimonious, particularly since the breakup of Czechoslovakia in January 1993. The two most disturbing issues are the treatment of the approximately 650,000 Hungarians in Slovakia and the construction of the Danube dam at Gabcikovo-Nagymaros. Both awaited resolution in early 1999. Many provisions of the basic treaty are not observed by the Slovak government, despite repeated Hungarian attempts to settle the issues.[7] Politicians in Budapest do not expect profound improvements so long as Prime Minister Mečiar and the nationalist parties that support him are in government.

The Hungarian-Romanian nexus was similarly strained—primarily owing to the treatment of the approximately two-million-strong Hungarian minority—under President Ion Iliescu's tenure (1990–1996). In September 1996 the basic treaty was finally signed, although not without grueling negotiations and numerous postponements. As US Ambassador to NATO Robert Hunter noted, the treaty was signed not "because they like each other" but because both governments realized that their chances of NATO membership would be increased with the agreement.[8] Since the December 1996 national elections that brought democratic forces and President Emil Constantinescu to power in Bucharest, relations between the two states have become more cordial, although some contentious issues remain.

Hungary's relations with Ukraine have been congenial, although the situation of the Hungarian minority in the Carpatho-Ukraine is considered unsatisfactory in Budapest. A treaty between the two countries was signed by the Antall government in December 1991.[9] Finally, mention must be made of Hungarian-Russian relations, though the two states do not share a border. Hungarian politicians have tried their best to assuage Moscow's fears about the diminution of Russian security after NATO's expansion.[10] Given the constraints created by the unpredictability of Russian domestic and foreign policies, Hungary has managed to maintain friendly relations with Moscow.

The War in Yugoslavia

The most important challenge to Hungary's security in the 1990s was the Yugoslav War. Hungary shares a border with both Serbia (where hundreds of thousands of ethnic Hungarians reside) and Croatia (home to a smaller Hungarian minority), and keeping the country out of the war was an obvious priority. This objective was jeopardized by Budapest's unambiguous sympathies toward Croatia, demonstrated by the clandestine delivery of Hungarian surplus infantry weapons to Zagreb in 1991. The revelation of this covert action by the Hungarian press increased tensions between Budapest and Belgrade.[11] During the war, violations of Hungary's borders were commonplace, with Croatian forces crossing over to engage the JNA from Hungarian territory. The Serbs, in turn, regularly infringed upon Hungarian airspace, most memorably when they accidentally dropped a bomb on the southern Hungarian village of Barcs (causing minor damage and no casualties). The call-up of thousands of ethnic Hungarians by the JNA did not make matters easier. As a preventive measure, the Hungarian and Yugoslav general staffs established direct contacts following the Barcs incident.[12]

As officials in Budapest clearly recognized, Hungary was not directly threatened by the war.[13] At the same time, hostilities so close to the border did call attention to Hungary's vulnerability, to the sources of potential danger to its security, and to its already small and swiftly decreasing defense budgets, which were causing serious problems in the Hungarian Defense Forces' (HDF's) ability to protect the nation. Since the conclusion of the Yugoslav War, Hungary has maintained good relations with Croatia. Budapest's nexus with Belgrade has been strained because Hungary allowed NATO forces to use its airspace and because the JNA conscripted ethnic Hungarians to serve in Kosovo.

Measures to Alleviate Security Concerns

The challenges to Hungarian security made enhancement of its defensive capabilities imperative. In the early 1990s, NATO membership seemed an elusive prospect, and so Budapest had to enhance Hungary's security in the short term.

The first step toward increasing national security was to devise a new military doctrine.[14] Debate over the doctrine flared up in the summer of 1990 and emerged on two fronts. On one front, the main political parties espoused different views of what constituted national interests. On the other, a professional dispute arose between the largely conservative military leadership and the amateurish representatives of the government (exemplified by the minister of defense, Lajos Für), who had no prior expertise or experience in defense matters. To make matters worse, the debate was conducted in an institutional vacuum, because after 1989 a number of military research centers were disbanded and most experienced members of the General Staff were ostracized owing to their association with the communist regime. The government itself had few experts, and the majority of the parties regarded independent think-tanks (which began slowly to emerge in the early 1990s) with distrust. The debate proceeded in civic organizations, periodicals, newspapers, and parliamentary channels.

As the discussion progressed, two contending views crystallized.[15] The first stressed Hungary's isolation in a region surrounded by hostile nations. Because of this situation, proponents argued, the country should possess strong armed forces capable of its defense. The opposite view denied the need for armed forces entirely. The protagonists of this ultra-liberal argument saw a domestic threat in the military and sought to guarantee the country's security through international agreements. In the end, these extremist views were defeated, and members of parliament agreed that Hungary was to have a smaller but more effective armed force.[16]

The new military doctrine is purely defensive, which has been reflected in the training of the HDF since 1989. The only objective of this defense concept is the protection of Hungarian sovereignty from any aggressor; weapons are to be used only in the case of external attack. The doctrine assumes the presence of sufficient military muscle to stall the advance of a potential aggressor and thereby win time without incurring heavy casualties and damage. Time gain is important because it could afford the possibility of resolving contentious issues through political negotiation; it could also enable Hungary's allies to offer military assistance.

According to the Ministry of Defense (MOD), the country's protection should rest on four pillars.[17] The first is the Euro-Atlantic security system, participants in which could collectively and mutually guarantee the security of the continent. Second are multilateral treaties made between the region's states, and third are bilateral agreements with neighboring countries. The fourth pillar is a small but capable military force that could arrest aggression against Hungary from any direction. The question of whether the HDF would be able to carry out such a function has been addressed, and there can be no doubt that the answer at present is negative. The question of whether a volunteer army might be the answer to the country's defense needs has been widely discussed since 1990. Most military experts agree that the costs of a professional army would be prohibitive for the foreseeable future.[18]

Military Diplomacy

Military diplomacy has played an important role in acquiring guarantees to Hungarian security. It was doubly valuable *prior* to NATO accession because it could yield tangible results contributing to Hungarian security in the short run and also advance Hungary's NATO candidacy. In concert with these considerations, military diplomacy switched into high gear in 1991 and has yet to slow down. The fruits of the myriad meetings, conferences, and negotiations have included a variety of bilateral military and security agreements with many states—most importantly with Hungary's neighbors.

It should be noted that military diplomacy is distinct from state-level diplomacy, and one may not always be reflective of the other. A fitting example is the relationship between the Hungarian and Romanian armed forces. Even in the early and mid-1990s, when relations between the two states were strained, the two armies maintained good relations.[19] The two defense ministries have kept close contacts on ministerial, General Staff, and lower levels and have signed several important agreements. A Romanian-Hungarian military treaty completed in December 1990 was aimed at strengthening confidence between the two armies and ensuring that political tension would not expand to the military sphere. In May 1991 the two countries were the first to sign an "open skies" agreement allowing for four annual unarmed surveillance flights over each other's territory.[20] The first trip of the new Romanian defense minister, Victor Babiuc, in 1997 was to Budapest, where he concluded an accord with his Hungarian colleague on the protection of military secrets. In March 1998 the two defense ministers signed an agreement to set up a joint, thousand-man-strong military peacekeeping unit. Prior to and following the July 1997 NATO conference in Madrid, Hungarian politicians (including Foreign Minister László Kovács) appealed to the alliance to include Romania (and Slovenia).

Although Hungarian-Slovakian military relations have developed less auspiciously, contacts between the two armed forces have been marked by less tension than have relations between the two governments. In July 1994, Hungarian Defense Minister György Keleti called on his Slovak colleague, Pavel Kanis, to defuse tensions. In February 1998, the two countries' defense ministers (Keleti and Jan Sitek) signed agreements on confidence-building measures, including cooperation in military aviation and anti-aircraft defense.[21]

Since 1990, Hungarian military diplomats have succeeded in improving the country's image and concluding a legion of defense agreements with other neighbors and with countries farther away. These cooperative arrangements range from a pact with Estonia that allows for the training of Estonian officers in Hungary to a treaty with France safeguarding military secrecy in hardware and data. In addition, Budapest's military diplomats succeeded in negotiating dozens of training programs enabling an ever larger number of Hungarian officers to study in the military academies and colleges of NATO member states.

Participation in International Organizations

Hungarian politicians understood that the formulation of the new defensive doctrine and bilateral agreements, although important, could provide no reliable security guarantees. Therefore, prior to the Madrid decision they attempted to improve the country's security situation through participation in international organizations. In the early 1990s politicians in Budapest—and in other central European capitals—had urged the endowment of the Conference on Security and Cooperation in Europe (CSCE, since then renamed OSCE) with concrete military content. They envisioned a new security arrangement for which CSCE could have provided a framework. CSCE was an ongoing conference, however, without troops or weapons, and not a security system. The only working security system for European democracies was NATO, which at that point was not prepared to welcome former communist states.

Although Hungary has been the originator of or active member in several regional organizations—such as the Central European Initiative and the Carpathian Euro-Region Group—none of these is designed for cooperation in security or defense matters. The most promising regional organization has been the Visegrád group (also including Czechoslovakia—later the Czech Republic and Slovakia—and Poland), which was co-founded by Hungary in 1991.[22] The Visegrád experiment has not lived up to its early promises owing to a number of sensitive issues among its members. To date, the establishment of a limited free trade zone has been its most tangible result. The Visegrád group was never intended to become a military pact, because all of its members saw NATO as the only satisfactory long-term solution for their security concerns.

The most important measure Hungary had taken to solve its security dilemma before 1998 was its vigorous and consistent pursuit of NATO membership. The new military doctrine, military diplomacy, and the government's approach to international organizations were all in service of this objective, which in many ways determined the direction of Hungarian foreign and military policy in the 1990s.

Hungary's Campaign for NATO Membership

Since the first democratic elections in Hungary in May 1990, the official view has been that membership in NATO is the primary channel through which Hungary can achieve integration with the West and promote its own security. This policy has been followed throughout seven years of unambiguous and concerted effort, crowned by NATO's official invitation to Hungary at the Madrid conference.

Selling Hungary to NATO

All three postcommunist governments assigned top priority to political and military integration with western Europe, a priority that enjoyed the support of every major parliamentary party. Every foreign and defense minister (respectively, Géza Jeszenszky and Lajos Für, 1990–94; László Kovács and György Keleti, 1994–98; and János Martonyi and János Szabó, 1998–) has actively promoted this goal.[23] This continuity is indicated by Martonyi's high regard for the efforts of his predecessors and Jeszenszky's recent appointment as the new Hungarian ambassador to Washington.[24]

Hungary was the first Warsaw Pact member to speculate about its potential membership in NATO (in February 1990) *and* to urge the WTO's dissolution (in June 1990).[25] In his maiden speech to parliament in May 1990, Prime Minister Antall called for Hungary's withdrawal from the WTO and expressed confidence that other member states would follow his lead. At the November 1990 CSCE conference in Paris, with Soviet President Gorbachev and Defense Minister Dimitri Yazov looking on, he announced that the WTO's political structure was soon to disappear.[26] By the fall of 1990, WTO foreign ministers had reached a consensus that the organization would stop functioning as a military alliance in July 1991.

On 20 February 1990, the last Hungarian communist foreign minister, Gyula Horn, detonated a political bomb by declaring that Hungary's membership in NATO was "not unimaginable in the none too distant future."[27] Western reactions to the announcement were guarded, and one might surmise that Horn was motivated in no small part by the approaching general elections—calculating that allusions to NATO while Hungary was still chained to the WTO might seem a courageous position to his countrymen.[28] Horn's Hungarian Socialist Party was trounced at the polls; Antall's new government embraced NATO membership as a top priority.

Hungary has organized hundreds of meetings, conferences, and visits between Hungarian politicians and military personnel and their NATO colleagues in order to convince the latter that Budapest was worthy of membership. In Budapest and other central European capitals, NATO's Partnership for Peace (PFP) program was regarded with misgivings because it was considered far short of the early enlargement decision these states had hoped for.[29] Still, Hungary signed up in February 1994 and, trying to make the best of the situation, put PFP in a positive light by portraying it as a useful step toward the attainment of full membership in the alliance.

In the meantime, Hungary tried to curry favor with NATO leaders in several ways. Budapest volunteered to participate in numerous peacekeeping activities; indeed, by early 1999 Hungary had become the twenty-fifth largest contributor to such operations.[30] At that time, unarmed Hungarian military observers were serving in Angola, Bosnia-Herzegovina, Georgia, Iraq, and Nagorno-Karabakh. In addition, a four-hundred-man engineering battalion was assisting IFOR/SFOR operations in Bosnia, a peacekeeping company was active in Cyprus, and a platoon of military police was stationed in the Sinai Peninsula. Budapest also supported the creation of joint peacekeeping units with Italy, Slovenia, Romania, Ukraine, and other countries. An important Hungarian contribution to NATO's success in bringing the Yugoslav War to a closure was the opening of a military base in southern Hungary (near the village of Taszár) to US forces.

Hungary also tried its best to convince its prospective NATO allies that it could be a valued contributor to the alliance. Although defense outlays were insufficient for the country's defense, units that were singled out for "early NATO compatibility" received priority treatment from the MOD. In addition, the military force structure was comprehensively reorganized to simulate the NATO model.[31]

Selling NATO to Hungarians

The campaign for NATO membership has been decidedly elite-driven and supported by all major political parties. Only extremist political forces (the Workers' Party on the left, MIÉP on the right) have opposed the government's alliance policy, but they enjoy limited political influence. At the same time—and in contrast to wide-based support for Hungary's membership in the European Union—a sizable segment of the population has been skeptical about the benefits of NATO membership.

Popular reluctance has several roots. First, with the exception of the interwar period, foreign troops have been stationed on Hungarian territory since 1526. Especially since the ill-fated, anti-Hapsburg War of Independence (1848–49), Hungarian territorial integrity has been associated in many people's minds with freedom from the presence of foreign troops. Second, the desire for neutrality is deep-rooted among many who are historically aware and believe that harmful alliances were largely responsible for the tragic events of twentieth-century Hungarian history. Third, the appalling conditions of the Hungarian military establishment, combined with slender state resources, make many citizens think about the financial burden NATO enlargement will signify. Finally, since 1990 the majority of Hungarians have not been concerned about any military threat to their country.[32]

Although the all-out government campaign to gain popular backing for NATO membership did not start until 1996, the number of supporters increased throughout the 1990s. Prior to 1994 (when chances of accession seemed remote), the ratio of supporters never reached 50 percent. Afterwards, their proportion increased to 52 percent in 1996 (57 percent of military officers),[33] 61 percent in summer 1997,[34] and 69 percent after the Madrid conference.[35] Taking nothing for granted, the Horn government conducted a major media campaign to convince people to vote for NATO in a referendum held on 16 November 1997. NATO's praises were written into soap operas, a game called "Natopoly" on CD-ROM was sent to all public high schools and libraries, and pro-NATO documentaries crowded television and radio broadcast time.[36] Thousands of newspaper and magazine articles extolled the benefits of NATO membership. Even the well-liked president, Árpád Göncz, addressed the country urging a positive vote.

The government insisted that the current 4- to 5-percent annual economic growth rate could be sustained and would be more than sufficient to permit the payment of Hungary's annual contribution to the alliance (believed to be set at $11.7 million).[37] Supportive US officials, such as Defense Undersecretary for Policy Walter Slocombe, who claimed that the military infrastructure Hungary had "inherited" from the WTO could be useful and lower the costs of accession, were widely quoted.[38] Proponents also made much of the expected positive economic impact of NATO membership—including job creation and enhanced foreign investment —even pointing to the infusion of $251 million into the economy of Taszár and its vicinity since the United States had begun to use the base there.[39] In the end, 85 percent of those who voted endorsed accession to NATO, thus saving their government from embarrassment. The turn-out was just shy of 50 percent, nearly double the 25 percent needed for validity.

NATO's Expectations

As President Göncz noted, Hungary's need for NATO membership was motivated by values shared with the West, by the desire to belong to a favorable security environment, and by the potential membership offered for creating a more cost-effective defense establishment.[40] Throughout the 1990s, NATO executives continually informed Hungarian leaders what the alliance needed from Hungary if it was to join up.

NATO leaders assume Hungary's continued political stability, further consolidation of its democracy, and firm civilian control over the armed forces. There are, however, a large number of specific expectations that Hungary will have to work hard to satisfy. These include, but are not lim-ited to, increases in military spending, conversion to NATO doctrines and planning, modernization of the HDF's arsenal, progress toward achiev-ing compatibility with NATO equipment, the development of coopera-tion with other NATO units, improvements in communications and air defense capabilities, reforms in military education and training, and a major increase in the number of English-speaking officers and NCOs.[41]

Although Budapest has agreed to NATO's demands, some potential problems have emerged even before actual membership. For example, during his September 1997 visit to Washington, Foreign Minister Kovács declared that Hungary's defense outlays would be lower than those requested by NATO, noting that they would be roughly equal to those of smaller NATO countries such as Belgium and Portugal.[42] He neglected to mention that the armed forces of those states were fully integrated into the alliance and were in incomparably better condition than the HDF. In July 1998, Prime Minister Victor Orbán ruled out the possibility of sending troops to Kosovo, owing to the presence of hundreds of ethnic Hungarian conscripts serving in the JNA.[43] MOD officials often noted disparities in the recommendations of American and western European politicians, on one hand, and NATO military and security officials, on the other.[44] For instance, US President Bill Clinton and Secretary of State Madeleine Albright were more flexible about defense budgets and put the emphasis on Hungary's political stability and its economic and social policies. In contrast, NATO military leaders and politicians such as US Defense Secretary William Cohen were more eager to ensure levels of military expenditures to remedy the HDF's deficiencies.

Given the geographical locations of the three new NATO members, Hungary constitutes an island in the alliance sharing no border with another NATO state. This is not expected to cause any political problems, but it could have negative military implications. Hungarian experts are quick to point out that the IFOR/SFOR operations gave rise to no special difficulties stemming from Hungary's location. In any case, in a potential conflict the two Hungarian neighbors that are not members of NATO—Austria and Slovenia—could provide a bridge to member states and would presumably to be supportive of NATO operations.

Budapest believes that it could most effectively promote NATO's programs and operations by belonging to NATO's Southern Command. This belief is considered justified by the notion that most potential crisis points lie in that direction (the Balkans, the Middle East). In addition, Hungarian officials suggest that in NATO's Southern Command they would not have to compete with the Czech Republic and Poland and could also benefit from their traditionally good relations with Italy and Turkey. In the southern region Hungary could also prove quickly that it intends to be a contributor, not just a beneficiary of the alliance. In this area, they surmise, the HDF's relatively high technical culture could be utilized more extensively than elsewhere.

Democratizing Civil-Military Relations

In all the formerly communist countries, the most important communist
legacies in the area of civil-military relations are armed forces that were
subordinated to the Communist Party, professional military personnel
who are heavily indoctrinated with Marxist-Leninist dogma, and vaguely
defined external and internal institutional functions for the armed
forces.[45]

Insofar as the Hungarian military is concerned, successful democratic
consolidation includes the following: (1) placing the military under the
authority and supervision of the elected government; (2) unambiguous
constitutional codification of the chains of command and areas of
responsibility over the armed forces between state institutions and within
the military establishment; (3) termination and prohibition of the activities of political parties within the armed forces, as well as an effective
ban on partisan political activities by active military personnel; (4) establishing the government's fiscal responsibility over defense expenditures
and the executive branch's accountability to the legislature over military
matters; (5) democratizing the military establishment itself, with special
attention to inculcating military personnel with fundamental democratic
values; (6) creating a pool of independent civilian experts to advise politicians on military and security issues; and (7) reforming military education and training. Despite some remaining shortcomings, during the
1990s Hungary successfully democratized its armed forces and established democratic civil-military relations.

Civilian Oversight Authority

The Hungarian constitution was amended in 1990 to subordinate the
military to the constitution and the president, who became commander-
in-chief of the armed forces, although he was not to exercise this prerog-
ative in peacetime. The military is responsible to, in descending order, the
president, the legislature, the cabinet, and the minister of defense.[46] In
April 1991 President Göncz caused a controversy by trying to interfere
with the day-to-day running of the MOD, but the Constitutional Court
quickly resolved to matter in favor of the latter.[47] Prior to 1993, the
defense establishment was divided into two parts: the relatively small

MOD and a separate Command of the Hungarian Defense Forces. This arrangement, devised by the last communist government to make it difficult for its successors to control the armed forces, resulted in the duplication of bureaucracies and precluded full ministerial accountability. In one renowned case, two separate Hungarian military delegations—one from the MOD and one from the HDF Command—each with the same purpose, visited Sweden at the same time, unbeknownst to each other.[48]

The Defense Law of 1993 drastically improved conditions for civilian control by creating the structural underpinnings for "balanced" civil-military relations.[49] The law subordinates the HDF's command directly to the minister of defense and clarifies other questions left open for interpretation. The minister—who remains accountable to the government and its head—supervises three state secretaries within the MOD who are responsible for political, administrative, and operational functions. (The state secretary for military operations is commander of the HDF.) The 1993 law also eliminated the duplication of functions and clearly defined areas of authority and accountability.

The legislature, through its Defense Committee, enjoys the most extensive control over the armed forces. This committee decides military doctrine, the functions of the military within the framework of security policy, the size and budget of the armed forces, and so forth. As the superior policy-making body, the government transmits its decisions to the MOD and, indirectly, to the armed forces. In addition, a new Defense Council was created whose activities are overseen by four individuals: the president, the prime minister, the chairman of the parliament, and the head of the Supreme Court.

Although the institutional structure for civilian control is adequate in Hungary, some practical problems remain. One of these is a lack of rigorous supervision within the MOD and the ministry's providing of insufficient information to the Defense Committee.[50] Incomplete communication between the MOD and parliament has thwarted the development of the legislature's supervisory role over the armed forces. In the first postcommunist government, the politicians chosen to lead the defense establishment were embarrassingly naive about defense matters, which frustrated the democratization of civil-military relations. This inexperience was particularly troubling before the 1993 structural reorganization, when the MOD was often "out of the loop" because the HDF Command (the bulwark of old-style senior officers) often got away with not informing the MOD about important developments in the armed forces.

On the financial level, the issue of the necessary transparency of military expenditures has not been satisfactorily resolved. Members of parliament are routinely left in the dark about the detailed breakdown of defense allocations. For instance, MPs may be told that the annual defense budget earmarks 21 billion forints (Ft) for the salaries and benefits of personnel, but they receive no figures broken down by individual units. In government budgets "defense" makes up merely 4 pages, supplemented by 120 pages of footnotes and explanations.[51] Another problem has been the conversion of political objectives into practical military tasks. The political directives of the government and the Defense Committee are often vague, and there is no concrete strategy or guidance available that would foster their interpretation by armed forces personnel.

The deficiency of internal control within the defense establishment has also been blamed for a number of scandals involving military personnel since 1990. These included the large-scale illegal sale and dilution of the army's fuel, financial embezzlement during the construction of a military hospital, and numerous other schemes.[52] More recently, the MOD's procurement office violated the principle of equal opportunity and fair competition over a contract for anti-missile systems. In February 1998 the Supreme Court ruled against the MOD and fined it Ft 15 million ($72,000).[53] At the same time, notwithstanding the MOD's perennial and justified pleas (buttressed by the arguments of foreign and domestic analysts), parliament has been effective in reducing military budgets and, in the process, drastically decreasing the HDF's capacity to defend the nation.

In sum, while the institutional structure of parliamentary civilian control over the armed forces in Hungary is adequate, the internal control mechanisms of the MOD are in need of further development. In large measure the problems have been due to general inexperience and the negligence and oversight of some high-ranking military officers.

Depoliticization and Democratization

The overwhelming majority of the armed forces welcomed the collapse of communism and the military's subsequent depoliticization.[54] In Hungary, the army's decommunization—the Main Political Administration and Communist Party organizations were disbanded, political officers dismissed or retrained, and so forth—was largely completed before József Antall's first postcommunist government took office in May 1990. Political activity may not be conducted in the armed forces, and active military personnel are not permitted to join political parties. The domestic function of the armed forces was settled by the 1990 Defense Law, which prohibited any role for the armed forces in domestic contingencies, with the exception of certain units that might be utilized for the defense of buildings housing public offices (such as parliament, ministries, etc.). The use of the military even in such cases is strictly limited to instances when these edifices are attacked by armed force.[55] As in other democracies, the HDF has been active in disaster relief operations.

The full democratization of civil-military relations requires the availability of civilian experts on defense and security matters who can provide knowledgeable and impartial advice to politicians and policymakers. One of the remaining shortcomings of civil-military relations in Hungary is the dearth of such experts, caused primarily by the lack of appropriate courses and programs in the civilian educational system. Most of those with the requisite knowledge and training are either active military personnel or persons with strong ties to the armed forces. Many of them are active in recently established think-tanks, some maintained by the MOD.[56]

The 1993 Defense Law laid the foundations of democratization in matters of personnel and strictly regulated the professional relationship between officers, NCOs, and conscripts. A particular source of problems in the past had been the habitual and generally overlooked hazing of fresh draftees by older conscripts. The 1993 Defense Law made such behavior illegal and subject to disciplinary action, allaying the fears of soldiers and concerned parents. In the same year, the Law on Religions reestablished the institution of military chaplaincy.[57]

Since 1989, HDF personnel have organized several independent associations and trade unions representing various interests to serve conscripted and professional soldiers alike. At times these organizations have resorted to public demonstrations in order to call attention to the plight of discharged officers and NCOs and to the extremely low remuneration of professional military personnel. Although the state and the MOD have fully accepted the legitimacy of these associations, most grievances remain unresolved because of meager MOD resources.

The Military Leadership

Postcommunist transitions are generally more traumatic for the armed forces than for other occupational strata. One of the problems is that the officers whom nascent democracies inherit from the past are tainted by their service of the Marxist-Leninist regime. This situation is nearly impossible to redress in the short term, because many military officers possess special skills unavailable elsewhere in the labor market. In Hungary, the few generals and officers who refused to pledge their allegiance to the democratic state were dismissed from the HDF along with political officers who could not be reassigned or retrained. By 1998, no general remained in the HDF who had received his promotion before 1989.[58]

The aforementioned problems in Hungarian civil-military relations may be partially ascribed to the questionable qualifications of postcommunist defense ministers. During the 1990s, three men led the MOD; all three were dubious choices, although for different reasons. Prior to his appointment, Lajos Für was a university lecturer specializing in the history of Hungarian agriculture. He had no expertise in military matters and no comprehension of the military profession. During his ministership (1990–94), Für devoted a great deal of energy to the design of new Hungarian uniforms (reflecting historical traditions), which, given their nearly prohibitive cost, in 1999 still awaited large-scale introduction. Für's interest in historic uniforms and traditional paraphernalia prevented him from concerning himself with many far more pressing and weighty issues. He evidenced neither conceptual clarity about key defense issues nor the ambition to understand them.[59]

Expertise was not what was missing from the resume of Für's successor.[60] Colonel György Keleti had retired after a twenty-eight-year career as a professional officer, some of it spent as a political officer. In 1990–94 Keleti served as the MOD's spokesman under Für. In the 1980s Keleti was a respected propagandist for the communist regime who was pegged to contribute the politically most sensitive parts of textbooks on national defense for secondary school students. "The main objective of capitalist armies is the annihilation of all progressive social systems," and "The most significant threat to world peace is NATO," opined Keleti in 1984.[61] That a high-ranking communist military officer wrote such nonsense in the mid-1980s is not particularly surprising. But his appointment by the socialist government as the defense minister charged with overseeing Hungary's campaign for accession to NATO demonstrated a lapse in judgment. (Then again, Prime Minister Gyula Horn and several other members of his cabinet had been equally ardent enemies of NATO and the West less than a decade earlier.)

Although little is known of János Szabó, an ISP politician who succeeded Keleti in 1998, his curriculum vitae divulges no prior defense-related background or interest.[62] According to his early speeches, Szabó planned to focus his energies on the resuscitation of Hungarian defense industries and on a limited reorganization of the MOD hierarchy.[63]

The classification and qualifications of MOD personnel are issues Szabó needs to address. In 1990–91, Für conducted a very limited purge of the high brass and subsequently made an effort to hire more civilians in the MOD. In contrast, Keleti surrounded himself with many of his old cronies. Although he accepted the policy of reducing the proportion of military officers at the MOD, Keleti made sure his advisers remained nearby, although reclassified as civilians. Another, related problem is that in the recent past a number of civilian experts employed by the MOD decided to put on uniforms and join the active military service, since military officers often receive perquisites (such as apartments) that are closed to civilians. In 1998 the majority of the MOD staff still consisted of either active or retired military officers (the latter were classified as civilians). Among the eighteen department chiefs of the MOD, twelve were active officers and six were civilians (of whom four were retired officers and two were true civilians).[64]

The State of the Hungarian Defense Forces

Postcommunist Hungary inherited a military establishment that had been prepared and outfitted as part of the Warsaw Pact's doctrine of coalition warfare. As such, it was fraught with an oversized command structure, strategic imbalances, antiquated armaments, organizational asymmetries, and apathetic professional personnel. The number of combat, logistical, and training units was excessive, and there was virtually no indigenous air defense capability.[65] Aside from these problems, the Conventional Forces in Europe Treaty and other international agreements limited the future size and composition of Hungary's military equipment.[66] In some of the most important and costly types of weapons, such as fighter aircraft and attack helicopters, the HDF's holdings were far below the permitted number. In others, such as main battle tanks and artillery pieces, the HDF possessed considerably more than the limit and was obliged to spend scarce resources on their disabling or destruction. In order to measure up to the challenges brought by its new security environment, Hungary needed to boost defense outlays to finance the needed restructuring of the HDF and the modernization of its equipment. Instead, military budgets plummeted along with the size, armament, and overall strength of the armed forces.

The Political Economy of the HDF

The transition from a centrally planned economy to one determined by market forces has caused major economic dislocations and adverse socio-political phenomena in Hungary. Prior to mid-1995, macroeconomic indicators were unimpressive. Military leaders repeatedly announced that it was impossible to maintain the country's defenses with the meager resources allocated to them. Still, defense budgets continued to decline. Quite simply, reducing defense budgets was good politics, particularly considering the government's fiscal priorities. In concert with these political preferences, Hungary's military budgets shrank from 3.5 percent of GDP in 1988 to 1.5 percent a decade later. As a result, the HDF became thoroughly impoverished.

Such inadequate defense outlays allowed virtually no procurement of new equipment and could not keep pace with the growing maintenance requirements of antiquated armaments. In recent years, less than 5 percent of the HDF's budget could be devoted to development and acquisitions. The HDF often lacks funds to purchase badly needed spare parts.

New uniforms were introduced in 1991, but the MOD has been unable to allocate the funds for their purchase for any units except those serving abroad. Indeed, year after year only half the needed money has been available for uniforms and related items.[67] The media have frequently criticized the poor nutritional value of soldiers' meals.[68] The vast majority of buildings in the HDF's care are in extremely poor repair. In one celebrated case, prior to US Defense Secretary William Perry's visit to the Taszár air base, HDF officers had all the buildings along his route repainted or draped with camouflage netting, because they did not want Perry "to see what NATO would be getting."[69] On several occasions in 1994 and 1995, the minister of defense voiced his fears that the MOD would be unable to pay salaries.[70] The press is full of reports describing widespread and long-lasting shortages in the HDF, from uniforms to fuel. Even with substantial reduction in the HDF's manpower, training has suffered owing to the lack of financial resources.

To contain the damage done by small defense budgets, the MOD has had to be attentive to its financial management. Under Für, a great deal of money was spent on useless or nonessential items, such as replacements for communist-era symbols and Western-made automobiles for MOD bureaucrats. Keleti pledged to improve the ministry's housekeeping by selling unused or underutilized MOD property and introducing new fiscal guidelines. By 1997 the MOD had succeeded in reducing its debt from Ft 1.5 billion to Ft 830 million.[71] Several recent investigations of the services have shown that the MOD's fiscal management has become more efficient.[72] The MOD has tried to make salaries and wages its main priority, given the exceedingly inadequate remuneration of military personnel. In 1993, for instance, 17 percent of officers, 46 percent of NCOs, and 57 percent of civilian employees lived below the officially established poverty line.[73] Since then matters have not improved perceptibly.

Spurred by the imperatives of NATO accession, in 1998 the government pledged to expand its military outlays by an annual 0.1 percent of the budget, to reach 1.8 percent by 2001. Given the HDF's needs, such budgetary expansion will guarantee no radical improvement in Hungarian defense capabilities without the additional infusion of funds from NATO.

Armed Forces Reform

Considering the inadequacy of resources, it is amazing that any improvement at all could be achieved in the HDF's restructuring. Surprisingly, a lot has been done.

Since 1990, the military's command structure has been streamlined and rationalized by abolishing the separation between the MOD and the HDF Command. The army's force structure has been significantly altered. Between 1989 and 1997, the number of active military bases and installations was decreased from nearly 300 to 81. Thousands of vehicles, weapons, and equipment of all kinds (24,000 tons of materiel in all) was relocated.[74] The previous concentration of bases in the western part of Hungary has given way to a more even distribution of forces around the country. The number and size of combat units inherited from the WTO have been cut, and those of rapid reaction forces—with an eye toward NATO membership—have been increased.

The HDF was the first former WTO army in which the corps-brigade structure was introduced in place of a system based on divisions. As a result of this reorganization, as of 1999 the HDF was divided into three military districts (headquartered in Tata, Cegléd, and Kaposvár, respectively) in addition to the Budapest Military District.[75] In the new system, three types of brigades are deployed within the military districts: rapid reaction (incorporating mainly professional soldiers), training (containing conscripts), and reserve.

One of the key military objectives between 1989 and 1997 was reduction of the army's manpower. As a result of this undertaking, the HDF shrank by approximately two-thirds. The number of HDF employees, including civilians, decreased by 64.2 percent, from 155,700 to 55,757. In terms of active military personnel, during the eight years of gradual force reductions the officer corps decreased by 51.5 percent, the number of NCOs by 33.4 percent, and that of conscripted soldiers by 70.7 percent (fig. 3.1; table 3.2).

Since 1989, the period of mandatory military service has also been reduced, first from eighteen to twelve months in 1991 and then from twelve to nine months in 1993. Moreover, there has been strong popular pressure for the further compression of service to six months. The new

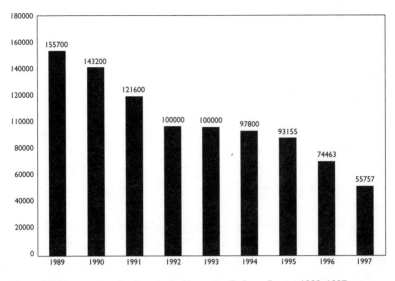

Figure 3.1 Manpower reductions in the Hungarian Defense Forces, 1989–1997.

TABLE 3.2
Size of the Hungarian Defense Forces, 1989–1997

Year	Officers	NCOs	Civilian Employees	Conscripts	Total
1989	17,800	12,700	33,300	91,900	155,700
1990	17,300	12,400	32,500	81,000	143,200
1991	16,800	11,900	27,600	65,300	121,600
1992	14,400	8,500	26,000	51,100	100,000
1993	13,700	8,300	25,660	52,340	100,000
1994	13,100	9,000	24,060	51,640	97,800
1995	13,308	9,603	23,894	46,350	93,155
1996	11,983	9,433	17,115	35,932	74,463
1997	8,634	8,453	11,789	26,881	55,575

government and the top brass agree with this objective, although some worry about the absence of the financial resources required by the more intensive training that must accompany the abbreviated training time.[76] Since 1989, there has been some political pressure for the abolition of mandatory conscription altogether. The present system is not entirely fair, considering that there are more young men in the eighteen-to-twenty-five age-group than the HDF can accommodate, and so thousands are excused from the extremely unpopular military service. The intro-duction of alternative service in 1990, which includes the possibility of service without arms or at civilian hospitals and charities, has not entirely solved the problem.

Aside from the additional fiscal burden an all-professional army would signify, the availability of qualified soldiers in sufficient numbers is also doubtful. In 1997 the MOD began to recruit professional soldiers because conscripted soldiers, owing to their limited service time, could not dis-charge many tasks requiring sophisticated skills. So far this project has met with limited success, given the shortage of eligible applicants. In August 1998, for instance, the MOD offered 5,100 contracts, but the number of qualified aspirants was considerably smaller, mainly due to the modest pay.[77] Still, the establishment of a professional army remains the long-term political objective.

There are few impartial reports on the HDF's performance. Following the fall 1994 British-Hungarian joint exercise, held under the aegis of the PFP program, HDF troops received favorable reviews from reliable ana-lysts, although communication problems were widely noted. The four hundred military engineers serving in Bosnia have also been favorably appraised.[78]

Training and Conditions of Military Personnel

The overall poverty of the HDF is duly reflected in the training, living standards, and quality of its personnel. During the communist period, the profession lost its earlier social esteem, despite the above-average pay and benefits of officers and NCOs. As supporters of the communist regime, professional soldiers were despised, and ordinarily only those with no other career alternatives entered the ranks. Since 1989, the profession has regained little of its lost prestige. First, in real terms the remuneration of military personnel has decreased substantially. Second, the number of career opportunities in the private sector has increased exponentially. Third, the HDF has raised demands on its personnel because of the new doctrine, the accession to NATO with the imperative language acquisition, and the shortened period of conscription. Fourth, as a result of force redistribution, many officers and NCOs have had to resettle, with their families, in distant parts of the country. Consequently, thousands of officers and NCOs have left the service, especially those who possessed qualifications and skills that enabled them to find more lucrative employment in the private sector. These were the individuals the HDF wanted least to lose.

At the same time, there have been some positive changes in the situation of officers and NCOs. First, the military is no longer associated with the WTO, the Soviet Union, and communism. Second, NATO accession brings not only new tasks and obligations but also benefits such as foreign travel and study and the increase in prestige expected from membership in the alliance. Third, the HDF has made a major effort to improve the housing conditions of its officers and NCOs through the sale of MOD-owned apartments on favorable terms. Fourth, the quality of officer and NCO training has improved by virtue of the termination of political indoctrination and an enhanced focus on professional matters.

Still, the living standards of the majority of professional military personnel are extremely low; many live in poverty. Their modest circumstances are especially conspicuous in an increasingly materialistic society and are reflected in the HDF's recruitment problems. Prior to 1989, attracting applicants to military colleges was difficult primarily for political reasons.[79] In the 1990s, in spite of low material rewards, the number of those interested in the occupation has increased. The most important problem has been that of attracting *qualified* applicants. In 1998, for instance, three times as many young men and women applied to the János Bólyai Military Technical College as the institution could accommodate, but after the rigorous academic and physical exams, only 60 percent of the available positions could be filled.[80]

Owing to the HDF's restructuring, hundreds of female civilian employees chose to be reclassified and entered the officer corps rather than lose their jobs. The training of female officer candidates at military colleges began in 1994. Female candidates generally score higher in their entrance exams to military colleges than their male counterparts.[81] In 1998, the first year in which female officers were graduated, 122 women were sworn in as second lieutenants. As of early 1999, 13 percent of the HDF's professional and contract soldiers were women. Their relative and absolute numbers have been increasing; in 1998 women constituted 5 percent of the officer corps and 23 percent of NCOs.[82] By all accounts, the MOD has been pleased with their performance.

Since 1990 the MOD has succeeded in reforming the system of military education. The top-level postgraduate education of HDF officers at the Miklós Zrínyi National Defense University has been transformed to emulate that of similar institutions in the United States. In military colleges, the training period has increased from three to four years. Curricula have been drastically overhauled to reflect political, societal, and military changes. Courses on Marxism-Leninism have been replaced by a focus on the military's role in democracies, and an emphasis on the Russian language has been supplanted by a stress on Western languages. The military leadership has managed to increase the proportion of civilian instructors and the compatibility of military institutions with mainstream universities and colleges to ease the transition of discharged or retired officers into civilian life. Thanks to the large variety of exchange programs offered by NATO member countries and other democratic states, the education of talented Hungarian officers in the West commenced soon after 1990. According to MOD sources, by 1998 more than a thousand Hungarian officers and NCOs had benefited from some exposure to Western military academies.[83] The main objective of these changes has been to inculcate professional personnel with democratic values and to professionalize their training.

At the same time, the resource-poor MOD has been unable to maintain, let alone improve, the training and preparedness of its troops. Freshly discharged conscripts often lament the amount of time wasted in idleness, which hurts morale. According to one interview, draftees spend more than half of their service time doing nothing, owing to poor organization and the shortage of weapons, ammunition, or fuel.[84] This observation is easily substantiated by looking at the preparation of Hungarian air force officers, particularly pilots. Reports mention no problems with theoretical instruction, but a host of complaints have been publicly aired regarding the inadequacies of the practical training. There are many aviators who fly no more than 30 hours per year, which is insufficient to maintain already acquired skills, much less to develop them.[85] According to Captain Gyula Vári, one of the forty Hungarian pilots flying MiG-29s, prior to 1989 the average flying time was 100 hours per year, although many pilots routinely flew 120 to 160 hours. In 1991 Vári was still allowed to log in 117 hours, but in 1997, as a result of consistent annual reductions, he was allowed only 63 hours. In 1998 Captain Vári was slated to fly 60 hours, 15 of them as an instructor pilot training a prospective colleague.[86]

Surprisingly, the Hungarian air force has been free of tragedies until recently. The MiG-29 that crashed in July 1998, killing its pilot, was the first major accident in several years. The subsequent investigation concluded that the mishap was caused by pilot error.[87] It is worth mentioning that when former Defense Minister Keleti was asked in February 1998 to comment on the brevity of flying time, especially in contrast to the 120–170 hours flown by many Western air force pilots, Keleti replied that although the average time Hungarian pilots spent in the air had fallen to fewer than 50 hours, dangers to their lives could be minimized by more thorough preparation and ground training.

In order to at least partly alleviate its recruitment and replacement difficulties, the HDF has established several military secondary schools. As of 1999 there are two military high schools, which are expected to produce a fair number of qualified candidates for military colleges. In addition, the MOD operates five secondary schools that train future NCOs. Instruction in all of these institutions has been designed to prepare officers and NCOs for the challenges presented by Hungary's impending NATO membership.

Finally, a few words should be said about the various social problems affecting HDF personnel. Morale has been low among professional soldiers, owing to insufficient remuneration, frequent relocation, and low occupational prestige. The majority of officers come from rural areas and the lowest income groups of society. Only 1–2 percent of those with an officer or NCO among their family members choose the military profession.[88] Social problems also affect conscripts, among whom drug abuse is reported to be rampant (an average of 35 percent use drugs while on furlough).[89] According to a study of the eleven thousand youths drafted in 1997, fewer than 5 percent were college graduates, and more than 25 percent had no more than eight years of education. Moreover, nearly 40 percent were unemployed prior to entering the armed forces.[90]

Equipment: Procurement and Maintenance

The vast majority of the HDF's weaponry is composed of old and obsolete Soviet-made equipment. According to Keleti, the necessary modernization of the HDF's armaments would require the government's entire annual budget.[91] During the 1990s, given minimal funds for procurement, maintenance and the best utilization of existing resources had to be the HDF's priority.

As far as its principal weapons are concerned, the HDF's main battle-tank fleet is composed of 797 units—597 T-55s (177 in storage) and 200 T-72M1s. The two air force regiments are equipped with 52 MiG-21s, 27 MiG-29s, and 59 Mi-24 attack helicopters. All of these weapons are Soviet-made, and their parts supply has been uneven at best. Since 1989 the HDF's acquisitions have included 100 T-72s from the surplus stock of the Belarusian army, 28 MiG-29s from Russia, more than 200 French Matra air defense missiles, some US-made communications equipment, dozens of Soviet-made BTR-80 armored personnel carriers, and a sizable German donation of arms (including 20 L-39 trainers, aircraft engines, and spare parts) from the arsenal of the former East German air force.

The HDF would have preferred to purchase only Western-made equipment, but it lacked the funds to do so. The reason for the procurement of so many Soviet-made armaments after the dissolution of the WTO is that Russia owed Hungary $1.5 billion, which cash-strapped Moscow chose to pay off with weapons. Hungary would have liked to buy F-16s, but during the Yugoslav War the United States did not allow the sale of advanced arms to countries in the region. Thus Budapest was forced to accept a Soviet offer of 28 MiG-29s in 1993. During the 1990s, Russia paid off some $800 million in debt with weapons; according to recent reports, the remainder of Moscow's obligations (around $700 million) will be paid off through military and civilian technology.[92]

The close of the 1990s found Hungary actively soliciting bids to modernize its air force equipment. The future purchase of new fighter planes has received a great deal of media attention, but the financial realities of such acquisitions are rarely examined. The cost of the thirty aircraft the MOD has been discussing would be approximately $1.5 billion, whereas the HDF's entire budget for 1997 was $511 million. Despite forecasted increases in defense allocations, the purchase of such expensive weapons seems to be beyond Hungary's means in the near future, especially considering other pressing concerns.

One such urgent task is the modernization of the HDF's vehicle fleet. The majority of jeeps, buses, trucks, and armored personal careers are 1970s vintage, and only one-third of the HDF's entire stock of vehicles is less than ten years old. All in all, more than sixteen thousand vehicles need to be replaced. The MOD has commenced the technical preparation of the Ft-50-billion ($240-million) project, which is expected to be completed in 2003. Because of the types of equipment needed, most of the bids will be won by foreign firms, although the MOD wants at least some of the vehicles to be manufactured in Hungary.[93]

The problems of the HDF's arsenal are compounded by the fact that the country's defense industry did not weather the postcommunist transition well.[94] Although Hungary has never had a robust defense industry, prior to 1990 this sector employed more than thirty thousand people. In the early 1960s the domestic arms industry concentrated on the production of ammunition and military vehicles, but by the late 1980s the emphasis had shifted to relatively modern electronics, 70 percent of which were exported, primarily to WTO states. The industry has yet to fully recover from the loss of over 80 percent of its traditional market since 1990. Since 1996 the small defense industry has become marginally profitable, though it is not competitive in world markets owing to the low technological level of its products.[95] The new defense minister has pegged the development of the arms industry as one of the MOD's major priorities.

Assessment

What does NATO gain by adding Hungary to the alliance? And what are the expected costs and benefits for Hungary itself? The picture that emerges from the foregoing analysis is decidedly mixed.

On the positive side, NATO will have a new member that has been one of the leaders of postcommunist democratization and economic transition in central Europe. Hungary has done a great deal to extricate itself from the post–Warsaw Pact security limbo. It has conducted a constructive foreign policy and devised a new defensive military doctrine. Its campaign for NATO membership has been intensive and consistent and has, by and large, enjoyed popular support. Since 1989 the political and military elites have established civil-military relations suitable for a democracy. Although some shortcomings remain, civilian control of the armed forces appears to be solid. Budapest has repeatedly expressed its willingness to send troops to wherever NATO might need them. This commitment should be qualified, however, owing to the presence of Hungarian ethnic minorities in every one of the country's seven neighbors, which makes sending Hungarian soldiers to them a sensitive issue at best. Hungary's strategic location may be considered both a curse and a blessing for the alliance. It will be a NATO island bordering on no other member state, and it is close to the center of Europe's most volatile region. The very same location, however, might prove quite useful for NATO, as demonstrated by the basing of IFOR/SFOR troops in Hungary since 1996.

At the top of the negative (or "dubious") column is a mighty handicap —the pathetic state of the Hungarian Defense Forces. Since the dissolution of the WTO, the HDF's responsibilities have increased dramatically. To measure up to the challenge, military budgets would have had to be substantially boosted to pay either for an increase in the army's size or for the preferred alternative: the technological modernization of the HDF's arsenal. Given the country's political and economic priorities, the opposite has transpired during the 1990s: year after year, the MOD's budget has decreased considerably, along with its personnel, the preparedness of its officers and men, and its overall strength. For the size of the country and its population, the HDF in 1999 is one of the weakest national military establishments in Europe.

The HDF's obsolete equipment, inadequate supplies, and low-tech training faithfully reflect the low priority Hungary's postcommunist governments have assigned to national defense. The prestige of the military profession is among the lowest in the region; since 1948 the army has been the bailiwick of the incompetent. Hungary's own resources now and in the foreseeable future will be inadequate to drastically alter the HDF's arsenal or the quality of its personnel. The large increases in budgetary outlays necessitated by the HDF's conditions are certain to be extremely unpopular, considering the state's slim resources. Lack of money is by far the biggest part of the HDF's predicament. At the same time, one should not dismiss Hungary's potential for a hostile entanglement with one of its neighbors (Slovakia, Romania, rump-Yugoslavia). To be sure, such an eventuality seems extremely unlikely as of early 1999, and NATO membership is expected to reduce its probability further still.

As the new Hungarian government well recognizes, the next period will be spent in the improvement of the Hungarian military and security apparatus for a smooth transition to NATO.[96] There will be many obstacles to master, ranging from issues of interoperability to language acquisition. The infusion of considerable NATO resources, know-how, and political support is likely to transform Hungary and its armed forces into a valuable asset for the alliance.

Notes

My thanks to Randel Zabel for assistance with the tables.

1. For an excellent review of the debate, see Adam Garfinkle, "NATO Enlargement: What's the Rush?" *National Interest* 46 (Winter 1996–97): 102–111.

2. See *Népszabadság*, 9 and 15 February 1989; *New York Times*, 11 February 1989.

3. See *Dátum*, 3 March 1990. To read General Lajos Morocz's "Katonai doktrínánk föbb tételei" (The major tenets of our defense doctrine) is to read an abridged version of the Soviet defense doctrine without the least pretension of consideration for Hungary's security. See *Magyar Tudomány* 33, no. 11 (November 1988): 833–842.

4. The data on eastern European armed forces come from recent issues of *The Military Balance, 1997–1998* (London: IISS, 1997) and from personal interviews with Czech, Hungarian, Polish, and Romanian diplomats and defense officials. For a recent Hungarian assessment, see *Napi Magyarország*, 6 June 1998.

5. On this issue see, for instance, *Radio Free Europe/Radio Liberty Daily Report* (hereafter RFE/RL DR) Part II, 2:147 (3 August 1998).

6. On Csurka and his political views, see Zoltan Barany, "Mass-Elite Relations and the Resurgence of Nationalism in Eastern Europe," *European Security* 3, no. 1 (Spring 1994): 162–181.

7. See László Valki, "Hungary and the Future of European Security," in Stephen J. Blank, ed., *European Security and NATO Enlargement: A View from Central Europe* (Carlisle Barracks, Pennsylvania: US Army War College, 1998), 108.

8. Hunter was quoted in the *Wall Street Journal*, 2 January 1997.

9. Alfred A. Reisch, "Central and Eastern Europe's Quest for NATO Membership," Radio Free Europe/Radio Liberty Research Report 2, no. 28 (9 July 1993): 36.

10. *Magyar Hírlap*, 27 May 1995.

11. The sale included twenty-four thousand Kalashnikov assault rifles that had belonged to the disbanded Workers' Guard. See Brigitte Sauerwein, "Defence Adequacy: The Hungarian Defence Forces," *Jane's Intelligence Review* 6, no. 10 (October 1994): 440.

12. Author's interview with Lieutenant Colonel János Szabó (Budapest, May 1993).

13. See the views of Defense Minister György Keleti in *Új Magyarország*, 19 May 1995.

14. This discussion draws on Zoltan Barany and Péter Deák, "The Civil-Military Nexus in Postcommunist Hungary," in Constantine Danopoulos and Daniel Zirker, eds., *The Military and Society in the Former Eastern Bloc* (Boulder, Colorado: Westview Press, 1999), 31–50.

15. On this issue, see Péter Deák, "Mi van a katonai viták mögött?" *Beszélö*, 21 September 1991, 9–11.

16. On this issue, see the interview with MOD spokesman Lieutenant Colonel Lajos Erdélyi in *Heti Magyarország*, 2 April 1993; and *Magyar Nemzet*, 19 November 1994.

17. See, for instance, the MOD's "A Magyar Köztársaság biztonságpolitikája" and "A Magyar Köztársaság honvédelmi politikája" on the Worldwide Web (hm.hu/HM/magyar_koztarsasag_vedelempoliti.htm), 1998.

18. In July 1998, parliamentary leaders of the Alliance of Free Democrats once again raised the issue in several press conferences. See, for instance, *Népszabadság*, 27 July 1998.

19. This impression was confirmed during several rounds of interviews the author conducted with high-ranking Romanian and Hungarian military officers and diplomats in Budapest and Bucharest in 1993, 1995, and 1996.

20. Reisch, "Central and Eastern Europe's Quest," 39.

21. RFE/RL DR II, 2:24 (5 February 1998).

22. See Joshua Spero, "The Budapest-Prague-Warsaw Triangle: Central European Security after the Visegrad Summit," *European Security* 1, no. 1 (Spring

1992): 58–83; and Zoltan Barany, "Visegrad Four Contemplate Separate Paths," *Transition* 1, no. 14 (11 August 1995): 56–59.

23. See, for instance, *Pesti Hírlap*, 8–9 January 1994; and *Új Magyarország*, 19 May 1995.

24. See *Magyar Nemzet*, 6 June 1998.

25. Zoltan Barany, *Soldiers and Politics in Eastern Europe, 1945–1990* (London: Macmillan, 1993), 132–133.

26. Reuters dispatch (Paris), 20 November 1990.

27. See *Népszabadság*, 21 February 1990. For commentary, see Miklós Szabó, "Improvizáció—a NATO tag Magyarországról," *Bészelö*, 3 March 1990.

28. See an interview with Lawrence Eagleburger, and a NATO spokesman's statement, in *Népszabadság*, 22 February 1990; and reports of the Budapest visit of West German Defense Minister Gerhard Stoltenberg, *Népszabadság*, 12 July 1990.

29. See Jeffrey Simon, "Post-Enlargement NATO: Dangers of 'Failed Suitors' and Need for a Strategy," in Stephen J. Blank, ed., *From Madrid to Brussels: Perspectives of NATO Enlargement* (Carlisle Barracks, Pennsylvania: US Army War College, 1997), 31.

30. Author's interview with Zoltán Martínusz, head of the Department of NATO Affairs at the Hungarian Ministry of Defense (Budapest, May 1998).

31. On this issue, see Thomas S. Szayna and F. Stephen Larrabee, *East European Military Reform after the Cold War: Implications for the United States* (Santa Monica, California: RAND, 1995).

32. See, for instance, Christian Haerpfer, Clair Wallace, and Richard Rose, *Public Perceptions of Threats to Security in Post-Communist Europe* (Glasgow: CSPP/University of Strathclyde, 1997).

33. *Népszabadság*, 26 February 1997.

34. RFE/RL DR II, 1:155 (7 November 1997).

35. *Népszava*, 29 August 1997.

36. See *The Economist*, 15 November 1997, 54.

37. *Világgazdaság*, 9 October 1997.

38. See, for instance, *Új Magyarország*, 30 October 1997.

39. *Népszabadság*, 8 April 1998 and 12 November 1998.

40. See Árpád Göncz, "The Least Expensive Way to Guarantee Security," *Transitions* 4, no. 7 (December 1997): 19.

41. For a more detailed discussion of this issue, see Christopher Jones, "NATO Enlargement: Brussels as the Heir of Moscow," *Problems of Post-Communism* 45, no. 4 (July–August 1998): 44–55.

42. RFE/RL DR II, 1:128 (30 September 1997).

43. RFE/RL DR II, 2:142 (27 July 1998).

44. Author's interviews with defense officials (Budapest, May 1998).

45. This section draws on Zoltan Barany, "Democratic Consolidation and the Military: The East European Experience," *Comparative Politics* 30, no. 1 (October 1997): 21–44.

46. See János Szabó, "Hadsereg és civil ellenörzés," *Társadalmi Szemle* 50, no. 4 (April 1995): 68–76.

47. See Zoltan Barany, "Civil-Military Relations in Comparative Perspective," *Political Studies* 41, no. 4 (December 1993): 605.

48. See the interview with former State Secretary of Defense Rudolf Joó in *A honvédelem négy éve, 1990–1994* (Budapest: Zrínyi, 1994), 164.

49. *Ibid.*, 38–47.

50. See, for instance, *Napi Magyarország*, 6 June 1998; author's interviews with MOD officials (Budapest, May 1998); and *A honvédelem négy éve*, 178.

51. Author's interview with Zoltán Martínusz.

52. See, for instance, *Magyar Nemzet*, 8 October 1993; and Reuters (Budapest), 9 October 1993.

53. *Magyar Hírlap*, 26 February 1998; and RFE/RL DR, 2:39 (26 February 1998).

54. See Barany, *Soldiers and Politics*, 119–122.

55. On this issue, see *Népszabadság* (Budapest), 29 October 1990; *Magyar Nemzet* (Budapest), 3 November 1990; and Endre Sík, "The Vulture and the Calamity (Or, Why Were Hungarian Taxi Drivers Able to Rebel?)," in János Mátyás Kovács, ed., *Transition to Capitalism? The Communist Legacy in Eastern Europe* (New Brunswick, New Jersey: Transaction, 1994), 275–289.

56. See, for instance, *Pesti Hírlap*, 7–8 May 1994.

57. *Magyar Hírlap*, 17 July 1998.

58. Author's interviews with MOD officials (Budapest, May 1998).

59. See, for instance, the interviews with Imre Mécs and Tamás Wachsler in *A honvédelem négy éve*, 174–178.

60. The pattern of inexperience was not broken under Keleti's term either; his deputy for political affairs (in the rank of state secretary), István Fodor, was a veterinarian.

61. *Honvédelmi ismeretek* (Budapest: Tankönyvkiadó, 1984), 76.

62. See *Szabadon választott: Parlamenti almanach, 1990* (Budapest: IPKV, 1990), 225.

63. MOD, Heti Sajtóösszefoglaló, 1998/44 (3 July 1998), www.h-m.hu/HM/cron/1998/19980703.html.

64. Author's interview with Zoltán Martínusz.

65. See Sauerwein, "Defence Adequacy," 438.

66. See *Los Angeles Times*, 4 November 1990; and *Financial Times*, 5 November 1990.

67. See *Magyar Hírlap*, 4 May 1998.

68. See, for instance, *Népszabadság*, 12 March 1997.

69. *Wall Street Journal*, 2 January 1997.

70. See, for example, *Új Magyarország*, 19 May 1995.

71. *Népszabadság*, 26 February 1997.

72. For results of the recent accounting probe of the air force, see *Népszabadság*, 21 July 1998.

73. *Magyar Honvéd,* 1 October 1993.

74. *Népszava,* 8 March 1997.

75. See *A honvédelem négy éve,* 71–78.

76. See *Népszabadság,* 4 April 1998; *Népszava,* 3 July 1998; *Magyar Hírlap,* 7 August 1998.

77. *Magyar Hírlap,* 7 August 1998.

78. *Die Süddeutsche Zeitung,* 3 December 1994; *Wall Street Journal,* 2 January 1997.

79. On this issue, see Zoltan Barany, "Military Higher Education in Hungary," *Armed Forces and Society* 15, no. 3 (Spring 1989): 371–389.

80. *Magyar Hírlap,* 28 July 1998.

81. See *Magyar Hírlap,* 28 July 1998.

82. *Magyar Nemzet,* 10 August 1998.

83. On this issue see, for instance, Captain Marybeth Peterson Ulrich, "When East Meets West: Fostering Democracy in Postcommunist States," *Airpower Journal* 9 (Special Edition 1995): 4–16.

84. *A honvédelem négy éve,* 69.

85. *Népszabadság,* 21 July 1998.

86. *Magyar Nemzet,* 29 July 1998.

87. *Magyar Hírlap,* 28 July 1998.

88. See the interview with military sociologist János Szabó in *Népszabadság,* 2 August 1993.

89. *Népszabadság,* 21 April 1998; *Magyar Hírlap,* 4 August 1998.

90. *Népszabadság,* 14 February 1997.

91. *Magyar Nemzet,* 15 October 1994.

92. RFE/RL DR II, 1:153 (5 November 1997).

93. *Magyar Hírlap,* 13 March 1998.

94. See for instance, *Heti Magyarország,* 7 January 1994.

95. See *Magyar Hírlap,* 12 November 1997 and 21 April 1998.

96. See the interview with Foreign Minister Martonyi, *Magyar Nemzet,* 6 June 1998.

4 The Czech Republic

A SMALL CONTRIBUTOR OR A "FREE RIDER"?

THOMAS S. SZAYNA

The Czech Republic's entry into NATO marks an important threshold in the country's postcommunist "transition." If the end point of the post-communist transition is defined as (1) the erasing of the legacy of Soviet-led forced detachment and communist autarkic estrangement of the country from its neighbors in Europe, (2) the setting in place of institutional means for the growth and prosperity of the Czech Republic within an increasingly unified community of democratic European states, and (3) the restoring of an international context for the Czech Republic in line with what has been "normal" for a millennium, then the incorporation of the Czech Republic into the dominant security organization in Europe amounts a milestone in the process. Although it will take decades for Czech prosperity to regain its pre–World War II parity with that of Austria or Bavaria, Czech entry into NATO accelerates the pace of the catching up, for it solidifies the irreversibility of the transition process and strengthens the country's candidacy for early European Union (EU) membership.

The lengthy road still left in order to erase the legacy of Soviet domination need not obfuscate the tremendous progress the Czech Republic has made so far. Indeed, the magnitude of the Czech transition can be seen in the sweeping changes of the 1990s. The Czech lands have moved from being a dominant component of the neo-Stalinist sham federal state of Czechoslovakia in 1989 to being a largely national Czech state and a functioning democracy. In terms of the depth of changes in the country's identity, the scope of the Czech transition exceeds that of the other two new NATO members, Poland and Hungary. Whereas all three countries went through the fundamental shocks of the end of communist regimes and their replacement by experiments in democratic political systems and free market economies, the lands currently forming the Czech Republic also went through a second fundamental shock, that of the Czechoslovak state's falling apart under the strains of the transition from communism just three years after the hard-line communists were ousted from power. Thus, besides the shock of the end of communism, the Czechs and the Slovaks also experienced a shock akin to those that befell the USSR and Yugoslavia (although without the strife that accompanied the breakup of the other two "federal" communist states).

The two successor states that emerged from Czechoslovakia, the Czech Republic and the Slovak Republic, diverged substantially in the paths their political transitions took soon after their split-up at the beginning of 1993. Whereas the breakup strengthened Czech efforts to join the dominant European security and economic institutions, similar tendencies weakened in Slovakia. Undoubtedly, Czechs had dominated Czechoslovakia, Prague housed the machinery of the federal state, and the transition to a Czech state faced fewer difficulties and proved less traumatic than the comparable transition in Slovakia, where some institutions truly had to emerge from scratch. But the fact remains that, as a new state, the Czech Republic has faced accession to NATO while grappling with establishing its own identity in contemporary, increasingly unified Europe.

After the ouster of communists from power, Czechoslovak policy had to adjust to dealing with security in terms of a newly sovereign federal state outside of an alliance framework. Then, upon the breakup of the country, the Czech security establishment had to consider security in terms of a smaller national state still outside of an alliance framework. Since 1997, Czech security experts have had to readjust their thinking again, away from national terms and toward planning as part of a genuine collective defense organization and a democratic security community. Since the Czech Republic gained independence, a sense of unreality has surrounded Czech defense planning, because the state has faced no military threats and it borders on neighbors with whom a military conflict seems unthinkable. The situation is different from that in Poland or Hungary, where instability in the former USSR (Belarus, Ukraine, and Russia) and the wars of the Yugoslav succession, respectively, have driven home the idea that conflicts have not ended and security has not been automatically assured despite the end of the Cold War.

For a variety of reasons, issues of safeguarding the security of the Czech state, outlining a defense strategy, and reorganizing the armed forces proved difficult for the Czechs and remained unresolved up until the invitation to join NATO in May 1997. Although Czech security and defense experts drew up blueprints of Czech security policy, the successive Czech governments have delayed adopting them formally. Similarly, Czech military planners have gone far in making the Czech armed forces more compatible with NATO's, but they have proceeded sometimes in an ad hoc fashion and without clear guidance and prioritization provided by the government. At the beginning of 1999, on the verge of Czech entry into NATO, aspects of security policy and defense strategy remained unresolved or only partially solved because of a series of weak governments and limited interest in security issues among political circles and the electorate in the Czech Republic.

In this chapter I attempt to explain some of the problems that have affected Czech thinking about defense and security. I begin with a discussion of the Czech defense establishment's assumptions about security, go over the Czech leadership's security policies, touch on the peculiar but widespread negative image of the military in the Czech Republic, and then trace the reform of the Czech armed forces. I conclude with a discussion of the role the country might play in NATO and the military contribution it might make to the organization.

Basic Czech Assumptions about Security

Although the Czech security and defense establishment on several occasions presented its vision of Czech national interests, potential threats to the country, and policies designed to deal with the threats, the Czech government repeatedly delayed its approval of a basic outline of national security and military strategy of the republic. A defense "white paper" was finally published on 17 February 1999—just a month before the country's scheduled formal membership in NATO. It presented official Czech views on security, outlined a state defense policy, and put together a set of guidelines for the military. The delay in issuing the Czech white paper on defense was peculiar and stood in contrast to the situation in Poland and Hungary.

The delay, however, meant neither the existence of deep cleavages within Czech society about the country's security orientation nor the absence of a consistent Czech policy of integration into Euro-Atlantic and European structures since the country's independence. Instead, the recognition of a benign security environment, a focus on economic transformation, and the low salience of security issues in the Czech Republic provide the most important reasons for the delays in tackling a basic security document. As has been borne out in public opinion surveys, the Czech electorate sees security in terms of the absence of a threat,[1] and in post–Cold War Europe, the geographical location of the Czech Republic makes the country highly unlikely to be threatened militarily. Since most Czechs seem to take security from external aggression pretty much for granted, membership in a military alliance has not generated any great enthusiasm or urgency among either the Czech population or the Czech political leadership.[2] In view of this sentiment, why have the successive Czech governments sought NATO membership?

The Institute of International Relations (IIR), an advisory body to the Czech Foreign Ministry, produced an elaboration of Czech national interests in 1993 and then, in 1997, its own version of a Czech security policy.[3] The two documents together amount to the most comprehensive, if not fully authoritative, Czech statements explaining the underpinnings of Czech security and defense policies, and the defense establishment has treated the two documents as de facto outlines of Czech policy.[4]

As the IIR's statement on security policy points out, establishing and sustaining a democratic political system and a functioning market economy are the fundamental goals of any Czech government. Such goals cannot be seen separately from the integration of the country into a larger, democratic, market-based European community. Moreover, as the IIR statement makes clear, the Czech Republic must play an active role in the further construction of such a community.[5] Since the EU and NATO form the two most important elements that allow for the development of such a community, in IIR's view Czech membership in both organizations emerges as crucial in securing the most basic goals and aspirations of

Czech society. Even in the absence of an authoritative Czech white paper on defense, it remains clear that all Czech governments since independence have subscribed to such a vision of basic principles underpinning Czech security policy. Scarcely a week has gone by since 1993 without some high Czech official's commenting that membership in NATO and entry into the EU constitute the two basic foreign policy goals of the Czech Republic. The goals are often couched in terms of a "return to Europe" or of "undoing past injustices." While not disputing the political and emotional significance of such claims, a more analytical perspective on Czech aspirations of EU and NATO membership focuses more on the gains that would accrue to the Czech state from such membership.

Since independence, every Czech (and post-1989 Czechoslovak) government has viewed integration of the country into the EU as the best way to secure its newly gained sovereignty and ensure its long-term prosperity and democratic development. From a rationalist perspective, in simple economic terms EU membership would make the country more competitive in the world economy, and the Czech Republic would obtain an abundance of aid and support from the EU to transform its economy effectively. And becoming part of an increasingly unified (politically and economically) European community, the Czech Republic would join the most affluent and powerful group of states in the world, thereby safeguarding its security for the foreseeable future.

A focus on the economic aspects of security has not been limited to the liberal economists who have played a dominant role in steering the country for the first five years after independence. Even some of the highest-ranking Czech military figures have argued that the economic security of the Czech Republic and its entry into the EU are just as important for the country's security as Czech military potential, if not more so.[6] Opinion polls have shown consistently that a majority of Czechs favor joining the EU as a full member in the shortest possible time.[7] Indeed, the Czech electorate sees EU membership as the standard by which to judge the success of the Czech transition away from communism and as a milestone in undoing the effects of communism upon the country (and the support stems from the economic as well as the emotional perspective of "rejoining Europe"). The strong popular support for EU membership stands in contrast to the substantially weaker support for NATO membership.[8]

The legacies of the communist system and the wide disparities in wealth and level of economic development between the Czech Republic and the affluent core of the EU have meant that the Czech Republic would not join the EU overnight. The EU's preoccupation with strengthening the ties among its existing members and those members' fears about admitting into their organization a country with a much weaker economy, as well as the range of economic, legal, and political adjustments needed to make the Czech Republic compatible with the EU, have delayed the country's likely entry into the EU until well into the first decade of the twenty-first century.[9] Such delays have complicated the Czechs' fundamental objective of "rejoining Europe" and have made it necessary to safeguard the country's transition during the stage of preparation for EU membership and accession negotiations with the EU. Several Czech security goals stem from such basic considerations: (1) ensuring that European integration does not unravel and that Germany remains firmly integrated in European structures; (2) preventing any possibility of Russia's imposing control over the Czech Republic or even thwarting its integration process; and (3) preventing regional problems from escalating to more serious security threats. All of these goals serve to keep the Czech drive to join the EU on track.

As the single most powerful state in Europe, Germany presents a potential security worry for most Europeans. The German "problem" seems to have been solved by making Germany unable to use its considerable power unilaterally and instead defining its security in terms of an integrated Europe. Czech views of the necessity of keeping Germany integrated do not differ greatly from the dominant views throughout Europe, though they have a special quality because of the history of Czech-German relations in the twentieth century and the proximity of the Czech Republic to Germany. The preferred Czech solution to the "German problem" emphasizes the continued vitality of NATO, for the alliance makes US involvement in European security affairs automatic and guarantees that Germany remains integrated in wider security structures. US leadership retains a crucial role for the foreseeable future, for no European state could play the role the United States does.[10] A European security pillar presents a reasonable option in the more distant future, but the Czech security establishment does not want to see plans for a European security pillar lead to the downgrading of US involvement in Europe any time soon.

Czech security experts recognize Germany's crucial role for the Czech Republic: "Germany was and always will remain the most important neighbor of the Czech nation."[11] Accordingly, they also see Germany's role in Europe as the most important security consideration for the Czech Republic. From such a perspective, NATO's persistence and Czech membership in NATO form the most important security goals of the Czech Republic. Put in different terms, the integration of the Czech Republic into a greater European security community (of which Germany is a member) holds out the possibility of transcending a persistent twentieth-century problem for the Czechs—that of being a "buffer state" between two large and sometimes aggressive powers (the USSR/Russia and Germany). Last but not least, Czech and German membership in the same alliance holds out the prospect of putting Czech-German relations on the same "normal" level as Dutch-German relations and finally putting the legacy of World War II to rest.[12]

Russia, as the main successor state to the former hegemon over central Europe in general—and the Czech Republic specifically—remains a hypothetical threat to the Czech Republic. If some of the elements unreconciled to the loss of Russia's superpower status came to power in Russia, they might conceivably launch an attempt to bring some of the former Soviet republics and perhaps even some of the former satellite states into a Russian sphere of influence. Increasingly, such a scenario seems farfetched, and Czech security experts treat it as such, but it remains plausible. The more likely effect of a Russian resurgence entails renewed confrontation in Europe and disruptions in the transformation and integration of the former communist states into the EU.[13] Czech membership in NATO would deter any hypothetical Russian expansionist designs on the country and would limit the level of any disruptions upon the country in case of Russian resurgence.

In Czech thinking, the potential threats from both Germany and Russia seem unlikely to materialize. If they were to do so, however, they would endanger the sovereignty of the Czech Republic fundamentally. In other words, such threats have a low probability but entail high potential cost. Regional, border, or internal conflicts seem much more likely as security threats to the Czech Republic in the foreseeable future.[14] But although such threats have a higher probability than does a fundamental challenge to Czech sovereignty, they would entail a lower cost to the Czech Republic if they were to materialize. Such threats also seem more likely in the unintegrated portions of Europe, primarily in the Balkans and the Soviet successor states, than in the immediate vicinity of the Czech Republic. The Czech security establishment sees a transformed NATO that deals effectively with such conflicts (deterring them and preventing their escalation) as being in the Czech interest. Since three of the Czech Republic's immediate neighbors (Germany, Austria, and Poland) are members of, or will shortly join, European security and economic institutions to which the Czech Republic aspires, a border war with Slovakia presents the only direct potential threat to the Czech Republic in the second category of threats. Although hypothetically plausible, the Czech security establishment sees such a threat as extremely unlikely, for no border or minority problems encumber relations between the two countries. Under Mečiar's tenure in Slovakia, however, the scenario became more plausible in terms of a resurgent Russia's using Slovakia to disrupt the former Soviet satellites, including the Czech Republic.[15]

According to Czech security experts, "soft" security problems such as organized crime, waves of refugees, and terrorism will form the most likely security threats in Europe for the foreseeable future, especially as they pertain to the Czech Republic and other states engaged in transforming their societies and economies away from communism. Such problems may affect the Czech Republic as a result of internal instability and unrest in the unintegrated portions of Europe. These threats have a high likelihood but would entail fairly low costs for the Czech Republic— primarily greater pressures on the state budget as a result of increased spending on police and housing for refugees, or as a result of delays in the economic transformation caused by the driving away of investors due to perceptions of increased risk. Although low in comparison with the costs of "hard" security threats, such costs might still become substantial when seen from the perspective of opportunity costs and delays in Czech integration into the EU.[16] Military means have secondary value in dealing with "soft" security problems, but such threats do make even more important the existence of an effective security organization that can provide expertise and material assistance to counter them. From such an angle, Czech integration into NATO and the EU will lead to a stronger state that can deal more effectively with "soft" security problems.

All of the security threats, from the highly unlikely fundamental problems to the more mundane and likely, have the common thread of highlighting the role of NATO in ensuring that Czech integration into the EU does not become sidetracked and in making sure that small states in Europe do not fall victim to aggression by the powerful (a pattern with a long history in Europe and one that the Czechs have experienced on a number of occasions in the twentieth century). NATO plays a role in maintaining a security environment in which the EU can continue to develop, and it deters or limits the manner in which a variety of security threats can affect the Czech Republic. But Czech membership in the alliance has the potential to enhance the country's role in shaping the security environment.

Although Czech officials agree in principle to the overall security goals outlined above, and although draft security documents prepared in the mid-1990s by the various Czech governments reflect the themes contained in the two IIR documents, successive Czech governments have paid limited attention to security and defense issues. The low level of interest in security issues has the potential to delay Czech integration into NATO and to make NATO's security guarantees more difficult to implement if the security environment were somehow to change for the worse. The next section provides an outline of Czech foreign and defense policies since the emergence of a sovereign Czech state.

Main Trends in Czech Security Policy

As a general rule, foreign and defense policies, including the identification of security threats, the importance attached to them, and policies designed to address them, stem from the domestic orientations of the ruling coalition in the given country. The Czech Republic fits the rule.

The Initial Postcommunist Period

The Czechoslovak "Velvet Revolution" took the form of a sudden rupture in November 1989. Within six weeks, former dissidents ousted and

replaced the hard-line communists associated with the Soviet intervention in 1968. The most famous dissident, the playwright Václav Havel, became president of the country in January 1990. The "founding elections"
in June 1990 revealed overwhelming public support for systemic change,
and the new government launched steps to replace the communist autarkic and authoritarian model with a market economy and a democratic
political system. The integration of Czechoslovakia into western European international institutions (the EC, now the EU) formed the international component of the domestic transition away from communism.

In terms of security, Czechoslovak efforts to safeguard the transition
concentrated initially on transforming the Conference on Security and
Cooperation in Europe (CSCE)—now the Organization for Security and
Cooperation in Europe (OSCE)—into a pan-European security organization that would transcend Cold War divisions and alliances. As part of
such a view, Czechoslovak foreign policy initially envisioned the dissolution of both NATO and the Warsaw Pact. Czechoslovak appreciation for
NATO and its continued role grew steadily, however, advanced by residual concerns about the future evolution of a unified Germany, fears over
the attempted coup in Moscow in August 1991, the violent breakup of
Yugoslavia in mid-1991, and then the breakup of the USSR. The wars of
Yugoslav succession especially put an end to the "romantic" stage in
Czechoslovakia's foreign policy thinking by demonstrating vividly that,
despite the end of the Cold War, security problems continued to exist, and
any effective all-European security institution would take time to develop.

Because of the need for Western diplomatic, economic, and financial
support to ensure the success of the Czechoslovak domestic transition, relations with the United States and western European countries (especially
the immediate neighbors, Germany and Austria) went almost overnight
from adversarial to close and friendly. Conversely, the new leadership
implicitly identified the USSR as Czechoslovakia's main potential threat
because of the possibility of the Soviets' attempting to reimpose a satellite
status on the country and constrain its reformist path. So long as Soviet
troops remained stationed in the country and the Warsaw Pact continued
to exist, a Soviet attempt to roll back the regime existed as a real threat.
Consequently, Czechoslovak leaders quickly negotiated a rapid withdrawal

of the Soviet troops stationed in the country (completed in mid-1991) and attempted first to curtail the ability of the Soviets to use the Warsaw Pact as a mechanism to deny full sovereignty to Czechoslovakia and then to end the pact altogether. After the breakup of the USSR in late 1991, the Czechoslovak security establishment identified Russia and Ukraine as sources of instability that could threaten Czechoslovakia's transformation.

Besides the complete shift in international orientation, the change of regimes also provided an opportunity for a change in relations with immediate neighbors. Driven by similar goals vis-à-vis the USSR, genuine cooperation and coordination of policies took place between Czechoslovakia, Poland, and Hungary. The cooperation built on earlier ties among the dissidents in the three countries, all of whom had assumed power. By 1991, the cooperation (spurred by Western encouragement) took on a formal nature, and the three countries became known as the Visegrád group (for the city in Hungary where the leaders of the three countries met and agreed to coordinate some of their policies).

The internal social strains of the transition away from communism exacerbated regionalist and nationalist tendencies in Czechoslovakia. The June 1992 elections led to a hopelessly deadlocked parliament—a civic-liberal and Christian-democratic coalition in favor of rapid market reforms emerged as the dominant political grouping in the Czech lands, while a populist-statist movement appealing to Slovak nationalism emerged as the dominant political grouping in Slovakia. Because of the rules concerning the passage of laws in the bicameral Czechoslovak parliament, the dominant Slovak and Czech groupings could each block any measure proposed by the other side. Recognizing the impasse and the futility of further debate, the two sides agreed to dissolve the federation and set up two independent successor states, even though a majority of Czechs and Slovaks favored a continued common state. During the later half of 1992, Czech and Slovak representatives negotiated the breakup, and the two new states came into being officially on 1 January 1993.

The Klaus Era

The Czech assembly, elected in the June 1992 elections, became the national parliament of the new Czech Republic upon its birth. For almost five years (from January 1993 until December 1997), a coalition of liberal, civic-democratic, and Christian-democratic parties formed a government led by Václav Klaus. Upon independence, Czech political institutions retained a great deal of continuity with former Czechoslovak structures. Havel became president of the new country, and the dominant pro-Western integrationist policy became even stronger. Even in terms of symbols, the Czech Republic represented the "true" successor state; for example, the Czechoslovak flag became the flag of the Czech Republic.

Upon independence, Czech foreign policy became a more radical variation of the earlier Czechoslovak policy. Klaus and his leadership previously had been uneasy with Slovak political trends and looked at Slovakia as unnecessary baggage that acted as a brake on Czech aspirations to become integrated into Western institutions. With the Slovak "baggage" discarded, Klaus felt free to implement the full range of policies needed for the Czech Republic to become integrated into Western institutions as soon as possible. Simple geography aided his goal. Upon independence, the Czech Republic became the westernmost of the former communist states in central Europe; more than half of its borders were shared with EU and NATO member Germany and soon-to-be EU member Austria. The Czech Republic also ceased to border any Soviet successor state. With the high level of development of the country and the successful reform measures in 1990–92, all the necessary factors seemed to be in place to push for a rapid Czech integration into Western international structures.

In a pattern similar to that of discarding the "baggage" that Slovakia represented, the Czech leadership downgraded regional cooperation in the Visegrád group (the Czech Republic, Slovakia, Poland, and Hungary) in favor of a unilateral attempt to join the EU and NATO. The rationale for such a policy stemmed from the Czech leadership's perception of the Czech Republic as the front-runner in the race with neighbors to join the Western institutions. Linking Czech fate with that of the other three countries only delayed Czech integration. Similarly, in terms of ties with Slovakia, the Klaus government quickly proved that it treated Slovakia like any other neighboring country and allowed a monetary union between the Czech Republic and Slovakia to break down soon after the two countries separated.

The other Visegrád members and, for their own reasons, the EU and NATO greeted the Czech "defection" from regional cooperation with resentment. Both the EU and NATO acted to curtail the Czechs' unilateral approaches. As a result, Klaus outwardly modified the Czech policy line, though without abandoning the goal of being the first of the former communist countries to join the EU. The acceptance of the Czech Republic into the OECD in 1995 as the first of the former communist states and the EU's invitation to the Czech Republic to begin accession negotiations (as one of six new countries) in March 1998 has borne out the determined Czech push for integration. Showing confidence in free market approaches, the Czech leadership also pursued a policy of regional trade liberalization, both by acting as a catalyst in the formation of the Central European Free Trade Area (CEFTA, at first consisting of the Czech Republic, Slovakia, Poland, and Hungary and later joined by Slovenia, Romania, and Bulgaria) and by negotiating a series of bilateral free trade agreements.

In the security sphere, the Czech Republic became physically more secure because of the increased distance between it and the former USSR. Whereas previously Czechoslovakia had bordered the former USSR (Ukraine), the Czech Republic became separated from Ukraine by Slovakia, and Russia became removed by two countries from the Czech Republic. In addition, because of the country's being geographically "wedged in" with the unified Germany, Czech planners could rely on substantial German assistance to deal with any hypothetical threat from Russia. Indeed, in view of the Czech Republic's lack of serious problems with any neighboring country, it became exceedingly difficult to come up with even hypothetical military threats.

Because of the perception of a benign security environment and a lack of military threats to the country, the Czech leadership initially did not lobby vigorously for membership in NATO. Prior to 1994, Czech officials certainly aimed for NATO membership but did not push the issue, because security concerns seemed secondary to them and they felt that a vigorous debate on NATO enlargement had the potential to cause problems in relations with Russia and unnecessarily worsen the security environment. However, after the alliance decided in late 1993 to enlarge eastward, and once the discussions about enlargement moved to specifics, Czech officials openly campaigned for inclusion in the first round. The Czech Republic joined the Partnership for Peace (PFP) program shortly after the latter's announcement, and it participated extensively in PFP activities, especially with German and US armed forces. The participation has had a clear motive—preparation for and early entry into NATO. In order to contribute to collective security efforts in post–Cold War Europe (and to deal with the secondary security threats on the continent), as well as to assuage some fears in NATO about the Czech leadership's limited attention to defense issues, the Czech Republic has participated in peace operations at a substantial level. The Czechs stepped up their earlier (Czechoslovak) involvement in UN peacekeeping operations and have deployed an infantry battalion as part of the IFOR/SFOR operation in Bosnia-Herzegovina.

As the debate over the first round of invitations to NATO escalated in 1995–96, Czech-Polish ties in the security realm improved. The improvement made sense because Poland's importance in central Europe grew after the breakup of Czechoslovakia. The Czech leadership realized that, for geostrategic reasons, NATO saw Poland as the most important country among the aspiring new members, and close Czech-Polish security ties opened up the prospect of simultaneous Czech-Polish integration into NATO.

Czech concerns about Germany probably also played a role in the improvement in Czech-Polish relations.[17] Although Czech-German relations remained close and good, legacies of the past inserted irritants and kept delaying the signing of a German-Czech treaty. Problems arose because of the intertwining of domestic German politics with the issue of compensation to ethnic Germans expelled from Czechoslovakia (mostly from Czech lands) shortly after World War II. Many of the expellees settled in Bavaria, and they have had a substantial influence on Bavarian politics. The junior partner in Helmut Kohl's coalition (which governed until 1998), the Bavarian-based Christian-Social Union, relied on the vote of the expellees, and as a result, the constituency has had an inordinate impact on German foreign policy. Although the issue really boils down to a German domestic problem, it has had the effect of alienating some Czechs and encouraging concerns about German designs. This, combined with the fact that much of the direct foreign investment into the Czech Republic since 1990 has come from Germany, has meant that residual fears among Czechs about the eventual nature of German influence over the Czech Republic have not disappeared. Both communist and extreme nationalist political forces in the Czech Republic have used fears of Germany to discredit the Klaus policy of integration. Ties with Austria have been free of major problems, though some irritants (including ones regarding expellees, similar to Czech-German irritants) have surfaced.

Czech relations with Slovakia have a special quality about them. On one hand, extensive and close ties remain between Czech and Slovak officials. On the other, postdivorce resentments and grudges have intruded into relations between the two states. Slovakia's uncertain political reform process (until the elections in the fall of 1998) raised a number of concerns in the Czech Republic. Most of all, Czech officials began to look upon Slovakia as a politically unstable and potentially threatening country (in the sense of causing refugee flows). One specific Czech concern revolved around the close ties between Russia and Slovakia and the potential Russian use of Slovakia as a tool to promote instability in central Europe. A clumsy Slovak attempt to create problems in Czech-Slovak relations shortly before NATO's May 1997 summit and thus to damage Czech entry into NATO provides one example of the pro-Moscow proclivities of the Mečiar leadership and his willingness to introduce irritants into Slovak-Czech ties. Another Czech concern stems from nationalistic policies in Slovakia and from Slovak-Hungarian friction. The Czech leadership has feared that tensions might escalate and cause a spillover of problems to the Czech Republic. Nonetheless, on the basis of extensive and continuing personal ties between individual Czech and Slovak politicians, administrators, and military officers, as well as disparities in power relations between the two countries, the Czech leadership views Slovakia as a problem but not as a military adversary. Czech officials treated the ouster of Mečiar from power in Slovakia with relief and even enthusiasm. All indications seem to point to close relations between the two countries for the foreseeable future, so long as liberal political forces remain in power in Slovakia.

Implicitly, Czech leadership has perceived Russia as an adversary because, most of all, Russian opposition to Czech membership in NATO has put an obstacle in front of a fundamental Czech foreign policy goal that underlies a whole range of the country's policies.[18] In addition, increasing signs of strength by communist and nationalist political forces in Russia raise the specter of renewed Russian attempts to expand its influence over central Europe. Finally, the uncertain political and economic situation in Russia and Ukraine has led to the proliferation of organized crime and drug smuggling rings that have established a strong presence in the Czech Republic. Dealing with such threats has become one of the foremost security problems for the Czech Republic.

Parliamentary elections in June 1996 weakened the Klaus-led coalition, and the government finally collapsed amid scandal, controversy, and internal bickering in December 1997.[19] The Klaus coalition, however, did steer the country successfully to the Madrid summit in July 1997 and managed to receive the invitation to join NATO. Had the Czech Republic not received an invitation at Madrid, the Klaus government probably would have fallen even sooner, not because of any great security concerns among the Czech electorate but because such a failure would have meant a symbolic stamp of disapproval by NATO regarding the pace of reforms in the Czech Republic. Had it happened, it would have slowed down the Czech drive to join the EU and relegated the Czech Republic to a "second tier" of countries emerging from communism.

Although successful in receiving the invitation to join NATO, the Klaus leadership had never paid great attention to security matters, and its activity in support of the NATO invitation had a forced feel about it. Befitting his own proclivities, Klaus seems to have perceived (probably correctly) that a vibrant economy and a strong currency provided the best ways to ensure security for a small country in contemporary Europe. But once NATO decided to enlarge, the Klaus government argued the Czech case sufficiently, despite widespread qualms in NATO about Czech military effectiveness.

After Klaus

A caretaker government of technocrats, led by Josef Tosovsky, succeeded Klaus for six months. Elections in June 1998 led to an impasse, because neither of the dominant parties—the civic-democrats led by Klaus and the social-democrats led by Miloš Zeman—won an outright majority, and neither could easily form a governing coalition. In a novel arrangement between two political archenemies, Zeman formed a social-democrat minority government with Klaus's acquiescence. The arrangement seems unlikely to work for the four years stipulated, and another round of early elections seems likely. The opposition scored successes in elections for the Senate as well as in local elections in November 1998. It appears that political volatility will continue during the Czech Republic's initial period of integration into NATO.

All indications point to the social-democrats' perpetuating Klaus's earlier policy of devoting only limited attention to security and defense matters. The social-democrats share the overall goal of EU membership, but their views toward NATO membership seem lukewarm. In the early years of the NATO enlargement debate, the social-democrats opposed enlargement. Even after the Madrid invitation, they advocated a referendum on the issue. Because of their constituency, the social-democrats may pay even less attention to security and defense issues and devote more resources to ameliorating the social disruptions connected with the Czech transformation rather than to defense. The economic slowdown that has affected the Czech Republic since 1997 makes the turn toward even less emphasis on defense more likely.

The Image of the Military

The low esteem in which the armed forces are held in the Czech lands—something that is borne out in all public opinion polls—has deep historical roots and represents a peculiar Czech problem. The issue has greatly affected the political role that the Czech armed forces have played in the country, and it has probably contributed to the political leadership's limited interest in defense and security. Quite simply, in a democratic political system, politicians will deal with issues of most interest to the electorate. If security does not seem threatened and the military seems unimportant, politicians have few incentives to pay much attention to such issues.

The strong anti-military and even pacifist outlooks common to people in the Czech lands have historical roots.[20] The last time the Bohemian (Czech) army fought a major battle in defense of its homeland was in 1620, during the Thirty Years War, when it suffered a crushing defeat at the Battle of White Mountain (Bílá Hora). Following the defeat, and the absorption of Bohemia and Moravia into the Hapsburg empire, the military became associated with foreign domination. The identification of German-speaking Austrians with the military during the rise of Czech nationalism in the nineteenth century strengthened the negative image of a soldier. The popular image of soldiers as bumbling fools also comes across in classic nineteenth-century Czech literature.

Despite the establishment of a Czechoslovak state in 1918, the Czechoslovak military never fought in its defense. Thus, the military could not point to any one "glorious fight" to form the core myth of its serving as the protector of state sovereignty. Indeed, the harnessing of the Czechoslovak military for Soviet ends and its participation in domestic crackdowns under the communist regime only strengthened the old negative images. The exploits of the Czechoslovak Legion during the Russian Civil War and the participation of a few Czechoslovak combat units on both eastern (primarily Slovak) and western fronts during World War II could not substitute for a battle in defense of the state. In popular perceptions, the military proved useless on the several occasions during the twentieth century when the Czechoslovak state came under threat.

The first such instance took place in 1938–39, when Nazi Germany threatened Czechoslovakia. In a pragmatic move, and after being abandoned by its allies (France and Britain), the Czechoslovak government surrendered to German demands even though the Czechoslovak armed forces rivaled, if not outclassed, the German military in quality of equipment and training, and even though the territory bordering Germany and Austria—forested, mountainous, and fortified—favored defense. The failure to fight stemmed from the political leadership's decision, and blaming the military seems misguided, but in popular imagery the military had failed the country. The second instance came in 1948, during the communist coup, when the Czechoslovak armed forces stayed in their barracks. Their inaction stemmed from a mixture of causes, including the genuine popularity of the communist party, the absence of anti-Russian outlooks among the Czechs and Slovaks, and the image of the USSR as the main force responsible for the defeat of Nazi Germany. Another instance came in 1968, during the Warsaw Pact intervention to crush the reformist "Prague Spring," when the Czechoslovak military again stayed in their barracks. Again, the popular image seems misguided, because by the late 1960s, the thoroughly Soviet-penetrated Czechoslovak officer corps had become internally paralyzed by the split among its ranks between those who supported the reformers and those owed allegiance to the hard-liners and the Warsaw Pact.

In popular perceptions, and despite the inherent inaccuracies, the military proved useless on all three occasions. Driving the point home, following the 1968 intervention the Soviets retained a permanently stationed group of forces in Czechoslovakia, deployed primarily in Moravia and Slovakia. (Prior to 1968, the Soviets had shown greater trust in Czechoslovakia as an ally and had not stationed forces in the country, unlike the situation in Poland, Hungary, or East Germany.) In this sense, to many Czechs and Slovaks, the period after 1968 took on direct similarities to foreign occupation.

Moreover, the communist regime used the Czechoslovak military in an internal security role, assisting internal security forces in putting down strikes in 1953 and in dealing with demonstrations on the first anniversary of the Warsaw Pact intervention in 1969. In keeping with the communist model, the regime used the military as a tool for the socialization of conscripts, and the heavy dose of Marxist-Leninist indoctrination in the Czechoslovak communist armed forces made them appear to be a main pillar of the regime. Finally, two large-scale purges of the officer corps (post-1948 and post-1968) eliminated all but the most compliant and loyal officers, making the military seem a place fit only for those fully devoted to the regime.

The country's more than forty years of subservience toward the USSR and the subordination of the Czechoslovak armed forces to Soviet goals had far-reaching effects on the social stature of the armed forces by deepening the anti-military outlooks and pacifistic proclivities already widespread in Czechoslovakia (particularly in the Czech lands) at the popular level. Especially after the 1968 intervention and the subsequent purges in the military, the Czechoslovak officer corps became perceived at the popular level as little more than a group of traitors serving a foreign power.[21] Despite the incentives offered by the regime, few young people chose the military as a career. Adding to the earlier negative image of soldiers, the officer corps became popularly perceived as a place for rejects unable to do anything else.

To top it all off, during the Velvet Revolution in late 1989, the Czechoslovak armed forces came close to intervening internally in defense of the communist regime. As the regime teetered on the brink of collapse, the defense minister, General Milan Vaclavik, ordered the armed forces to prepare for possible intervention. Although the regime capitulated and never gave orders to implement the plans, the top leadership of the armed forces proved ready to intervene.

In light of all the foregoing, many calls emerged after 1989 advocating the abolition of the Czechoslovak armed forces altogether. A process of decline in the prestige of the armed forces took place in the other Soviet satellite states as well. But anti-military outlooks and low regard for the military clearly went farthest in Czechoslovakia, because they built on earlier proclivities. Only Hungary came close to the Czechoslovak case in this sense.[22]

A historically conditioned distrust of the military certainly exists in the Czech Republic, but treating it in a deterministic fashion misses the point. Many other militaries have gone through periods of popular distrust and low prestige (for example, the US armed forces after the Vietnam war), yet have managed to recover public esteem rapidly. Although unfavorable popular myths have contributed to suspicion of the armed forces in the Czech lands, less abstract problems, such as widespread hazing practices among conscripts and low pay and poor conditions for professional soldiers, have kept the suspicion at high levels. An efficient, people-oriented, capable Czech military associated with defense of the democratic system could break quickly with the earlier negative images. That the Czech military has had to overcome strong negative preconceptions, however, has increased the importance of leadership, resources, and a well-designed plan of action for changing the armed forces. Until 1998, none of these elements had sufficiently materialized in the Czech Republic.

Military Reform

The Czech Republic has followed the general line of military reform in postcommunist central Europe. Specifically, this has entailed drastic declines in the size of the military (structure and personnel) and in defense budgets in comparison with pre-1989 levels and a switch to territorial-type deployment of the armed forces. The budgetary cutbacks have eroded the armed forces' combat capabilities because the extent of equipment and personnel reductions has not matched the extent of the drop in funds available under market conditions. The limited attention paid by the Czech political leadership to security and defense issues and the public's low esteem for the military have combined to worsen some of these problems.

The Czechoslovak Period

After the Velvet Revolution, the new Czechoslovak leadership instructed the military to change its planning, overall size, and force structure and to weed out personnel with suspect loyalty to a sovereign and noncommunist Czechoslovakia. The new political leadership directed the military to abandon planning against NATO in favor of planning against a threat from—theoretically—any direction. It also called on the military to institute a process of verification for the entire officer corps. By September 1990, some 15 percent of professional soldiers had left the armed forces, including more than half of all generals. All officers went through an interview process in order to remove the most undesirable elements.

Initially, General Milan Vaček, a communist holdover, served as minister of defense and directed the changes in the military. Luboš Dobrovský, a civilian and former dissident, replaced Vaček in October 1990. Dobrovský speeded up some of the reforms initiated by Vaček and reinvestigated Vaček's personnel verification process. He also implemented reforms of the defense ministry, separating it from actual troop command.[23] The impasse in Czech-Slovak negotiations, however, affected the functioning of the military—as it did all other Czechoslovak state institutions—resulting in only the initial implementation of Dobrovský's reforms. Although the military establishment tried to stay out of the political-ethnic tensions, a sense of uncertainty over the future of the country and the military affected the functioning and reform of the armed forces.

After the June 1992 elections and the decision to divide the country, the Czech and Slovak representatives agreed to divide the military at a two-to-one ratio in favor of the Czechs, roughly approximating the territorial and population ratios of Czechs and Slovaks. In a compromise choice, a Slovak general, Imrich Andrejčak, became the last Czechoslovak defense minister and presided over the division of the armed forces. Interestingly, the actual split-up took place without any major problems or bickering over specific weapons systems, as Slovak and Czech officers worked out the technical issues of the division of military assets. The absence of problems showed that Czech and Slovak officers did not look upon each other as potential adversaries; they followed orders on the division of the country, though few of them either helped initiate or supported the breakup.

In an overall sense, the Czechoslovak military as an institution suffered greatly in the initial years after the regime change in 1989. The government slashed the defense budget by approximately 50 percent between 1989 and 1991, the officer corps went through two rounds of a humiliating personnel verification process designed to ensure loyalty to the country rather than to a foreign power, the basic tenets of Czechoslovak military planning changed, and the military's very existence became publicly and vocally questioned in the media and in the parliament. And yet, throughout this period (except during the crisis in November 1989), no signs appeared that the military contemplated any challenge to the new political authorities. One may question the extent of direct control the new civilian leadership actually had over the military, but problems in extending that control stemmed mostly from the civilians' lack of interest in and, especially, lack of expertise about the military. As an institution closely identified with the old regime, the military became discredited and weakened along with the delegitimation of the old regime.

The Czech Armed Forces in the Klaus Era

The Czech Republic inherited two-thirds of the partly transformed Czechoslovak armed forces. But more than the further reduction of the armed forces, what changed for the Czech defense establishment was the strategic context for military planning. No longer bordering on the potentially unstable Ukraine, distanced from the ethnic Hungarian problems, and surrounded by four friendly states—against whom Czech planners found it inconceivable that they would fight in the foreseeable future —military planners seemed at a loss for plausible threats. The Czechoslovak "all-azimuth" defense attempted to adjust to a situation of nonthreat planning, though implicitly the political leadership saw a security threat from the former USSR. But nonthreat planning in the Czech Republic truly meant an almost complete lack of identifiable military threats. Under such circumstances, the role of the military really became one of providing a credible deterrent to an unspecified, hypothetical military contingency.

In 1993–94, the Czech defense establishment debated vigorously the preferred role for the armed forces in the new state and the strategy for the country's defense.[24] In accord with the fundamental goal of integration into Western security structures, all Czech military reform plans stipulated preparation of the armed forces for eventual entry into NATO. The first Czech strategic concept regarding the defense of the Czech Republic, prepared by the chief of staff, General Karl Pezl, in 1993, already envisioned Czech entry into Western security structures and the country's dependence on NATO reinforcement to deal with any major threat to its territory.[25] A long-range concept for the transformation of the Czech armed forces through 2005 followed, but it failed to win governmental approval. Indeed, the parliament failed to approve any of the concepts advanced by the Ministry of Defense. Only a general, four-page National Defense Strategy, hastily approved by the parliament in March 1997 in order to satisfy NATO requirements just prior to the Madrid summit, existed as a guideline for military planning as of early 1999.[26] Yet the vagueness of the document made it unsuitable to provide much guidance for military planners. As the Czech Republic entered the final stage of preparation for entry into NATO, more than five years after becoming independent, it still had no basic document outlining a security policy and military strategy.

The limited attention the parliament gave to security, its lack of expertise about the military, and its treatment of the armed forces as an unimportant institution certainly played roles in this awkward state of affairs,

but the leadership of the Ministry of Defense under the Klaus governments deserves much of the blame. Throughout the Klaus era, a minor
coalition partner, the Christian-Democrats (KDU-CSL), held control of
the defense portfolio. Three members of the KDU-CSL held the post of
Minister of Defense successively under the Klaus coalition governments:
Antonín Baudyš (January 1993–September 1994), Vilém Holáň (September 1994–June 1996), and Miloslav Výborný (June 1996–December
1997). None of them excelled in security issues, and none proved to be a
particularly skilled or able manager. Each tinkered with the organizational structure of the ministry,[27] and each began his tenure questioning
the previous verification processes within the armed forces (Baudyš presided over another round of verification, or screening, of the entire officer
corps in 1993–94). Each man ended his short tenure amid scandals and
tensions within the coalition.

Upon independence, the Czech armed forces had an active personnel
strength of ninety-three thousand, less than one-half the strength of the
Czechoslovak armed forces just three years previously. The blueprint for
the evolution of the Czech armed forces until 2005 stipulated a reduction
of the active force to sixty-five thousand, and the military reached that
level in 1995.[28] The plan envisioned a gradual professionalization of the
armed forces and maintenance of the existing conscription system only
to train soldiers for the territorial forces. The concept also envisioned a
transition from a division structure to one consisting of corps and brigades deployed fairly evenly in Bohemia and Moravia. In terms of force
structure, the plan stipulated seven mechanized brigades (at various levels of readiness), one rapid reaction brigade (at a high level of readiness),
support units, and a territorial force organized into fifteen brigades. In
1996–97, the Czech defense leadership scaled down aspects of the 2005
plan, reducing the readiness level of some of the units and abandoning
some of the support and territorial formations altogether. The air force
shrank to five main operating bases. Plans envisioned the modernization
of some MiG-21s, the procurement of an indigenous light attack jet, the
L-159, and the phasing out of most of the rest of the aircraft. In 1995–96,
the Czech Republic exchanged all ten of its MiG-29s for eleven Polish
multipurpose helicopters.

The initially large Czech defense budget shrank steadily after Czech independence, both in absolute terms and as a percentage of gross domestic product (GDP). From 2.3 percent of GDP in 1993, it slid to 1.7 percent in 1997. In real terms, Czech defense budgets since independence have hovered in the range of $800 million to $1 billion (fig. 4.1). The declining budgets took their toll on readiness by reducing the proficiency and training of the Czech armed forces; the air force was hardest hit. Indeed, as a result of a series of aircraft crashes in 1997, a group of air force officers sent an open letter to President Havel warning of the impending end of the Czech air force if current trends continued. Most of all, the low availability of funds delayed the procurement of new equipment or prolonged the acquisition cycles for items essential to the military's effective integration into NATO, such as communications equipment, in spite of the priority given to integration into NATO.

Corruption and scandals have accompanied the Czech acquisition and procurement process. Most of all, because of the limited expertise of the top leadership in the Ministry of Defense and the inattention to security and military affairs by the parliament, Czech procurement decisions during the Klaus governments lacked coherence. Evidence uncovered after the Klaus government fell shows that the changes in plans to

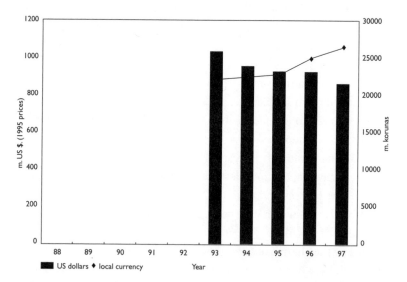

Figure 4.1 Czech Republic military expenditures, 1988–1997. Source: SIPRI, 1998.

modernize the MiG-21s, the controversy over modernization of the T-72 main battle tanks, and the ongoing procurement of the L-159 attack jet all stemmed more from intra-coalition politics, electoral considerations, and personal gain than from any clear military strategy. Of course, such rationales come up in other NATO countries (including the United States, as the case of the B-2 bomber shows) but they usually go hand in hand with the more common pattern of genuine competition and fair bidding. The latter pattern seemed in short supply in the Czech Republic during the Klaus era.

US and NATO officials noticed the readiness, training, and equipment problems just outlined. Even prior to the invitation to the Czech Republic to join NATO, as part of the Partnership and Review Process, Czech defense officials regularly consulted with NATO officials regarding the interoperability objectives to which the Czechs had agreed. And after the invitation, the Czech military filled out a detailed Defense Planning Questionnaire that served as a basis for coordinating the national plans of all members within the alliance. The wealth of information about the Czech military's shortcomings, combined with the incipient Czech entry into the alliance, led to strong criticisms of the Czech defense establishment by NATO. US defense officials even lambasted the Czech defense establishment publicly for insufficient progress in planning its integration into NATO,[29] contributing to the dissension and recriminations within the Klaus coalition in 1997.

In terms of civil-military relations, no questions arose concerning the dominance of civilians in the security sphere in the Czech Republic during Klaus's tenure. By any measure, the military complied fully with the directives of the civilians in the Ministry of Defense and accepted the liberal model of civil-military relations.[30] During Klaus's tenure, however, the civilians did not exhibit tremendous talent or skills in guiding the Czech military.[31] At the political level, the Czech leadership paid insufficient attention to military and security matters, and the parliament abdicated some of its responsibility. The civilians' treatment of the military also shows deep distrust of it among some of the ruling circles in the Czech Republic, an unhealthy phenomenon that has the potential to make the Czech armed forces less effective.

After Klaus

The two defense ministers who followed the KDU-CSL's hold on the ministry attempted to make progress in reforming the armed forces and preparing them for NATO. In doing so, they had to undo some of the mess they inherited from their predecessors under the Klaus governments. The defense minister during the caretaker Tosovsky government, Michal Lobkowicz, proved to be the most able administrator in the Czech defense ministry up to that time. Under Lobkowicz's tenure, the Ministry of Defense put together a conceptual outline for the development of the Czech armed forces until 2003, with guidelines until 2008.

The plan, approved just before the 1998 elections, amounted to a Czech blueprint for integration into NATO.[32] In terms of active force size, the armed forces were to shrink to fifty-six thousand personnel, with the professional component reaching 60 percent of the force. Conscription was to continue, with a twelve-month term of service. One rapid deployment brigade, two mechanized brigades, support units, and territorial forces were to make up the ground forces. Plans for the air force stipulated continued use of five main operating bases and a full transition to the L-159, supplemented by as-yet-unannounced, NATO-compatible, multipurpose aircraft (one of the following: F-16, F-18, JAS Gripen, Mirage 2000-5). If the Czech air force hoped to operate supersonic aircraft, the Czechs would need to purchase new aircraft by 2002, since the service life of the existing supersonic aircraft would run out in 2003. However, the enormous funds required for such a purchase remained elusive.[33] In view of the other pressing needs facing the armed forces, the persistent plans for procurement of supersonic, multipurpose aircraft seemed misguided and driven more by a desire for prestige than by any real military need. Suspecting corruption behind some procurement decisions under previous defense ministers, Lobkowicz launched investigations of some high-profile orders. In addition, he cancelled a number of programs and put others on hold, including the modernization of the main battle tanks.[34]

The current minister of defense, Vladimír Vetchy, began his tenure in July 1998, and it appeared that he would preside over the initial period of integration of the Czech armed forces into NATO. Vetchy's appointment represented a clear departure from those of previous defense ministers. A former professional soldier (having served in the armed forces since the late 1970s), he was more knowledgeable about and experienced with the military than his predecessors had been. Vetchy also was a member of the communist party in the 1980s; as an officer, he was expected to join the party and was pressured to do so. Such a background stood in sharp contrast to those of the earlier ministers who presided over the verification campaign in the Czech officer corps.

Shortly after assuming his position, Vetchy placed Lobkowicz's defense plans through 2008 on hold for another review. Some of the differences in emphasis that Vetchy outlined included a move away from the eventual full professionalization that Lobkowicz had envisioned and greater attention to personnel and training than to procurement. Earlier plans called for procurement to amount to 20 percent of the defense budget, but reaching that goal seemed ambitious in view of the readiness shortcomings of the Czech armed forces. Most of all, Vetchy expressed chagrin over the inattention, mismanagement of resources, and corruption in the defense ministry during the Klaus administration.[35]

Because of the criticism of the Czech armed forces by NATO officials during the ratification debates in 1997–98, the Czech government obliged itself to increase its defense budget gradually (by 0.1 percent of GDP annually), so that it would amount to 2.0 percent of GDP in 2000. In 1998, the Czech parliament fulfilled its promise and raised the defense budget to a level of almost 1.9 percent of GDP. The move took place under pressure and amid criticism from NATO at a crucial time in the ratification process. Whether the new social-democrat-led government would abide by the agreement remained unclear. The fall of the Czech GDP by 0.7 percent in 1998 and increased pressures on the state budget threatened to make it difficult to keep the promise.

In terms of civil-military relations, no problems arose under Lobkowicz, nor had any arisen under Vetchy as of early 1999. Indeed, the administrative skill and genuine concern for the military that Lobkowicz showed seems to have made a good impression upon the armed forces and may have elevated the military's image of civilians.

Future Needs

The Czech armed forces have achieved compatibility with NATO in terms
of their structure, but important elements still differentiate them from
NATO's armed forces and make Czech operations in an alliance framework difficult. Insufficient progress in building a noncommissioned
officer corps, continued lack of English language skills, unfamiliarity
with NATO procedures and concepts, and low readiness and limited
training (especially combined arms training) form the most important
shortcomings.[36] Some of these, such as lack of English language skills and
unfamiliarity with NATO procedures, will gradually fade away over the
first decade of the twenty-first century as a new generation of Czech NCOs
and officers enters the armed forces having already learned English in ele-
mentary and high school and having gained familiarity with NATO doctrine in Czech military educational institutions. Other shortcomings, such
as the weakness of the NCO corps and the need for higher readiness, will
require greater resources and sufficient administrative skill to overcome.

Although real, the equipment deficiencies of the Czech armed forces
do not necessarily constitute as important a problem as those just listed.
Rather than a massive spending spree, a far better solution lies in the
selective upgrading of equipment, focusing primarily on making current
equipment more lethal and accurate. Most of all, the elements listed
above require a financially realistic, well-thought-out, long-term plan of
integration, based on a consensus among the mainstream political parties in the Czech parliament. Otherwise, the measures will have an ad hoc
quality about them and do little to address the overall goal.

The Czech defense establishment also has to tackle the military's image
problem. With skilled managers and administrators, a more libertarian
than authoritarian style of leadership, and improvements in social conditions for conscripts, the Czech armed forces could overcome the negative
stereotyping they face in society and perhaps reverse the relatively low
rate of staff retention.[37] But the entire way of thinking about individuals
in the armed forces will need to change within the defense establishment.
Rather than treating individuals as unimportant, the armed forces will
need to reorient toward focusing on the individual soldier and making
him feel valued, well trained, and supplied with appropriate equipment.

Such a change would truly mean a shift away from a communist-style military to a NATO-style military charged with upholding the security of a democratic community.

For a variety of reasons (poor leadership, insufficient attention to security and defense by the country's political leadership, ingrained anti-military outlooks, adjustment to a newly independent state and the breakup of the former federal state, and so forth), the Czech defense establishment fell behind that of Poland and even Hungary in terms of preparations for joining NATO and now has some catching up to do. It made substantial strides in the first half of 1998, but the momentum seemed uncertain under Vetchy's tenure at the Ministry of Defense. Despite the Czech Republic's peculiar problems regarding the military, the country remains wealthier than Poland or Hungary (in per-capita GDP), and if it were to invest in defense at GDP levels comparable to those of Poland and Hungary, it has the potential to have a military as good as, if not better than, those of the other two new members. If the Czech defense budget reaches and stays at the agreed-upon level of 2 percent of GDP, and if skilled administrators with realistic and well-thought-out plans run the defense establishment, no bar exists to the Czech armed forces' becoming a small but high-quality force valuable to the alliance within a decade.

The Czech Republic in NATO

What does NATO gain with Czech membership, and what kind of role will the Czech Republic play as an alliance member? For reasons simply of small size and an economy still adjusting to competitive market pressures, the Czech Republic can play only a minor role in the alliance for the foreseeable future. Just as Belgium and Portugal are not major military or political actors in the alliance, neither will be the Czech Republic. Regionally, the country can play an important role regarding NATO's actions vis-à-vis Slovakia. Shortly after the change of governments in Slovakia, the Czechs and Slovaks agreed to upgrade their military cooperation, and further ties are likely to develop. The Czech Republic may also be able to play a useful role regarding some of the smaller candidates for NATO, such as Slovenia, Lithuania, and Latvia.

Militarily, the Czech armed forces plan eventually to provide one rapid deployment brigade for NATO's projection missions; elements of the brigade are to become fully compatible with the alliance shortly after accession. A possible joint Czech-Polish-German unit (along the lines of the Polish-Danish-German corps, though probably of division size) might eventually form part of NATO's main defense forces. And the entry of the Czech Republic provides the alliance with access to infrastructure and geostrategic depth. In case of contingencies in Poland, the infrastructure in the Czech Republic can play an important role in supporting NATO operations. The same applies to possible NATO operations in the Balkans or eastern Europe. Of course, NATO might have had access to facilities in the Czech Republic in any case, without Czech membership, but the upgrading of the Czech infrastructure to compatibility with NATO's will proceed faster with membership because of NATO's infrastructure funds.

Despite the Czech Republic's small size, its contribution to NATO's missions could become highly valuable politically. Future NATO (or NATO-based) operations will probably take the form of "coalitions of the willing," and because of the Czech Republic's strong pro-US stand, Czech units would probably participate alongside US units even if many other NATO members declined to participate. During discussions of potential NATO action in Kosovo in 1998, the Czech Republic made preparations to contribute forces. It also made plans to provide a combat service support unit to a potential US-led contingency in the Persian Gulf in 1998. Thus, in an operation in which only a few NATO allies participate alongside the United States, the political value of the central Europeans' participation would outweigh their small military contribution. In addition, together with Poland, the Czech Republic can play a useful role in hypothetical alliance operations in some of the Slavic-speaking countries of central and eastern Europe. The IFOR/SFOR operation has already shown evidence of the value of the Poles and Czechs; because Czech and Polish speakers find Serbo-Croatian intelligible, Czech and Polish troops assigned to IFOR/SFOR have managed to understand conversations among Serbs and to prevent certain situations from escalating. Finally, some of the Czech special support units, such as chemical defense troops, could augment NATO forces if needed.

Does the Czech military contribution to NATO fall below reasonable levels? The real issue concerns which standards to use in measuring the Czechs' contribution and their role in the alliance. Some of the criticism aimed at the new members of NATO has focused on the supposedly poor quality of their armed forces. Often, the United States or Germany provides the standard of comparison in such judgments. But such comparisons miss the point, because the US and German armed forces are the most modern and best equipped in the world, and any military would look inferior when compared with them (especially with the United States). The standard to use in assessing the new members' contribution should be reasonable and should not exceed what the alliance expects of its current members. The Czech Republic has population and territory similar in size to those of current NATO member Portugal, although its economy remains substantially smaller than Portugal's. Consequently, aiming for an eventual contribution at a level close to Portugal's seems reasonable as a goal for the Czech Republic. The Czech Republic already matches the Portugese contribution of one brigade for NATO missions. If the Czechs implement their plans for improved training and equipment of the NATO-earmarked unit, then their contribution will be at least on a par with that of the Portugese.

In view of anti-military outlooks in the Czech Republic, the country's enviably good relations with its neighbors, and the already demonstrated Czech tendencies toward limiting expenditures on defense, will the Czech Republic move toward "free riding"—defined as spending less than 1.5 percent of GDP on defense—within the alliance? The Czech Republic seems likely to be an average or below-average NATO member in terms of contribution, but not a free rider in the near term. Keeping in mind that, in the post-Cold War period, the mean for European NATO countries in defense spending has fallen to about 2 percent of GDP and may decline further, then the Czech Republic will fall near the middle among European NATO members in terms of spending on defense. In at least the short-term (until 2003), a number of factors make Czech free riding unlikely. Most of all, for purposes of making NATO membership effective, the Czech leadership needs to demonstrate that it takes alliance commitments seriously in its initial period of membership. That entails making reasonable progress in meeting target force goals (NATO's mechanism for coordinating the military plans of members). Without such progress, doubts will surround NATO's commitment to the new member, in effect making alliance membership hollow and the concomitant deterrent less credible.

In addition, the Czech Republic has a strong interest in making the initial round of NATO enlargement successful in order to keep the door open to Slovakia (and Austria). If the initial round of enlargement is assessed a failure, it will delay or even put in doubt further enlargement of the alliance. The Czech Republic's long-term security interests entail the integration of neighboring countries into European multilateral structures, in order to remove the possibility of even secondary or tertiary threats to Czech territory emanating from Slovakia. That incentive probably will moderate any Czech proclivities toward early free riding.

Beyond the short and medium term, if a benign security environment continues to hold, a Czech tendency toward free riding might increase. By that time, however, the Czech armed forces will probably have gone a long way toward becoming successfully integrated into the alliance, making lower defense expenditures less salient. In any event, with the growth of the Czech economy, the defense budget may still increase in absolute terms despite decreases relative to GDP.

In summary, from a NATO perspective, the benefits that Czech membership brings to the alliance cannot be separated from the criteria used to assess what is reasonable and expected from current and future members. The Czech Republic is likely to be among the more pro-US members in the alliance. It is likely to contribute small but potentially politically important forces to future NATO operations. The size and usefulness of the contribution will vary according to the speed of integration of the Czech military into NATO. With skilled leadership at the Czech defense ministry, greater attention to defense matters by the Czech government, and well-targeted assistance measures, the size and effectiveness of the Czech military contribution will increase. But perhaps the most important benefit of Czech entry into NATO is the further erasing of the legacy of Soviet communist domination in Europe. That was the political goal and the main motive for NATO's enlargement; the alliance did not enlarge for military reasons. Any strictly military gains resulting from the first round of enlargement are little more than marginal benefits in view of the enormous political gains accruing to the United States as it leads the process toward a more integrated, democratic, and unified Europe that will be a US security partner for the foreseeable future.

Notes

1. Roman Blasek, "Perception of Security Risks by the Population of the Czech Republic," *Journal of Slavic Military Studies* 11, no. 3 (September 1998): 89–96.

2. Analysts and policymakers have noticed the low level of Czech enthusiasm for joining NATO. The Czechs' seeming reluctance has provided ammunition to those skeptical about NATO's enlargement and has raised doubts among others about what kind of member the Czech Republic will be. See, for example, Robert H. Dorff, "Public Opinion and NATO Enlargement," in Stephen J. Blank, ed., *NATO after Enlargement: New Challenges, New Missions, New Forces* (Carlisle Barracks, Pennsylvania: Strategic Studies Institute, US Army War College, 1998), 5–37.

3. *Czech National Interests* (Prague: Institute for International Relations, 1993); *The Security Policy of the Czech Republic* (Prague: Institute for International Relations, 1997).

4. The IIR documents have received substantial coverage in the main Czech military theoretical journal, *Vojenské Rozhledy*. See Antonín Leška, "Bezpečnostní aspekty českych národních zájmú" (The security aspects of Czech national interests), *Vojenské Rozhledy* 2 (1993), no. 10: 28–38. The guidelines for Czech security policy proposed by the IIR are implicit in numerous articles in *Vojenské Rozhledy* in 1997–98.

5. *Security Policy of the Czech Republic*, 47–48.

6. Major General Emil Antušák and Petr Svozil, "Současná evropská bezpečnost a národní zájmy ČR" (Present European security and national interests of the Czech Republic), *Vojenské Rozhledy* 5 (1996), no. 6: 3–7.

7. The eagerness of the Czech population to join the EU has not changed substantially since 1993, with generally about three out of four Czechs in favor. For example, an August 1998 poll (by STEM) showed a level of support for EU membership of 72.5 percent in the Czech Republic. Newsletter from the Czech Embassy in the USA, September 1998, http://www.czech.cz/washington.

8. For time-series public opinion poll data on support for NATO membership in the Czech Republic, see Štefan Sarvaš, "Attitudes of the Czech Public toward National Security, the Military, and NATO Membership," *Journal of Slavic Military Studies* 11, no. 3 (September 1998): 56–88.

9. The Czech Republic is one of five former communist countries invited for "fast-track" negotiations on membership in the EU. However, it increasingly appears that earlier optimistic expectations of joining the EU in 2002–2003 may be pushed back to 2005 or later.

10. *Security Policy of the Czech Republic,* 50; *Czech National Interests,* 28–29.

11. *Security Policy of the Czech Republic,* 16; *Czech National Interests,* 25.

12. *Security Policy of the Czech Republic,* 16; *Czech National Interests,* 27–28.

13. *Security Policy of the Czech Republic,* 14.

14. *Security Policy of the Czech Republic,* 14–18. In this sense, Czech views are in agreement with other NATO countries' views of probable threats to European security. See Stanislav Jurnečka, "Konflikty Nízké a Středni Úrovné" (Low- and mid-level conflicts), *Vojenské Rozhledy* 2 (1993), no. 4: 4–14.

15. Since the Czech Republic was invited to join NATO in 1997, discussions of Czech defensive operations in *Vojenske Rozhledy* have portrayed only cases of defense against aggression coming from the territory of the Czech Republic's two non-NATO neighbors, Austria and Slovakia. Of course, such scenarios are hypothetical and implausible, in view of the Czech Republic's good relations with Austria and the post-Mečiar government in Slovakia. But they do represent vividly the fact that the Czech Republic faces few threats; its planning sometimes verges on the unreal. See Milan Kubeša, "Způsoby použití armády české republiky" (Ways of deploying the army of the Czech Republic), *Vojenské Rozhledy* 7 (1998), no. 1: 46–55.

16. *Security Policy of the Czech Republic,* 61–63.

17. *Czech National Interests,* 25–26.

18. Explicit public references to Russia as somehow an adversary of the Czech Republic are rare. But implicitly, the instability in Russia and its early post-imperial stage is a cause of concern to the Czech security establishment. See *Security Policy of the Czech Republic,* 40–41.

19. František Turnovec, "Votes, Seats, and Power: 1996 Parliamentary Election in the Czech Republic," *Communist and Postcommunist Studies* 30, no. 3 (1997): 289–305. The elections resulted in the Klaus-led coalition's being one vote short of a majority, but Klaus managed to hold onto power for over a year with the help of a maverick opposition party member.

20. Czech sociologists acknowledge the historical roots as a contributing reason for the poor prestige of the Czech armed forces. See Sarvaš, "Attitudes of the Czech Public."

21. Survey research has demonstrated the huge drop in the prestige of professional soldiers in the aftermath of the 1968 Warsaw Pact intervention. See Jiří Hodný, "The Prestige of Professional Czech Soldiers in the Eyes of the General Public," *Journal of Slavic Military Studies* 11, no. 3 (September 1998): 97–104.

22. A Eurobarometer survey in 1994 showed that among the former non-Soviet Warsaw Pact countries, the Czech armed forces scored lowest in terms of trust, gaining 4.1 on a 7-point scale (with 7 being maximum trust). The figures for other countries were Romania, 5.5; Poland, 4.8; Bulgaria, 4.6; Slovakia, 4.4;

and Hungary, 4.3. See data in William Mishler and Richard Rose, "Trust, Distrust, and Skepticism: Popular Evaluations of Civil and Political Institutions in Postcommunist Societies," *Journal of Politics* 59, no. 2 (May 1997): 418–451.

23. For more detailed information, see the chapter on Czechoslovakia in Jeffrey Simon, *NATO Enlargement and Central Europe: A Study in Civil-Military Relations* (Washington, D.C.: National Defense University, Institute for National Strategic Studies, 1996), 191–210.

24. In 1993, the Czech defense establishment put forth many interesting and innovative ideas regarding an optimal manner of providing for Czech security and the Czech military's role in it. The main Czech professional military journal, *Vojenské Rozhledy,* contained numerous discussion articles on strategies for defense of the Czech Republic and the concept of evolution of the armed forces. For examples, see Emil Antušák, "Další kolo reorganizace armády před námi" (The next stage of reorganization of the army is ahead of us), *Vojenské Rozhledy* 2 (1993), no. 3: 3–6; Otakar Vlach, "Možnosti a účinnost obrany České Republiky po rozdělení ČSFR" (Possibilities of effective defense of the Czech Republic after the division of the CSFR), *Vojenské Rozhledy* 2 (1993), no. 1: 27–34; Antonín Rašek, "Systém obrany České Republiky a jeho tvorba" (The Czech Republic's defense system and its construction), *Vojenské Rozhledy* 2 (1993), no. 3: 27–39.

25. "Koncepce výstavby armády ČR do roku 1996" (A concept for the building of the army of the Czech Republic until 1996), *Vojenské Rozhledy* 2 (1993), no. 7: 5–26.

26. "Národní obranná strategie" (The national defense strategy), *Vojenské Rozhledy* 6 (1997), no. 2: 3–12.

27. For more detailed information, see the chapter on the Czech Republic in Simon, *NATO Enlargement and Central Europe,* 213–251.

28. For a detailed look at the Czech military shortly after independence, see Stéphane Lefebvre, "The Army of the Czech Republic: A Status Report," *Journal of Slavic Military Studies* 8, no. 4 (December 1995): 718–751.

29. Frank Kramer, the US assistant secretary of defense, was brutally frank in meetings with Czech defense officials in September 1997 and has not shied away from expressing some criticism in public.

30. One of the best definitions of the principle of civilian control of the military is this one: "First, the ends of government policy are to be set by civilians; the military is limited to decisions about means. In other words, the military are to be policy implementers, not policymakers. Second, it is for the civilian leadership to decide where the line between ends and means (and hence between civilian and military responsibility) is to be drawn." Kenneth W. Kemp and Charles Hudlin, "Civil Supremacy over the Military: Its Nature and Limits," *Armed Forces and Society* 19, no. 1 (Fall 1992): 7–26, quote on 8–9.

31. For an insightful look at Czech civil-military relations, see Marybeth Peterson Ulrich, "U.S. Assistance and Military Democratization in the Czech Republic," *Problems of Postcommunism* 45, no. 2 (March–April 1998): 22–32; and Marybeth Peterson Ulrich, "The Democratization of Civil-Military Relations in

the Czech Republic," in *The Military and Society in Post-Communist Countries,* Constantine Danoupoulous, ed. (Boulder, Colorado: Westview Press, 1998).

32. For more about the Czech plans, see "Country Briefing: The Czech Republic," *Jane's Defense Weekly* (May 20, 1998): 18–27.

33. The cost of twenty-four new F-16 or F-18 fighter aircraft and their support package is more than $1 billion, an amount that exceeds the entire annual defense budget of the Czech Republic. The US has offered the no-cost, five-year lease of a handful (less than a dozen) surplus F-16s or F-18s to begin the process of Czech transition to NATO-type aircraft. The Czechs had not accepted the offer as of early 1999. See "Military Aviation Review: Czech Republic, Free U.S. Fighters," *World Airpower Journal* 30 (Fall 1997): 5.

34. The tank modernization scheme demonstrates the ad hoc feel to the whole process of Czech procurement and modernization during the Klaus era. Moving to a light force appropriate for NATO projection missions does not necessitate tanks. Even a credible deterrent to a potential threat to the territory of the Czech Republic entails effective and cheap anti-tank weapons, but not necessarily tanks. Yet the Czech ministry of defense awarded contracts to a consortium of companies for the modernization of tanks. A more prudent course of action would have entailed the preparation of an appropriate strategy for defense first, proceeding then to procurement of equipment.

35. Interview with Vladimír Vetchy, *Pravo,* 7 November 1998, 17, in FBIS-EEU-98–335, 1 December 1998.

36. For an excellent and comprehensive elaboration of the training problems faced by the three new members of NATO, see David M. Glantz, "Military Training and Education Challenges in Poland, Hungary, and the Czech Republic," *Journal of Slavic Military Studies* 11, no. 3 (September 1998): 1–55.

37. The Czech military has the worst record of the three new NATO members in retaining young officers trained at military educational institutions in current NATO countries (though none of the three has done particularly well in retaining such personnel). In late 1997, the problem gained wide publicity because of the departure of Lieutenant Petr Vohralík from the Czech military. As the first Czech graduate of the US Army Academy at West Point, Vohralík was portrayed as an example of the "new look" of the Czech armed forces and the officer corps; a Czech military weekly aimed at young officers and conscripts even featured a lengthy interview with Vohralík (*A Report* 14 [1997]: 8–9). Vohralík's departure and his highly critical remarks about the state of the Czech armed forces amounted to a major embarrassment for the Czech military.

5 NATO Enlargement

POLICY, PROCESS, AND IMPLICATIONS

SEAN KAY

In March 1999, Poland, Hungary, and the Czech Republic took their respective seats as the newest members of the North Atlantic Treaty Organization (NATO). In this chapter I examine the decision-making dynamics that framed the various rationales for the policy of enlarging NATO. I then assess the implementation of the policy as of early 1999 in order to consider its prospects for success. My central conclusion is that NATO enlargement originated from a diverse group of policy objectives. Its implementation to date shows that not all supporters are likely to be comfortable with the outcome of policy decisions stemming from the admission of three new NATO members. On its own, NATO membership for Poland, Hungary, and the Czech Republic was a logical reflection of post–Cold War European security dynamics. NATO's method of implementing the enlargement policy, however, may not necessarily be what all advocates of enlargement—including the three new members—initially hoped to achieve.

Why NATO Enlargement?

NATO enlargement was a European idea—or, more specifically, a German initiative. The impetus for the policy stemmed from the German government of Helmut Kohl in mid-1993. Germany hoped to use NATO membership to stabilize countries to its east and thus enhance its economic investments there, engage the United States deeply in post–Cold War European security, and ensure that any future front lines in Europe emerged far to its east. Ultimately, Germany accelerated NATO toward enlargement in order to reaffirm its own postwar self-restraint in security policy. As one high-level German official put it: "Insofar as the Germans like happy neighbors, they also think that the presence of the United States is an insuring element, a stabilizing component to prevent our neighbors from perceiving that something might happen.... This is what you objectively call a stabilizing factor.... So it has not only to do with an outside threat, it's an internal balancing element inside the European security structure as such."[1]

Early German initiatives were not well received by the other NATO allies. By August 1993, senior NATO officials had signaled discomfort with the policy. At the core of their concern was deep worry over its military implications and its impact on Russia. In Washington, D.C., NATO enlargement gathered some early support at the RAND Corporation, among the policy planning staff of the Department of State, and at the National Security Council. Senior decision-makers in the Department of State, however, and particularly those at the Department of Defense, opposed the policy. By the fall of 1993, a general consensus was reached within the US government and among the NATO allies that immediate enlargement would be self-defeating and damaging to the alliance. As a result, NATO's Partnership for Peace (PFP) program—one of reaching out to the east, short of providing security guarantees—was agreed to in January 1994.[2]

Nevertheless, the idea of NATO enlargement had prompted intense debates over four independent themes advanced by policy advocates: grand strategy, the spread of stability, the building of democracy and a Western-oriented community of states in Europe, and collective security.

NATO had always been a tool of grand strategy, and containment of external aggression against member states its primary utility. Some advocates of NATO enlargement saw the policy as an effective way of perpetuating NATO's classic role in keeping the Americans in, the Germans down, and the Russians out. In this view, NATO enlargement would extend and sustain American involvement in post–Cold War European security. The end product would be the extension of American influence into the region between Germany and Russia in order to prevent future security competition between a growing power in Germany and a declining power in Russia. Of equal concern to some supporters of NATO enlargement was a lingering Cold War view that Russia remained a threat.

Historical fear of Russia was an important (though not the sole) factor that drove applicant countries toward NATO. Indeed, some senior US officials saw the enlargement of NATO as a hedge in the event that democracy collapsed in Russia and Moscow chose a more confrontational policy toward the West.

For some advocates of NATO enlargement, the policy was a tool for spreading stability—that is, shaping the international security environment in central and eastern Europe by linking membership in NATO with specific policy outcomes within or among states. By bringing new members toward the multilateral NATO defense planning process, states might learn about each other and be socialized into new patterns of behavior. This would reduce uncertainty and therefore the costs of national defense in new member countries. Through this expansion of multilateral planning, NATO would lower the costs of collective defense or out-of-area activities such as peacekeeping as it added new members with shared interests. Moreover, by specifying membership criteria, NATO would shape the international security environment in central and eastern Europe.

The United States endorsed five criteria for NATO aspirants to meet before being considered for membership: democratic elections; individual liberty and the rule of law; demonstrated commitment to economic reform and a market economy; adherence to Organization for Security and Cooperation in Europe (OSCE) norms and principles involving ethnic minorities and social justice; resolution of territorial disputes with neighbors; and establishment of democratic control of the military. Collectively, NATO required new members to provide adequate resources and assume the financial obligations of joining and to establish interoperability with NATO structures. Additional membership criteria included transparency in defense planning, parliamentary oversight of national defense structures, minimal standards of defense planning to operate with NATO structures, and a commitment to leaving the door open to further enlargement.

To some advocates of NATO enlargement, the policy was based on a moral imperative to spread democracy in postcommunist Europe. By expanding the "democratic club" of nations within NATO, the organization would reify its internal fabric by including like-minded states with similar values and interests. As new democracies emerged from the collapse of communism in eastern Europe, NATO enlargement would consolidate the process. It would thus contribute to a building of community in Europe that would broaden the idea of "the West" on the continent. As the US Department of Defense concluded in its *Report to Congress on the Enlargement of the North Atlantic Treaty Organization: Rationale, Benefits, Costs and Implications:* "The purpose of enlargement is to integrate more countries into the existing community of values and institutions, thereby enhancing stability and security for all countries in the Euro-Atlantic area."

Finally, some supporters of NATO enlargement saw the policy as a means of promoting a new architecture for European security based on the concept of collective security—in contrast to NATO's traditional purpose of collective defense, limited to alliance members. Collective security is an institutionalization of balance-of-power arrangements organized on the principle of all against one. Advocates of collective security posit that states can organize to punish violators of agreed-upon international norms. According to this principle, NATO membership would contribute to European security by facilitating the internal management of crises among aspiring members such as Hungary and Romania. At a more general level, some advocates promoted NATO enlargement if it were open to all qualified European states—including Russia. From this perspective, Russia should become a full member of NATO in order to institutionalize collective security in twenty-first-century Europe.

Measuring Success

Measuring the success of NATO enlargement is difficult, considering the variety of rationales behind the policy. As the other chapters in this book show, the three new NATO members have made considerable progress along their paths to membership. Moreover, through parliamentary ratification, sixteen previous members of NATO have welcomed the new members into the alliance. Nevertheless, to fully assess the long-term success of NATO enlargement will require years of observation. What follows is an initial effort to examine the ways in which NATO enlargement was being implemented at the time of NATO's fiftieth anniversary summit, held in April 1999. I organize the discussion in terms of the four major themes just outlined: grand strategy, the spread of stability, the building of democracy and community, and collective security.

Grand Strategy

Some advocates of NATO enlargement are left with a conundrum: NATO has expanded to include the three countries many supporters wanted, but strategic goals have been poorly served by what will be a hollow military commitment to the new members. The price of success has been to give Russia an informal veto in NATO decision-making, which has accelerated trends toward making collective security NATO's de facto policy. The strategic case for enlarging NATO may have had fundamental shortcomings because it treated NATO as a traditional alliance rather than as an organization that is undergoing a dramatic transition away from its policy of collective defense. The historical rationale for NATO enlargement may have been weak for two key reasons.

First, this approach ignored disintegrative trends in the alliance that emerged with the absence of the Soviet threat. Although the United States attained consensus for the normative goals of NATO enlargement, key European countries would have been uncomfortable supporting enlargement in the absence of an accommodation with Russia. Two members that each share a border with Russia—Norway and Turkey—were among the least enthusiastic supporters of NATO enlargement. Britain, France, and Italy were not especially excited by the policy, either. Ironically, Germany, which accelerated NATO enlargement in 1993, seemed to insist in 1997 that an accord with Russia be reached at any expense, including substantial NATO concessions over infrastructure development in new member states.[3] The cost of this grand strategy for post–Cold War European security has been a gain for Russia over the instrument of implementation—NATO.

Second, those who advanced strong principles of collective defense as reasons for enlarging NATO were guided by perception and historicism rather than by a careful assessment of capabilities, threats, and trends. If Russia is a threat to central and eastern Europe, then the region would be more secure with a line drawn, in theory, at Russia's border. Thus the three Baltic countries and Ukraine would be primary candidates for membership. Enlargement to include Poland, Hungary, and the Czech Republic invites the creation of a gray zone of security competition farther to the east. Whereas Germany might view its security as dependent on events in Poland, Warsaw may, in part, view its security as dependent upon events in Lithuania, Belarus, and Ukraine. By stressing a limited enlargement, NATO may have contributed to a security vacuum more dangerous than the one enlargement has solved. For example, absent a credible military guarantee to defend Poland's borders, NATO's area of interest has now spread to include stability in one of the most unstable countries in eastern Europe—Belarus.

Hypothetical threats aside, advocates of collective defense incorrectly assumed that Russia was a threat to central Europe. Russia's own internal assessments are said to conclude that only after substantial downsizing of the Russian armed forces, combined with years, if not decades, of economic growth, could the Russian military mount a conventional challenge to central and eastern Europe by 2025.[4] Ironically, NATO enlargement may have given conservative forces in Russia justification not to reduce the overall size of the armed forces and proceed with serious military reform. Although at face value this possibility appears to validate Western concerns about the quantitative Russian threat, it ignores the qualitative disaster of the Russian military. Indeed, NATO enlargement may reduce the prospect for military reform that might allow Russia to become a major threat to Europe in years to come. While this might reduce the immediate danger of aggression against a new NATO member, the delay in military reform in Russia also diminishes the possibility that Moscow will adopt a Western-style military or invest in programs to increase the security and stability of its nuclear weapons arsenal. Ultimately dismissing alarmist notions of a Russian threat, NATO military planners assumed in 1997 that new members could be reinforced with a mobilization of two divisions—an impressive drop from the six assumed in 1996.

Arguments favoring the enlargement of NATO in order to deter Russian threats thus had little value. A more plausible threat-based case for NATO enlargement was available, however, but was rejected by the

United States. Threats ranging from instability in the Balkan region to the proliferation of weapons of mass destruction in the Middle East or North Africa made a strong case for Romanian membership.[5] For example, a scenario in which, hypothetically, large-scale instability in the Persian Gulf forced the United States to look for alternative energy sources would likely shift American strategic priorities to the oil-rich Caspian Sea region, possibly leading to security competition between the United States, Iran, and Russia. In such a scenario, Romania's membership in NATO would provide a critical base for US operations by assisting extended deterrence and supporting force projection. Given uncertain trends in Turkey's political development, Romania could become critical to the security of the alliance's southern rim. Because this scenario is as plausible as a Russian threat to central Europe, it is worth questioning why the United States opposed Romania's entrance into NATO in 1997. A majority of European NATO members, for a variety of reasons, pushed strongly for Romanian membership, thereby placing the United States in a very small minority. Only when the Clinton administration tersely insisted that it would not support Romania's entry did the allies drop their insistence on its (and Slovenia's) membership.

The event most damaging to the strategic case for NATO enlargement was the negotiation of the NATO-Russia Founding Act, which gave Moscow a voice in NATO debates in exchange for its grudging acceptance of enlargement. At the highest level, rejection of the goal of containing Russia was paramount to the decision-making involved in NATO enlargement. As US President Bill Clinton said at the signing ceremony for the NATO-Russia Founding Act in Paris in May 1997:

> The historic change in the relationship between NATO and Russia grows out of a fundamental change in how we think about each other and our future. NATO's member states recognize that the Russian people are building a new Russia, defining their greatness in terms of the future as much as the past. Russia's transition to democracy and open markets is as difficult as it is dramatic. And its steadfast commitment to freedom and reform has earned the world's admiration.[6]

The president added that "this new NATO will work with Russia, not against it.... By reducing rivalry and fear, by strengthening peace and cooperation, by facing common threats to the security of all democracies, NATO will promote greater stability in all of Europe, including Russia.... We are determined to create a future in which European security is not a zero-sum game—where NATO's gain is Russia's loss, and Russia's strength is our alliance's weakness."[7]

This approach led to a variety of concessions by the United States and its NATO allies to Russia regarding new members. Though officially a restatement of existing NATO policy as codified in the 1995 *Study on NATO Enlargement,* these concessions were designed to help ease Russian concerns over NATO enlargement. First, NATO agreed that it saw no reason to deploy nuclear weapons on the territory of new members or any need to change any aspect of NATO's nuclear posture or nuclear policy—and it saw no future need to do so. Specifically, the act said: "This subsumes the fact that NATO has decided that it has no intention, no plan, and no reason to establish nuclear weapon storage sites on the territory of those members, whether through the construction of new nuclear storage facilities or the adaptation of old nuclear storage facilities." Nuclear storage sites were defined as facilities specifically designed for the stationing of nuclear weapons, including all types of hardened above- or below-ground facilities (storage bunkers or vaults) designed for storing nuclear weapons.[8] The language addressing nuclear weapons infrastructure and related storage facilities was added by American and NATO negotiators at Russia's insistence during negotiations over the NATO-Russia Founding Act.

Second, NATO agreed that there would be no quantitative change in force levels in new member states that might negatively affect the existing Conventional Forces in Europe Treaty. Both NATO and Russia agreed that they would prevent a potentially threatening buildup of conventional forces in central and eastern Europe. There would be no significant force buildup by new members, and there would be no substantial deployment of NATO forces on new member territory that might shift the balance of power.[9] NATO agreed that "in the current and foreseeable security environment, the alliance will carry out its collective defense and other missions by ensuring the necessary interoperability, integration, and capability for reinforcement rather than by additional permanent stationing of substantial combat forces."[10]

As a result, NATO's deterrent value for a new member such as Poland will be based on a promise of reinforcement and intervention rather than on the actual presence of troops to deter an attack. Reinforcement is the centerpiece of NATO's New Strategic Concept of 1991. NATO planning emphasizes multinational force projection, supported from extended lines of communication and reliance on deployable and flexible logistics support capabilities for crisis management. The stress is on smaller, more mobile, and, in particular, more rapidly deployable reaction forces that can quickly reinforce interoperable national forces in the event of a collective defense requirement. The strategic environment in 1991, however, allowed NATO to rely on the forward defense of Germany through the continued stationing of American armed forces. Thus the US Department of Defense concluded in 1995: "Forward deployed conventional and nuclear forces are the single most visible demonstration of America's commitment to defend U.S. and allied interests in Europe."[11] In the post-enlargement NATO, forward deployment of conventional and nuclear forces has been abandoned in favor of a reinforcement status in Germany. The United States now has a forward political commitment to defend Poland but no forward deployments to make such a commitment credible.

Perhaps more problematically for the new NATO, any decision to reinforce a new member during a crisis carries a risk of escalation that would raise fears in Russia that the premises on which Moscow had accepted NATO enlargement were being violated. Such concerns would inevitably affect the NATO consensus process and be as likely to divide as to unite current NATO allies over defense of the new member. Indeed, there has already been a worrisome decline in the willingness of the public in Germany (from which reinforcement would most likely have to flow) to support the defense of new allies. In 1996, some 61 percent of Germans felt that NATO enlargement would benefit European security. In 1997, the number was down to 38 percent. An opinion poll found that 51 percent of Germans surveyed would vote against Poland's joining NATO when the question was worded this way: "Keeping in mind that our country must defend any NATO member that comes under attack, please tell me how you would vote if there were a referendum tomorrow on including Poland in NATO." Only 23 percent of Germans believed that NATO should not be swayed by Russian concerns about acceptance of new members.[12]

In the absence of a strong security guarantee to the new NATO members, the decision-making surrounding NATO enlargement may have failed to meet a major strategic goal—to hedge between German and Russian security competition. Were Poland to feel threatened, and were the absence of an immediate security guarantee to divide NATO into inaction, Germany might still opt to act unilaterally to protect its interests to the east. Absent a strong NATO presence and a credible guarantee to Poland, the old claim that NATO's mission is to keep the Americans in, the Russians out, and the Germans down may have lost a degree of value. Indeed, NATO must now explain why, if it does not need American troops deployed in Poland, it does need US troops stationed in Germany.

Third, NATO agreed to create a Permanent Joint Council (PJC) for regular consultation with Russia inside NATO headquarters. Such consultation includes regular meetings at the ambassadorial, ministerial, and heads-of-state levels. The PJC can establish committees and working groups and will hold regular meetings for military representatives and chiefs of staff no less than twice a year, in addition to monthly meetings at the military representative level. Russia has established a mission to NATO headed by a representative of ambassadorial rank; it includes a senior military representative for purposes of strengthening military cooperation between NATO and Russia.

The NATO-Russia Founding Act stipulates that its provisions neither "provide NATO or Russia, in any way, with a right of veto over the actions of the other nor do they infringe upon or restrict the rights of NATO or Russia to independent decision-making and action.... They cannot be used as a means to disadvantage the interests of other states."[13] This statement led to public-relations assertions that Russia would have a "voice but not a veto" in NATO's decision-making process. In testimony to the Senate Foreign Relations Committee on 7 October 1997, US Secretary of State Madeleine K. Albright noted that "the NATO-Russia Founding Act gives no opportunity to dilute, delay, or block NATO decisions. NATO's allies will always meet to agree on every item on their agenda before meeting with Russia."[14] Albright added: "The Founding Act also does not limit NATO's ultimate authority to deploy troops or nuclear weapons in order to meet its commitments to new and old members. All it does is restate unilaterally existing NATO policy."[15] To critics of this key aspect of NATO's transformation, Albright's reassurances did not reflect great sensitivity to the way NATO works in its consensus process.

Russia does not have a "veto" over NATO decisions because no country has a formal veto; NATO makes decisions by consensus. A vote, which would enable a formal veto, is held only if unanimity on a particular decision already exists within the alliance. Thus, it is in the consensus process that effective veto power lies—and that is where most of the influence and bargaining takes place in NATO. Russia's presence will inevitably affect that process because it has been granted an increased capacity to lobby individual NATO members to be sensitive to Moscow's concerns. At a minimum, cohesion and coherence in NATO will be affected by this new institutional architecture. NATO will have to attain consensus among all nineteen members before going to the PJC on any given issue. The inevitable result will be administrative disarray that could lead to institutional gridlock and bureaucratic redundancy in daily operations or, especially, in a crisis.

NATO's post–Cold War consensus was sorely tested by Balkan issues and by the NATO enlargement process. As a result, NATO risks assuming an institutional architecture under which confusion reigns while state interests conflict. As the analyst William Hyland concluded: "That Russia will have 'a voice but not a veto' is a naïve incantation.... Moscow will have more of an opportunity to influence every NATO decision, including military strategy, than the new members themselves."[16] A leading supporter of NATO enlargement, Henry Kissinger, conceded: "I confess that, had I known the price of NATO enlargement would be the gross dilution of NATO, I might have urged other means to achieve the objective."[17] This school of enlargement advocates must now rely on a diluted alliance and collective security to sustain its strategic objectives in central and eastern Europe.

The Spread of Stability

The United States and its allies have attempted to use NATO enlargement as a tool to promote stability in postcommunist Europe by linking membership to specific actions or policies on the part of aspiring members. The results so far have been mixed. At the operational level, this became clearest in the area of military criteria for membership in NATO—there were none. Consequently, the transaction costs of consensus-building in NATO are likely to be increased by adding new members. NATO's capacity to spread stability throughout central and eastern Europe may be diminished if the consensus process now makes crisis management more difficult. Cohesion issues within NATO will also be aggravated by a growing split in the trans-Atlantic relationship over the costs and burden sharing involved in NATO enlargement.

Arguments for linking NATO membership to policy outcomes were undermined by the timing of the decision to proceed with enlargement, which was driven primarily by political calculations by President Clinton. The basic decision to expand NATO was not related to domestic political calculations, but the timing of implementation was. Initially, Clinton and senior US officials opposed the policy, seeking to defer discussion of enlargement by initiating the Partnership for Peace. Only National Security Advisor W. Anthony Lake and a handful of other key advisors actively pushed for NATO enlargement in 1993 and 1994. When congressional Republicans included NATO enlargement in their 1994 Contract with America, Clinton accelerated NATO toward enlargement as an attempt to claim the issue for himself. Yet only during the 1996 presidential campaign did Clinton make a firm commitment to set a timetable for enlargement. Decisions relating to the sequencing of NATO enlargement negotiations and parliamentary ratification were guided not by specific policy goals but by a desire to have the project completed for the symbolically important fiftieth anniversary of NATO in April 1999. Canadian prime minister Jean Chrétien spoke for many of the NATO allies when he stated at the Madrid summit in 1997 that the Clinton administration had no strategic vision for Europe and that America's two-year campaign to enlarge NATO was "done for short-term political reasons, to win elections."[18] At no point did President Clinton make an effort to explain why

NATO enlargement had been deemed a bad idea in the administration's interagency process in 1993–94 but a good idea in late 1996.

The linkage approach to NATO enlargement was nonetheless strong. Its strength lay in NATO's combining membership criteria with specific policy outcomes in or among aspiring member states. Once these countries become NATO members, however, there is no guarantee that they will ascribe to the criteria with which enlargement was linked. This is not to say that there is reason to expect new member's policies to diverge from their current directions. Rather, the concern has more to do with NATO as an international organization. NATO is a nonregulative institution that is heavily dependent upon the exercise of American power in order to function. Independent institutional leverage to shape state behavior is absent among members but high for those seeking to get in. By articulating membership criteria, NATO was able to get aspiring countries to conform to important norms and procedures—for example, in the areas of civil-military relations and negotiation of border disputes. The challenge for NATO now will be to sustain these trends within a nonregulative institution.

NATO's strength depends on the exercise of American power and influence. Absent that, its institutional attributes alone have yet to be shown to guarantee peace. For example, from 1967 to 1974, Greece was governed by a military junta that came to power using a secret NATO counterinsurgency plan. Despite the wishes of the Scandinavian members of NATO to have Greece considered for sanction by the alliance, they could get no consensus in the North Atlantic Council even to debate it. Turkey's record as a democracy is highly questionable. As recently as the summer of 1997 (just before the Madrid summit), the Turkish military forced the elected government to give up power. As US National Security Advisor Sandy Berger said, briefing reporters before the summit: "There's no exit door from NATO.... Once you come into NATO, there's no door on the back that says, this is the door for countries that didn't make it."[19]

Interestingly, NATO's enlargement criteria ignored the most important aspects of what NATO does. NATO is, at its core, a military organization, but it established no military or strategic criteria for assessing membership qualifications. For example, in Hungary 63 percent of the public has signaled its opposition to using Hungarian forces to defend another NATO ally if attacked. Although NATO has no need or plans to station nuclear weapons in new member states, it is a principle they must accept. Yet 96 percent of Hungarians oppose the stationing of nuclear weapons on their territory. Moreover, 88 percent of Hungarians oppose an increase in defense spending to pay for membership if it comes at the expense of social spending.[20] The 1997 Hungarian defense budget was about 1.3 percent of gross national product (GNP)—far short of the 2.2 percent that American officials estimate Hungary will have to spend in order to achieve the lowest level of integration into NATO.

For its part, the Czech government cut defense spending some 20 percent between 1997 and 1998. Senior Czech officials have promised the United States that they will increase their defense spending over the next several years to meet the requirements of integrating into NATO. Such an increase would be by 20 percent, which would get the Czechs back to where they were before they began cutting defense spending, which was about 1.8 percent of GNP.

According to Jeffrey Simon, an effective advocate of enlargement as a linkage tool to promote military reform in central and eastern Europe, Hungary has considerable work to do to restore military prestige, build social support for the military, and construct a viable military institution. Simon notes that parliamentary oversight of the military in Hungary is limited, that Hungary lacks an interagency organization that could formulate and coordinate a national security policy, and that no public record of defense policy or the state of the Hungarian Defense Forces is provided by the Hungarian Ministry of Defense.[21] Although the armed forces of Hungary include thirty thousand conscripts, their time spent in service is limited to nine months.[22] Credible forces will include only professional and limited-contract soldiers, with conscription time reduced in order to free monies to pay for basic training and the upkeep of forces. In 1997, the Hungarian government sought to contract forty-five hundred soldiers, but by August only twenty-two hundred places had been filled. Most soldiers were unemployed young men with a general education through the American equivalent of the eighth grade. Seventy percent of Hungarian professional soldiers hold a second job to make ends meet.

The Czech Republic has similar military problems, if not worse.[23] Only Poland has presented a credible and effective plan to modernize its armed forces over a fifteen-year period. Ultimately, it would be inappropriate to measure these new NATO members by comparing their armed forces with those of current NATO countries. It is possible, however, that with a more extended linkage period, more could have been achieved in terms of guaranteeing a high degree of force modernization, implementation of defense spending goals, and specific policy commitments.

Institutionally, the transaction costs of NATO consensus-building may be increased by adding new members. In the current security environment, these countries have every reason to show that they will be good allies over time, particularly by closely mirroring American policy goals. But it would be inappropriate to assume that new members will always share the same immediate interests as their allies. When asked in October 1997 whether NATO enlargement would dilute the institution's ability to carry out future tasks, the recently retired SACEUR General George Joulwan could offer only, "[That] is a point that needs to be debated over the next year or two."[24] For enlargement to succeed in lowering transaction costs, it may be necessary to keep additional pressure on new or future NATO members to contribute to overall alliance goals and ensure that NATO can expand and maintain cohesion simultaneously.

Out-of-area, or "non–Article 5," missions, such as the IFOR/SFOR operations in Bosnia, are symbolic of the idea that there is a "new NATO." The new NATO is defined by increased European responsibility for security matters and nontraditional military activities such as peacekeeping.[25] Many senior central and eastern European government officials note privately, however, that they do not want to join the "new NATO"—they seek the "old NATO" of collective defense and a hard American security guarantee. But there is no strong collective defense element to NATO enlargement as practiced. Therefore, the process of adapting NATO's military structure to become more efficient for force projection will be complicated. For example, it is in the interest of new members to promote NATO military planning in a way that makes their immediate regional security concerns a high priority and to use their new leverage as NATO members to bargain for that position. NATO's bureaucratic time and energy may thus be diverted away from current challenges to the south and toward a more Cold-War-oriented dominance of the central European region. As F. Stephen Larrabee, an early and articulate advocate of NATO enlargement, now maintains: "There is very little work being done on NATO's southern strategy, even though everybody agrees that is where the next war could happen.... The alliance is being expanded into central Europe, where the threat has vanished, yet nobody seems to know if it can cope with the multiple risks present in the Mediterranean."[26]

Further complicating NATO's ability to project stability, the allies agreed, as part of the enlargement package, to conduct further rounds of NATO enlargement. Only three of eleven candidate countries were admitted to NATO membership in the first round, and pressure for further expansion will be intense. The recently retired chairman of the US Joint Chiefs of Staff, General John Shalikashvili, concluded:

I think that NATO as now organized must have some limits, but I don't know what they are. What do I mean by that? On the political side we have the mechanisms in the NATO North Atlantic Council and the NATO Defense Planning Committee ... military committees of unanimity. There might be a natural law that says there's a limit to how many nations can make tough decisions in that kind of mechanism, and if you go beyond that, must you somehow change that?[27]

At the political level, therefore, NATO enlargement at best complicates governance matters within the alliance. While the "new NATO" reflects a collective desire to spread stability in Europe, the alliance's political and operational ability to sustain such a goal is in decline.

The political dynamics in NATO most complicated by the enlargement decision-making process involved financial burden sharing. In calculating the financial burden, the United States government assumed that overall costs would range from $27 billion to $35 billion over a ten-to twelve-year period.[28] Among the countries involved, new members would pay 35 percent of costs, current European members would pay 50 percent, and the US would pay about 15 percent.[29] This assumption was rebuked by French President Jacques Chirac at the Madrid summit, where he said that France would spend nothing on NATO enlargement. The German government was also adamant that enlargement costs be kept to a minimum. British officials working in the Ministry of Defense suggested that NATO enlargement might actually reduce the amount Britain contributed to NATO infrastructure costs. Complicating this dynamic, American members of Congress insisted that the European allies bear the primary cost burden of NATO enlargement.

The European NATO allies were strongly critical of the US cost study, which some viewed as prescribing unnecessarily high costs in order to market US arms in central and eastern Europe. Actually, US Department of Defense officials had urged new NATO members not to purchase expensive new weapons systems. Instead, they stressed education and training in NATO doctrine, procedures, and command-and-control, interoperable communications systems, and integration into air defense structures. "Soft" interoperability—specifically, in language, procedures, and doctrine—is viewed by NATO military planners as a fundamental requirement of early integration. Nonetheless, some of the strongest American advocates of NATO enlargement have pushed to export large and expensive weapons systems to new NATO members. For example, Bruce L. Jackson served as president of the US Committee to Expand NATO and was at the same time director of strategic planning for the Lockheed Martin Corporation, the world's largest weapons manufacturer. Offering a potential market of about $10 billion for fighter jets alone in new member countries, NATO enlargement was obviously an appealing policy for US arms manufacturers.

A credible collective defense commitment to new NATO members would require greater costs than were initially estimated. Indeed, current cost assumptions for NATO reinforce the conclusion that the security guarantee that new members will get is questionable. As Walter Steutzle, a former high-level defense planning official in the German government, asserted: "If you are serious about providing equal security, the basic defense needs of the new members will raise the enlargement bill to $70 billion."[30] Nonetheless, in October 1997, US Secretary of Defense William

Cohen announced to the US Senate Appropriations Committee that estimated enlargement costs would be lower than anticipated. The administration asserted that the initial US cost study had assumed that four
countries would be invited to join NATO, instead of only three, and the
infrastructure of the new members had been found to be in better shape
than expected. Therefore, the shared direct costs of NATO enlargement
would be only $1.3 billion over ten years (a figure reduced from $5 billion
in a spring 1997 NATO study; the initial US study had assumed shared
direct enlargement costs of $9–12 billion).[31]

These costs are assessed as the specific costs of integrating the new
members into common NATO programs such as air defense and headquarters. They exclude the costs of making the new members' militaries
compatible with Western standards. There is serious reason to question
the finding that new members' militaries were in better shape than
expected. NATO had been working with these militaries on their territory
in one way or another since 1994. Since no major programmatic changes
had taken place in the new member countries between February 1997
and the issuing of the NATO report that fall, the claim that the US and
NATO did not know the state of infrastructure in these countries was
acknowledged off-the-record by NATO officials as dubious.[32]

During NATO's negotiations with the three new members in the fall of
1997, alliance officials grew increasingly concerned about the status of
the armed forces in these countries. According to a classified NATO study
leaked in Brussels to the magazine *Defense News*, NATO's internal view of
the three new members departed substantially from the public rhetoric
that justified the low-end cost assessments.[33] NATO Defense Planning
Questionnaires (DPQs) completed by the three invitees in October–
November 1997 raised serious concerns in NATO about the scope and
depth of problems in the new member states and demonstrated flaws in
the cost assumptions of the policy. The NATO study identified the Czech
army's equipment as "old and approaching obsolescence" and noted that
none of the ships in Poland's navy was "capable for command and control
or joint or combined operations." The DPQ assessments concluded that
vast segments of each new member's infrastructure were obsolete, un-
secured for communications, and generally incompatible with NATO.

The internal NATO study also revealed serious air force command-and-control problems in Hungary's thirty-two-page DPQ report. NATO noted that some 70 percent of the country's pilots carried out only fifty hours of training per year, with another 30 percent flying only thirty hours per year. Poland's forty-three-page report, titled "Defense Review Committee Assessment of Plans of Poland," opened by stating that the country's army faced "widespread and significant interoperability deficiencies" that, if not corrected, would "substantially limit its combat capacity." The NATO report was especially critical of Poland's naval readiness, because only a few ships were "capable of more distant deployment beyond Poland's coastal region and the Baltic Sea," and "only limited improvements" would occur during the five-year period of national planning under review. Additionally, the Polish DPQ noted that there was no tactical ballistic missile defense capability for any of the Polish army's surface-to-air missile systems, while the air force suffered from low levels of combat readiness, lack of mobility in its air defense systems, limited airlift, and very limited tactical reconnaissance resources.

The NATO reviews of the three new members' DPQs raised acute concerns among military planners about the ability to meet basic NATO planning requirements for new members with low-end cost estimates. For example, the Polish DPQ showed that no Polish air base had adequate cargo-handling equipment, and none of the air force's radar, communications, or navigation equipment could exchange data with NATO's. Because of its size, Poland's share of the additional NATO infrastructure money will be $649 million over ten years, with the Czechs and Hungarians receiving approximately $260 million each. Such expenditures will be sufficient to help buy communications equipment that the three new members need and will help their armed services' radar and command systems to interface with NATO's. However, the internal NATO study did not suggest that infrastructure was better than expected. Indeed, Poland's DPQ showed that none of its fifty-five military airfields was connected to a fuel pipeline system. Internal NATO estimates assume that constructing a single mile of pipeline will cost as much as $300,000 in the Czech Republic and more in Poland, where distances from airfields to existing fuel lines are greater.

Ultimately, the acceptance of a low-end cost study was a concession by the United States to its allies. This became the official NATO cost study, which had been delayed because of a trans-Atlantic split over priorities. Europe (and Canada) wanted the lowest possible cost figures, whereas Washington insisted on higher numbers to provide at least minimal credibility to the collective defense provisions of the NATO treaty. Accepting the European position was a dramatic shift for American diplomats. In May 1997, a US official in Brussels commented, "We've laid it on the line about costs to our allies.... They're low-balling the cost and that's not acceptable."[34] However, the remaining costs of elevating new members to mature capability would still require additional funding on a bilateral level. For example, Polish officials indicated they would require (while not formally requesting) up to $2 billion in credits to purchase multipurpose aircraft. Additionally, the RAND Corporation estimated that to equip five divisions and ten air wings already in NATO so that they could rapidly reinforce the new members in a crisis, and to stockpile supplies and ammunition in the new countries for the reinforcement's use, would cost $22 billion.

For this reason, a General Accounting Office (GAO) audit of NATO enlargement costs concluded that the administration's estimates were "quite speculative" and that "while not an added cost of enlargement, such assistance would represent a shift in the cost burden from the new member countries to the countries providing assistance."[35] According to the GAO study, the ultimate costs of NATO enlargement will be contingent on several factors. Specifically, NATO has yet to define its future strategy for defending the expanded alliance, the force and facility requirements of the new member states, and the way in which costs of expanding the alliance will be financed. Additionally, the absence of an assessment of long-term security threats and the promise of further expansions make cost assessments highly contingent.

NATO enlargement, for the short term, may also exacerbate an increasing military disfunctionalism within NATO and thus further increase the costs of spreading stability. European defense investment has declined precipitously and impedes the ability of European countries to participate in power projection missions. European dependence on the United

States is leading to a strategic imbalance in NATO, particularly in areas of high technology. Current European members of NATO can barely communicate with the US military. For example, in the summer of 1997 NATO conducted a Mediterranean exercise (IVITEX '97) that included more than twenty-five ships from the United States, Greece, the Netherlands, Germany, Italy, France, and the United Kingdom. The goal of the exercise was to test the communications links of the naval forces and to establish a common ground for communications. The commanders were forced to use the lowest common level of communications technology to ensure uninterrupted communications across the different navies, which was a substantial diminution from the technical capabilities contributed by the American forces.[36] The chairman of NATO's Military Committee, General Klaus Naumann, complained that "the United States is moving with unparalleled velocity toward the kind of high-tech military equipment that has no match in Europe.... I am beginning to worry that one day we will wake up and find that our armies can no longer work well together."[37] As of early 1999, NATO could mobilize only 2 percent of its overall combat potential in twelve hours—a decline from 70 percent at the end of the Cold War. As European allies continue to struggle with monetary union criteria, prospects are slim that this burden-sharing dilemma will be resolved in the near future.

In theory, NATO enlargement could diminish this problem. Because they inherited a Soviet military legacy, the three new NATO members will have to undergo substantial force modernization. And because they are likely to be investing in defense infrastructure as part of their military integration into NATO, they may become more compatible with American forces than some current allies are. However, as these countries reorient their priorities toward membership in the European Union after having attained NATO membership, they are equally likely to choose not to invest in defense modernization. Either way, new NATO members may have some difficult economic choices to make in the years to come—especially if the real challenges to their security and stability come not from traditional sources of power but from economic chaos and instability in the global market.

NATO faces a new institutional challenge as a result of the enlargement process. There is a particular danger that NATO is confusing institutional interaction within the alliance with concrete actions that actually increase international security in Europe. One senior NATO official worries about "institutional gridlock and bureaucratic redundancy" resulting from the expanding institutional mechanisms of managing NATO enlargement.[38] In fact, NATO officials are often left exasperated over how to make the new institutional architecture work or how it would respond in a serious crisis.[39] NATO's mandate and missions have been expanded substantially, but without a corresponding increase in resources or personnel to help implement the changes. Secretary General Solana concluded in 1997 that "if this pace continues, it is hard to predict what NATO will be like just three years from now."[40]

Building Democracy and Community

The relevance of NATO's goal of building democracy and community in postcommunist Europe is mixed, but this goal was the dominant force behind the implementation of the enlargement decision. It is important, however, to differentiate between NATO and democracy in Europe. Austria, Finland, the Republic of Ireland, Sweden, and Switzerland are democracies that do not require reinforcement of their identity by joining a military alliance—though it is possible that some of them might seek to join NATO for other reasons in the future. Nonetheless, rewarding democratic reformers for the impressive efforts they have made toward democracy and lasting peace in central Europe was a critical rationale for NATO enlargement. Thus, NATO enlargement might be viewed as a fundamentally political act rather than a military or strategic one.

There are some marginal risks associated with this policy objective. Confidence in democratic and market reformers in the new member states will certainly be enhanced by the symbolic affirmation of those countries' return to Europe via NATO membership. Political leaders in the new NATO states, however, may not have prepared their publics sufficiently for the budgetary implications of NATO membership. Absent a strong base of public support for defense investment, there is a risk that the substantial costs of military integration might force the new members to adapt their budgetary priorities away from economic reform programs, leading to public displeasure with reform-oriented politicians. For domestic political reasons, new members may ignore defense investment and thus make themselves, from a military perspective, "second-class citizens" in NATO. Nevertheless, the prospect of shifting budget priorities in central Europe has raised high-level concern in the International Monetary Fund (IMF), which is responsible for guaranteeing credits and loans that finance economic reform among the aspiring members. In June 1997, the IMF managing director personally warned US Treasury Secretary Robert E. Rubin that increased defense spending by new NATO members could negatively affect the IMF's engagement with them. Yet officials from the Czech Republic and Hungary have informally signaled that they hope to purchase F-16 or F-18 fighter aircraft costing some $8 billion. If they do, the expenditure would exceed the combined defense budgets of all three new member countries.[41]

At the core of this dilemma is a tension between NATO enlargement as a political act and the fact that NATO is, at its core, a military organization that requires substantial contributions from its member states. Czech President Václav Havel maintained that NATO must redefine its aims and purpose before admitting new members. "The expansion of NATO should be preceded by something even more important, that is, a new formulation of its own meaning, mission, and identity," Havel asserted.[42] NATO's mission has changed, but it is still primarily in the military business, and new members will be expected to contribute to its military functions and to build public support for its military role. As German Defense Minister Volker Ruehe asserted, the three new members "have to make their own contribution—this concerns not only financing but also public opinion so that we can be sure that if there's a crisis their populations will be willing to carry the burden."[43]

Despite warnings by countries left out of NATO membership and by opponents of the enlargement policy, NATO's enlargement has not harmed democracy in those countries left out—including Russia. There, reformists consolidated power in the Yeltsin administration in the months immediately following the Madrid summit. If they failed to sustain reform, it was due to internal political and economic crises in Russia and not to NATO enlargement. If anything, NATO enlargement was a net gain for Russia, which now has a voice in NATO policy and was also invited to participate with the transformed Group of Seven industrialized countries, now the Summit of the Eight. American and allied backing for Russia's admittance to this exclusive club of democratic powers was largely a concession to Russia's worries that NATO enlargement would isolate it from the international community.[44]

Although one senior Romanian official warned in advance of the Madrid summit that rejection of Romania as a NATO member would leave the country with a sense of abandonment by the West on a par with that resulting from the Yalta accords, Romanians continued with economic reform programs and democratization efforts, albeit faltering ones.[45] A senior Estonian official warned that a failure to join NATO might force the Baltic countries to reevaluate their 1991 decision to align with the West, but this has not happened.[46] Nevertheless, NATO does risk endorsing a double standard by declaring that membership should not be decided by where a country sits on the map while privately being guided by geostrategic concerns in the case of the three Baltic countries. A high-level Baltic official wants NATO to be honest if it is not serious about inclusiveness for those who have met political criteria. He asserts tersely that "if, in reality, whether you are in NATO is dependent upon where you are located, then NATO should say so."[47] Indeed, holding out a false promise of NATO membership to the Baltic countries only encourages them to waste scarce resources by lobbying and conducting public-relations programs in NATO countries.

NATO enlargement is also a half-step toward community building because it risks undermining NATO's existing Partnership for Peace program of cooperative outreach to interested non-NATO countries in central and eastern Europe. Though it was initially perceived as a sort of waiting room for NATO membership, the Partnership for Peace eventually took on a life of its own. Through a variety of programmatic activities, NATO worked at the ground level to build trust among the central and eastern European militaries while enhancing civilian control over the armed forces and transparency in defense planning.

To compensate for the rejection of aspiring members, NATO promised an "enhanced" Partnership for Peace program that would include making

PFP more operational and oriented toward real-world contingencies, strengthening its political consultation elements, and involving partners more in its planning and decision-making. Overall, common NATO funding for the PFP in fiscal year 1997 was a mere $16.4 million. Direct American assistance to facilitate partnership programs under the "Warsaw Initiative" Foreign Military Financing program is provided by funding grants to partners primarily for training and the purchase of nonlethal equipment in the areas of communications, language, and search-and-rescue, as well as computers, personnel equipment, and command-and-control centers for a Regional Airspace Initiative. From 1996 to 1998, the annual US allocation to these programs grew from $53.1 million to $94.0 million. The fiscal year 1999 budget request, however, signaled a decline, to $80.0 million. At the very time an enhanced PFP was being celebrated, rhetoric outpaced the investment of resources that would actually make it credible.[48]

The PFP has been weakened in part because its three main drivers were Poland, Hungary, and the Czech Republic. Enlargement will inevitably consume NATO resources away from the PFP and toward integrating the new members into the alliance. When asked how the United States intended to provide resources for an enhanced PFP, one senior State Department official suggested that "these partners will have to mobilize their domestic interest groups in Washington" in order to assure funding.[49] US Senator Richard G. Lugar maintained that "neither NATO enlargement nor PFP is well understood in the Senate, and it will be hard to make an enhanced PFP credible without resources."[50] Without an *increase* in PFP funding, the credibility of NATO's open door to promote further democratization among aspiring countries is in doubt. According to a high-ranking NATO military official: "Enhanced PFP is lip-service.... Militarily, NATO has already reached the maximum of what it can sustain in PFP, as resources are at the limit and funds and staff are beyond limits."[51]

The Partnership for Peace was among the most creative aspects of NATO's post–Cold War adaptation. It is the main NATO program that can functionally promote the spread of an undifferentiated Western community at the military-to-military level by blurring the distinction between NATO members and nonmembers. Arguably, if the goal of NATO enlargement is to extend a Western community based on shared democratic principles, then funding equal to, if not greater than, that provided to the three new members should go to the PFP from the United States and its allies (including the new NATO members). This is especially true because the three countries that were invited to join NATO were those least in need of the confidence that membership would bring in order to help consolidate democracy. Nevertheless, they will inevitably be the primary focus of resource investment as they are integrated into NATO.

NATO has sought to accommodate the non-invitees who still aspire to NATO membership by eliminating the North Atlantic Cooperation Council (NACC) and replacing it with a new Euro-Atlantic Partnership Council (EAPC). The NACC was created at American initiative in 1991 to build non–collective defense consultation and socialization among NATO and non-NATO states. Its comprehensive work plan on information sharing for peacekeeping played a critical role in preparing PFP countries to complement and work with NATO troops in the IFOR/ SFOR operations in Bosnia-Herzegovina. Criticized by US officials as an anachronism of the Cold War (even though it was established in 1991), the NACC was absorbed by the EAPC, which was presented as a new alternative to NATO membership. The initial premise behind the EAPC was to create an elevated level of partnership for countries that formally sought NATO membership. Not wanting to create a third tier of participants in the NACC, however, the EAPC assumed the identity of the NACC. Acronyms changed, but with no qualitative difference.

In sum, the two main programs consistent with the building of democracy and community in central and eastern Europe are diminished by NATO enlargement. As a result, this goal of NATO enlargement is a glass both half full and half empty. It is half full because the countries that were admitted are stable democracies. It is half empty because the countries that most need the confidence to build democracy were left out.

Collective Security

Trends in NATO are toward collective security. Although NATO has no legal responsibility to function as a general European collective security system, states in Europe are increasingly treating it as such—especially Russia. However, rather than institutionalizing an emerging pattern of collective security power dynamics, Europe has proceeded in an ad hoc manner toward collective security. By first seeking to build interlocking institutions in 1991, the United States, Canada, and Europe sought an integrative approach to create a security architecture and deter aggression in the Balkan region. When that failed, Europe moved toward an ad hoc arrangement in which NATO would be a tool for the UN or OSCE as a peacekeeping force. When that arrangement, too, failed to end the Balkan conflict, Europe resorted to an informal concert arrangement with the five-power Contact Group, for which NATO became a means of collective security—not a determinant of it.

NATO's own trend toward collective security was accelerated by the decision to give Russia a voice in NATO decision-making. Moreover, its members increasingly view NATO's mission as being defense not only of territory but also of values. As Czech President Václav Havel asserted: "The new European security system must be built by democratic forces.... The North Atlantic Alliance is, as recent experience has shown, the most appropriate means of ensuring the collective security of our values."[52] By broadening NATO's fundamental purpose beyond that of collective defense, the alliance's responsibilities are being increased to include intervention within states when stability is challenged—as the summer of 1999 demonstrated in Kosovo.

Kosovo was especially instructive regarding NATO's post-enlargement evolution. As Serb forces attacked ethnic Albanians, who represent 90 percent of the population in this Yugoslav region, they were conducting aggression within a sovereign state. Collective intervention by NATO would represent a test of its new mission. Could members justify intervention in a sovereign state—and if so, under what legal mandate? With regard to the overall enlargement package, it was interesting to note that in August 1998, none of the new NATO allies sent forces to participate in NATO-PFP exercises in Albania designed to signal NATO resolve to halt the Serb assault. Even more importantly, Presidents Clinton and Chirac agreed in an August 1998 telephone conversation that at the time NATO could not intervene in Kosovo without Russian support. Formally, NATO was not reflecting the principle of collective security and did not claim to do so, but in practice its members behaved as if collective security was the organizing principle for European security and NATO was the channel for it. At the same time, the power dynamics that have undermined previous state efforts to build collective security architectures constrained NATO's ability to act when the crisis grew to proportions that threatened regional stability in the Balkans.

For advocates of NATO's transition toward collective security, this pattern of state behavior implies that NATO should include Russia as a member in order to better reflect underlying power dynamics. Yet for advocates of collective security, the promise remains unfulfilled. NATO ignored the premise of collective security between Hungary and Romania by leaving Romania out of the enlargement process. Russia lingers in a waiting room in which it is formally given a lower legal-institutional status than Belgium, Luxembourg, or the Czech Republic in affecting European security. The informal veto granted to Russia may not satisfy Moscow over the long term. Conversely, there is no reciprocal provision in the NATO-Russia Founding Act that would dismantle the PJC if Russia violated international norms of behavior—for example, in its near abroad. A "voice but not a veto" works both ways regarding Russia, and there is no mechanism for sanction against Russia within the NATO-Russia architecture. Thus, for collective security to be complete, Russia would have to join NATO as a full member, and the principle of collective defense would have to be eliminated—or placed in reserve.

Among NATO countries there is public support for the idea that Russia should be a member of NATO. In one 1997 survey, 68 percent of Americans who were questioned indicated that NATO should be expanded to remove the outdated divisions of the Cold War and help bring Europe together. Only 22 percent believed NATO should be expanded to make it larger and more powerful so that it could more effectively deal with the possibility of a threat from Russia. Most significantly, 52 percent of those surveyed favored NATO membership for Russia. Support was even higher when stability in Russia was made a prerequisite. Fully 65 percent agreed that "once Russia has shown that it can be stable and peaceful for a significant period, we should try to include it in NATO."

Only 30 percent believed that "there are too many ways that our interests might come into conflict with Russia in the future and there is always the chance that Russia may go back to being aggressive.... Therefore it is not a good idea to include Russia in NATO."[53] When asked whether Russia should join NATO or be excluded from membership, people in the new member countries responded favorably, with the Czech Republic at 50 percent, Hungary at 46 percent, and Poland at 42 percent in support of Russian membership.[54] US President Bill Clinton suggested that "no European democracy should be excluded from ultimate consideration.... My personal position is that should apply to Russia as well."[55]

Advocates of collective security see Russia remaining in an inadequate and dangerous "halfway house" as a result of the overall NATO enlargement package. Moreover, just as some advocates of collective defense might be surprised that their policy advocacy has instead advanced trends toward collective security, so might the new and old members of NATO wonder whether they are getting what they signed up for. It would be ironic if, in seeking to join NATO in part over fears of Russia, central and eastern Europeans have caused the institution to evolve toward something other than what they thought they were getting into and devoting resources toward. This trend toward collective security may eventually raise a fundamental question, given the historical track record of the institutional form: If NATO is becoming a general collective security system for Europe, is it still the best alternative for guaranteeing peace and security—including preventing the possibility of security competition within the West?

What Next for NATO?

NATO enlargement was an important political dynamic shaping the post–Cold War European security environment. Indeed, it was a logical extension of the "new NATO." The alliance's institutional role now involves a variety of new goals, including rebalancing the organization between US and European military responsibilities, outreach to the East, peacekeeping, and organizing to respond to nontraditional threats such as the proliferation of weapons of mass destruction and related missile technology. Yet NATO enlargement, placed in the context of competing expectations and goals, raises important questions about the future effectiveness of NATO. Some supporters of the enlarged alliance might worry especially that the security guarantee to new members is tenuous and that Russia has been granted a strong say over the NATO consensus process. The rationales for enlargement with the most relevance to its implementation—building democracy and fostering collective security—challenge the very foundations of NATO as a collective defense organization.

New NATO members may not especially like the further implementation of the existing enlargement policy. Poland, no doubt, did not join NATO to see it transformed into a collective security institution with an enhanced Russian voice over Warsaw's own security interests. Thus, NATO will have to assess more concretely what collective defense means in the new security environment. Its policy of reinforcement, adopted in the 1991 New Strategic Concept, relied on forward-deployed American troops and nuclear weapons stationed in Germany. In the post-enlargement NATO, forward deployment no longer exists. Any security challenge to new members would be a sore test of NATO's ability to build consensus for "Article 5" missions, and any decision to reinforce a new member could be destabilizing to overall European security.

As a result, new NATO members will still have to rely on self-help for their territorial defense. The main benefit they will get from NATO is technical expertise to aid in modernizing their armed forces as they become deeply integrated into the NATO culture of conducting security relations. This *is* an important and substantial gain for the new members. At the same time, their leaders should make clear to their publics exactly what they will get from NATO—and what they must contribute as responsible members. In the run-up to the process of parliamentary ratification of enlargement, Hungary and the Czech Republic made a number of commitments to NATO regarding long-term goals, including planned increases in their defense budgets. But global economic trends that might make the economies of the new NATO members vulnerable in the absence of European Union membership may put such goals at risk. Therefore, it is in the interest of the US and its NATO allies to see that these countries become EU members at the earliest opportunity. EU membership will lock in an institutional framework that will ensure that the new NATO members can be the contributors to security they aspire to be.

From an American foreign-policy and security perspective, the need to make EU membership a high priority creates a short-term dilemma. First, as the new NATO members seek to join the EU, they will have to satisfy French and German political leaders—in the area of common foreign and security policy, among other things. If, as is increasingly the case, French and German policies diverge from America's, the new members may have to make hard choices about their strategic alliance with the United States and their economic interests in EU membership. Second, as these countries set a high priority on meeting the criteria for EU membership, they will be challenged to sustain increases in defense investment programs as they implement further economic restructuring. Ultimately, NATO requires considerable commitment from its members, who must make the security relationship credible at a military and political level. Poland, Hungary, and the Czech Republic are strategic contributors to NATO just by their location on the map. Making sure that they are operational contributors to NATO as an institution will require a sustained commitment and considerable leadership.

NATO is confronted by a new challenge raised by the values-laden democratic mission and the collective security dynamics in Europe that drove the enlargement process. NATO is a union of sovereign states. But if NATO is orienting itself around a premise that it must secure the values of its members, then questions of military planning and strategic agendas arise. Just how far would NATO go to "secure" democracy? There is a common misconception about NATO that a member (old or new) could be suspended if it violated institutional norms and rules in either its foreign or its domestic policy. There is no such provision in NATO. The treaty allows only for a state to withdraw voluntarily from the organization. A state not playing by the rules can wreak considerable havoc on NATO by blocking consensus and inhibiting effective decision-making. If NATO's new mission is based on a concept of values rather than of territory, then in theory the allies must be prepared to intervene in a state if democracy is threatened. If NATO were really serious about this new mission, it would have to change its operational mandate and submit such changes in mission to parliamentary ratification.

Because prospects for such a development are poor, NATO must clarify exactly what it can and cannot do to enhance democracy. NATO can contribute to a general sense of reassurance and confidence in the reform processes of new member states, especially in the area of civil-military relations. It can also serve new and aspiring members by promoting a security culture that facilitates the peaceful resolution of international disputes through transparent defense planning and political consultation. Thus NATO can reduce the need for new members to worry about the intentions of their allies. By broadening the Partnership for Peace with substantial increases in funding and closer access to NATO defense planning procedures, NATO can expand this security culture further by blurring the distinction between members and nonmembers such as Russia, Ukraine, and the Baltic states. If it is successful, then pressure to conduct additional NATO enlargements for political reasons—at the expense of strategic criteria—may decline.

For the relationship between NATO and Russia (and between NATO and Ukraine) to succeed, the partnership will have to receive a greater bottom-up emphasis at the political and military level. Immediately following the Madrid summit, interest in Washington in developing the NATO-Russia partnership declined. Many advocates of enlargement viewed the relationship as having fulfilled its purpose—that is, ensuring the completion of a limited enlargement process. Yet Western-style military reform for Russia and Ukraine is a core interest for both old and new NATO members and will thus require an increase in political attention and resources at the operational level. If a culture of trust and direct cooperation in areas of shared interest can be developed, then these by-products of the enlargement decision will enhance security in Europe. On the other hand, if trends in NATO toward military dilution, strategic imbalance, and collective security continue, then Russia may have been granted an unprecedented opportunity to negatively affect decision-making in the alliance, an opportunity that was not reciprocated in terms of Western influence in the former Soviet Union. Ultimately, knowing how to build a positive and energetic relationship with Russia will be as important as knowing what circumstances might require NATO to dissolve cooperation with Russia.

NATO enlargement has, to date, played a positive role in shaping the security environment in central and eastern Europe. NATO enlargement, however, was an important *process,* not an end in itself. NATO must now explain exactly what its broader foundations are if its relevance is to be sustained in the twenty-first century. This is critical to justifying to the United States Congress the long-term stationing of American troops on the continent—on which any credible defense of new members will rest. If forward defense is not required in Poland, then it is that much more important to establish a clear rationale for the maintenance of US forces in Germany. NATO is an institution in transition, and sustaining its strategic foundations, particularly the core US-German security partnership, will be essential in the twenty-first century if NATO is to maintain its strategic viability. Building upon this bedrock of post–Cold War European security will be especially important if trends in NATO toward collective security continue and the enlargement door truly does remain open.

The problems with the policy do not necessarily lie in its well-intentioned goals, but rather in its implementation, which overpromised what NATO enlargement would deliver and established trends in NATO toward collective security. For example, presidential talking points and congressional testimony by senior US officials appeared designed to appeal simultaneously to supporters of enlargement who wanted to expand the alliance on the basis of anti-Russian containment and those who wanted to use NATO enlargement to integrate Russia into a general European collective security system. As a result of such divergent policy rationales, NATO enlargement must be viewed as part of an overall package that requires vision, leadership, and orchestration if it is to work. NATO enlargement, the NATO-Russia Permanent Joint Council, an enhanced Partnership for Peace, and the Euro-Atlantic Partnership Council each had strong foundations independently. Making them function together will require increased staff energy and budgets at a time when national investments in NATO are in decline. NATO has become overcommitted, understaffed, and underfinanced. Sifting through this increasingly complex institutional dynamic will be one of the greatest challenges to both old and new member states in the early twenty-first century.

Notes

1. Off-the-record comments, Washington, D.C., February 1996.

2. For further detail on the decision-making dynamics that led to NATO enlargement, see James Goldgier, "NATO Enlargement: Anatomy of a Decision," *Washington Quarterly* 21, no. 1 (Winter 1998): 85–102; and Sean Kay, *NATO and the Future of European Security* (Lanham, Maryland: Rowman and Littlefield, 1998).

3. Based on the author's interviews with senior US and European officials, 1994–1997.

4. Author's interviews with US officials, November 1997.

5. For discussion of threats to NATO's southern regions, see *Allied Command Structures in the New NATO* (Washington, D.C.: National Defense University Press, 1997). Also see Romanian Ministry of Foreign Affairs, *White Book on Romania and NATO,* 1997.

6. "Remarks by President Clinton at NATO/Russia Founding Act Signing Ceremony," the White House, Office of the Press Secretary, 27 May 1997.

7. *Ibid.*

8. "Founding Act on Mutual Relations, Cooperation and Security between NATO and the Russian Federation," NATO Office of Information and Press, May 1997.

9. This was a sensitive concern for the Russian negotiators. As the Russian ambassador to the United States claimed in a speech in April 1997, at the annual SACLANT Seminar, "enlargement will mean added to NATO: 731 fighter bombers, 1,300 to be reduced will be replaced by 3,400 Soviet-made tanks in Poland, Hungary, and the Czech Republic; 290 airfields, 550 weapons depots; and Visegrad tactical aviation will be able to bring missiles directly to the west of Russia."

10. "Statement by the North Atlantic Council," NATO Office of Information and Press, 14 March 1997.

11. Department of Defense, *United States Security Strategy for Europe and NATO,* June 1995, 27.

12. "German Public Endorsement of NATO Enlargement Declines Sharply," *USIA Opinion Analysis* (April 1997): M-55-97.

13. NATO Information and Press, May 1997.

14. Statement by Secretary of State Madeleine K. Albright to the US Senate Foreign Relations Commttee, 7 October 1997.

15. *Ibid.*

16. William G. Hyland, "NATO's Incredible Shrinking Defense," Paper presented to a CATO Institute Conference, "NATO Enlargement: Illusions and Reality," 25 June 1997.

17. Henry Kissinger, "The Dilution of NATO," *Washington Post,* 8 June 1997.

18. J. F. O. McAllister, "If You Buy That, We Know a Bridge in Brooklyn," *Time* 150 (21 July 1997): 16.

19. "Transcript: Berger, Cohen, Talbott Briefing on NATO Summit," *United States Information Agency,* 2 July 1997.

20. "Hungarian Public Widely Opposed to Military Spending Increase," *USIA Opinion Analysis* (21 April 1997): M-66-97.

21. Jeffrey Simon, "New Challenges in Hungarian Civil-Military Relations," paper presented at an international conference on civil-military relations in Budapest, Hungary, September 1997.

22. Also see Sebastian Gorka, "Hungary Reinvents its Defence Force," *Jane's Intelligence Review* (May 1997): 197–200.

23. See Christine Spolar, "Applicants Offer Lots of Heart but Few Arms," *Washington Post,* 17 June 1997; and George Jahn, "Money Woes Plague NATO Invitees," *Associated Press,* 16 November 1997.

24. "Transcript: Joulwan Interview on NATO Enlargement," *USIS Washington File* 2070, 29 October 1997.

25. See Sean Kay, "The New NATO and the Enlargement Process," *European Security* 6, no. 4 (Winter 1997): 1–16.

26. William Drozdiak, "Sixth Fleet Keeps Watch in Mediterranean Region's Turbulent Seas," *Washington Post,* 16 August 1998, A28.

27. Transcript: interview with reporters from the *International Herald Tribune, USA Today, Defense News,* and *Jane's Defense News,* 16 June 1997.

28. Other estimates, such as that of the RAND Corporation, saw likely costs of $40–60 billion, whereas the Congressional Budget Office estimated costs as high as $120 billion.

29. This conclusion was based on the assumption that force projection defense of new members would require already-agreed-upon modernization by current NATO member forces—which the US had completed.

30. William Drozdiak, "NATO Expansion 'On the Cheap' May Have Surcharge," *Washington Post,* 12 March 1997, A22.

31. William Drozdiak, "NATO: U.S. Erred on Costs of Expansion," *Washington Post,* 14 November 1997, A22.

32. Author's interviews, spring 1998.

33. Brooks Tigner, "NATO Papers Belie Modest Expansion Costs: Classified Reports Reveal Deep Deficiencies in Polish, Hungarian, Czech Republic Militaries," *Defense News,* 8 December 1997, 1. All references to the DPQs come from this article.

34. Brooks Tigner, "New NATO Cost Rift Threatens to Erode Support," *Defense News,* June 1997.

35. "GAO: NATO Expansion Price Tag Unknown," *United Press International*, 23 October 1997.

36. See Brian Bender, "Naval Exercise Highlights NATO Interoperability Challenge," *Defense Daily*, 1 August 1997, 190.

37. William Drozdiak, "NATO Finds an Expansive Sense of Purpose," *Washington Post*, 6 July 1997, A1, 19.

38. Author's interview, spring 1997.

39. Author's interview, spring 1997.

40. William Drozdiak, "Ex-Antagonist Leading Alliance to New Century," *Washington Post*, 6 July 1997.

41. Jeff Gerth and Tim Weiner, "Arms Makers See a Bonanza in Selling NATO Expansion," *New York Times*, 29 June 1997, A1, 4.

42. Open Media Research Institute, *Daily Digest*, 29 April 1995.

43. Sean Kay, "Budapest Needs to Get Serious about NATO," *Wall Street Journal Europe*, 6 October 1997, A6.

44. See Hans Binnendijk and Sean Kay, "Measuring NATO's Outreach," *Washington Times*, 21 August 1997, A17.

45. Off-the-record discussion with a senior Romanian official, Washington, D.C., June 1997.

46. Off-the-record discussion with a senior Estonian official, Washington, D.C., April 1997.

47. Off-the-record discussion with a high-level Baltic official, spring 1997.

48. The Department of Defense contribution to exercise and support programs received increased funding between 1996 and 1997, from $40 million to $49 million. In 1998 the budget fell to $37.5 million, in part necessitated by an undistributed administrative reduction in all Office of the Secretary of Defense defense-wide O&M funding. The 1999 budget request was for $54 million, though that was not guaranteed at the time of writing.

49. Off-the-record discussion with a senior State Department official, March 1997.

50. On-the-record discussion with Senator Richard G. Lugar, March 1997, at the annual SACLANT Seminar.

51. Off-the-record discussion, spring 1997.

52. Václav Havel, "NATO and the Czech Republic: A Common Destiny," *NATO Review* 45, no. 5 (September–October 1997): 8.

53. Steven Kull, "The American Public, Congress and NATO Enlargement, Part I: Is There Sufficient Public Support?" *NATO Review* 45, no. 1 (January 1997): 9–11.

54. United States Information Agency, "NATO Enlargement: Public Opinion on the Eve of the Madrid Summit," May 1997.

55. "Remarks by the President in Photo Opportunity at Meeting with Members of Congress and National Security Team, Madrid, Spain, 7 July 1997, " the White House, Office of the Press Secretary.

Conclusion

MAKING THE PIECES FIT

ANDREW A. MICHTA

The 1999 enlargement of NATO concluded the first post–Cold War phase of restructuring of the European security system. The move has proved that the United States is committed to remaining directly involved in the security realm on the European continent after the Cold War, and it has established NATO as the primary security organization in Europe for the foreseeable future. It has broken down the organizational barrier between the former communist and noncommunist states and, as such, has advanced the process of erasing the effects of the Cold War in Europe. Though problem areas remain, on balance the 1999 enlargement decision holds promise. In the geopolitical sense, NATO enlargement has contributed to stabilizing central Europe. It has also laid the foundation for a new security dynamic in the region. The next requisite step is to bring Poland, Hungary, and the Czech Republic into the European Union.

In the long term, the 1999 NATO enlargement has the potential to move central Europe away from its historical pattern of instability and great-power competition and toward further integration into Western political and economic institutions. The post-1999 integration process will serve as an important test of whether the emerging security architecture will water down NATO's core defensive role or whether NATO can indeed build on the enlargement to preserve the alliance as the linchpin of the post–Cold War trans-Atlantic system. This will depend on how well Poland, Hungary, and the Czech Republic integrate themselves into NATO and on how successfully NATO resolves its internal debates about future missions.

The New Allies

The success of democratic transition in Poland, Hungary, and the Czech Republic cannot be reduced to a single factor; however, the prospect of NATO membership was a further inducement to the establishment and consolidation of democracy in the region. In the case of Poland, the political criteria for NATO membership framed the boundaries of civil-military relations and established patterns that were emulated by subsequent governments. In the Hungarian and Czech cases, the prospect of NATO membership encouraged non-antagonistic relations with neighbors and contributed to the sense of external security the countries needed in order to proceed with democratic reforms. In early 1999, the three new entrants ranked among the most successful postcommunist democracies.

Although they joined NATO as a group, Poland, Hungary, and the Czech Republic are three very different countries. They share the experience of communist domination and the attendant loss of sovereignty during the Cold War. Likewise, they are united in their determination to take their place among Western democracies. They differ in terms of size, population, culture, and economic and military potential. Poland, with a population almost twice that of the other two combined and situated at the heart of central Europe, outranks Hungary and the Czech Republic in its potential significance to future NATO missions. Hungary's primary significance lies in its strategic position along the southern axis, facing unstable southeastern Europe and the Balkans, though this aspect of Hungary's contribution may be questioned in light of Romania and Slovenia's absence from the alliance. The Czech Republic is the most insulated of the three, exposed to hypothetical security threats only along its border with Slovakia.

All three new entrants still have some way to go to complete the restructuring of their militaries, to institute effective modernization programs, and to integrate their armies with those of the alliance in order to become meaningful contributors to NATO—a task that may not be finalized until 2005 or later. In order to transcend fully the legacy of decades of Soviet control, Poland, Hungary, and the Czech Republic will also need to complete the generational turnover at key military positions in their countries, strengthen the English language skills of their personnel, and develop a military ethos on a par with that of the armies of Western democracies. If the experience of East Germany can serve as a guidepost, a successful transformation of the postcommunist military culture requires considerable investment in training and education, as well as the strengthening of the military's prestige. Rebuilding the armies of the three new NATO allies will require time to bear fruit, but it should accelerate in step with the progressive consolidation of democracy in these countries.

Military reform proceeded at a different pace in each of the three entrants. In the case of Poland, in 1991 and 1992 the process was initially retarded by the continued presence of the Northern Group of Soviet forces, and then by struggles between the president and the parliament over a new constitutional framework. (The Russian forces left Poland in 1993; they departed Hungary and Czechoslovakia in 1991.) In the case of Hungary, lingering structural problems within the defense ministry and the need for further constitutional reform required improvements in civilian control over the military, which, though adequate, needed to be consolidated to meet NATO standards. In the case of the Czech Republic, the reform program was complicated by the disintegration of the Czechoslovak federal state, even though the "velvet divorce" was accompanied by a relatively smooth breakup of the federal armed forces. Though NATO will provide the necessary common framework, the responsibility for further steps in the reform process in the years to come lies squarely with each individual new member.

These problem areas, however, should not diminish the overall record of achievement of the three. Through military reform, by sending their officers to study in the West, and through cooperation within the Partnership for Peace program in preparation for joining NATO, Poland, Hungary, and the Czech Republic have laid the institutional foundations for building NATO-compatible militaries. In the coming years we should expect to see their officer corps progressively acculturated to NATO's procedures and practices. Further consolidation of civilian control over the military should follow.

The most significant reforms in the area of personnel that will be crucial to building NATO-compatible militaries by the three new entrants include creating a genuine Western-type NCO corps, further reducing the ratio of senior to junior officers (eliminating the "inverted pyramid" inherited from the Warsaw Pact era), gradually professionalizing the armed forces as budgetary limits permit, providing adequately for the individual soldiers, and continuing the shift away from the authoritarian pattern of command. The new allies have begun to tackle some of these tasks, but much remains to be done to complete the process.

Another important area in which to gauge the future value of Poland, Hungary, and the Czech Republic to NATO lies in their willingness to spend sufficient resources to make a contribution to the alliance commensurate with their size and economic potential. So far only Poland has demonstrated a sustained commitment to invest more in military modernization, while Hungary and the Czech Republic have neglected defense investment, cutting defense spending and thereby raising justifiable concerns in Brussels and Washington that the Hungarians and Czechs might become NATO's "second-class citizens" by their own making, and that they want to "free ride." Although it is true that, considering the pressing needs of their continued economic transitions, it would be unreasonable to expect Poland, Hungary, and the Czech Republic to launch radical modernization programs for their armed forces, NATO has every right to expect them to contribute equitably. The critical task for the three armed forces is to raise the effectiveness of their existing weapons through investment in "C3" (command, control, communications) equipment in order to take advantage of the surveillance and reconnaissance assets of the alliance. The Poles and the Czechs have begun to invest in such equipment, but Hungary has lagged behind. In the coming years, all three will need to spend more on C3 systems if they are to function effectively in multinational alliance operations. The next five years will show whether the new allies' rhetoric about commitment to NATO security will translate into real procurement and acquisition. Indeed, NATO's credibility with the US Congress will depend on it, and the record will have considerable impact on how US lawmakers view future proposals for NATO enlargement.

One way to assess the new allies' budgetary contribution is to set targets for their defense burden, expressed in terms of defense budgets as a

percentage of GDP. For the new entrants to become meaningful contributors, they will need to approach a defense burden close to the NATO
mean—approximately 2.2 percent of GDP in 1998—and, more importantly, they will need to spend the funds more efficiently from the standpoint of NATO compatibility. By 1999 only Poland had showed that it was
willing to commit the resources necessary to ensure the requisite degree
of compatibility with NATO. Hungary and the Czech Republic were
below these levels. Though spending close to the NATO mean for defense
is not a magic bullet, Washington and Brussels would do well to treat it
as a gauge of how determined the new entrants are not to become "free
riders" in the alliance.

Continued military reform in Poland, Hungary, and the Czech Republic requires their commitment to a sustained level of defense burden of
at least 2 percent of GDP. They should focus on enhancing the readiness
and training levels of their armed forces through increased expenditures
on operations and maintenance, as well as through a long-term and carefully targeted procurement program. They should place high priority on
the acquisition of equipment designed to integrate their armed forces
into the alliance—especially "C4ISR" systems (command, control, communications, computers, intelligence, surveillance, and reconnaissance).
Showcase programs, such as the often-discussed purchase of high-
performance, multipurpose aircraft (which would effectively consume
the entire defense budgets of the three entrants), should best be handled
through leasing arrangements similar to one explored by Poland and the
United States in late 1998.

In the coming years, the target size of the Polish, Hungarian, and Czech
armed forces ought to be carefully reviewed once again. Although the
three have already been substantially reduced in comparison with the
armed forces of the Warsaw Pact era, further reductions in personnel
might be warranted. The new allies need to consider realistically their
military reform objectives against the limitations of their current defense
outlays and NATO's budgetary allocations for enlargement. For example,
although the ultimate goal of the three is to maximize the professionalization of their armed forces, they cannot expect to move away from draft-
based armies any time soon if they remain committed to the current size

of their armed forces. Hence, the push to reduce the term of conscription to fewer than twelve months in the Czech Republic, or to six months in Hungary (while maintaining current force levels), raises serious doubts about the quality and combat readiness of these forces.

An alternative and more effective approach would trade quantity for quality by investing the available resources into a smaller military. This would increase professionalism while allowing Poland, Hungary, and the Czech Republic to reduce further the term of the draft. The Polish case illustrates this dynamic. If Warsaw remains committed to the current size of its armed forces, it is unlikely that the 30,000 troops it plans to contribute to NATO missions will be of consistently high quality. However, if the idea of reducing the armed forces below the 100,000 level (mooted by senior Polish officers in 1998) were implemented, Poland could provide NATO with a smaller contingent of well trained and equipped personnel. Such a high-quality force of approximately 18,000 men would make Poland's contribution to NATO more meaningful. It would also give Poland a higher standing among NATO allies than will be achieved by the larger but lower-quality force it currently plans to contribute.

Poland, Hungary, and the Czech Republic have the potential to make a significant military contribution to the alliance, but as yet their value to NATO's force-projection missions is marginal. In the short term, the core assets that the three bring to the alliance lie in the political rather than the military arena. The three countries must play an important role in achieving NATO's foreign policy objectives and keeping the future enlargement option open. In this respect, they can contribute to the US "peacetime engagement" effort in the context of the enlarged Partnership for Peace program.[1] By taking an active role in PFP initiatives with their neighboring partners, Poland, Hungary, and the Czech Republic can make a difference. Initiatives such as Hungarian-Romanian military cooperation or the Polish-Lithuanian joint military unit will help engage the non-NATO states in a meaningful dialogue on security issues. In the coming years, the enhanced Partnership for Peace program may prove to be the most effective tool of American influence in postcommunist Europe.

If the idea of a democratic security community evolving around NATO and reaching out into the former communist states is to come to fruition, the new allies must be seen as bridge builders across the region. Since they are among the most pro-American states in Europe, they can provide a conduit for extending Washington's influence farther east and southeast. As the contributors to this book have argued, Poland's ability to successfully manage its relations with Ukraine and Lithuania (and to some extent with Russia), Hungary's relations with Slovakia and especially with Romania and Ukraine (including active participation within the PFP) and the Czech Republic's relations with Slovakia will be a significant test of the efficacy of NATO's 1999 enlargement decision and of the new members' ability to be contributors to, not merely consumers of, security. In the political arena, the extent of the new allies' positive contribution to NATO will lie in their ability to bring closer the states left out of the first round of the enlargement process. If the process remains open, and if NATO's assertion that enlargement will continue in the future remains credible (even if the next round of enlargement is not expected anytime soon), then the policy will have contributed to the further systemic transformation of Europe's new democracies.

The New Alliance

NATO's evolution is a work in progress. Whereas during the Cold War NATO's mission focused on the defense of its territory, by 1999 the American position on the future mission of the alliance had shifted to emphasize the defense of shared interests. As part of the redefinition, NATO shifted its primary emphasis to the "non-Article 5 outer core missions."[2] In 1999, Poland, Hungary, and the Czech Republic entered a NATO alliance that continued to seek consensus on its post–Cold War purpose. In the 1990s NATO steered progressively in the direction of collective security, conflict prevention, and peacekeeping. The IFOR/SFOR operations in Bosnia and the 1998 threat to use NATO air power in Kosovo were symptomatic of this trend. However, allied consensus on how far NATO should go to strengthen the organization's proactive outlook remained in question. Between 1991 and 1999, the sixteen NATO members debated the scope of their new mission, the territory to which NATO should limit itself, and whether it should act independently of other international organizations. In 1999, misgivings about NATO's new identity further complicated the task of successfully integrating the new central European allies, raising the question of whether the "new" NATO was the kind of alliance Poland, Hungary, and the Czech Republic had aspired to join.

At the base of the continued disagreement within NATO over its mission lay the divergence of national interests between the United States and its principal European allies in the absence of the singular, overwhelming external Soviet threat of the Cold War era. Increasingly, the American vision for NATO as a security-projecting organization based on shared interests but not limited exclusively to Europe (and dealing with issues such as terrorism and weapons of mass destruction) came into conflict with the European vision, with its more limited regional focus. The protracted argument among the allies over the 1999 New Strategic Concept in preparation for the April 1999 summit underscored this issue.

The principal decisions that will determine NATO's role and its continued viability into the twenty-first century rest on the allies' ability to reach an agreement on the scope of NATO's new mission. That decision will have a direct effect on the place the new entrants will have in the alliance, as well as on their own procurement decisions and long-term defense policies. In 1998–99, the hotly debated question in Brussels and in allied capitals was the scope of NATO's security-projecting missions and the territory to which they should be confined. The American view was that NATO's future role should be extended to cover allied missions outside of Europe and focused on missions in areas of broadly defined "shared interests." For the Europeans, the emphasis was on Article 5 and Article 4 missions on the continent. The differences were further underlined by France's initial push to create a European Security and Defense Identity (ESDI) outside of NATO. The American proposal to create Combined Joint Task Forces to include NATO and possibly non-NATO forces and to be controlled by either NATO or the Western European Union was a compromise solution to decrease the growing tension between the European and American visions of the alliance, as well as to lower the cost of continued US commitment to European security. Though the French position was moderated by the German and British preference to build the ESDI by further strengthening the Western European Union through the creation of a European corps, the disagreement over the nature of the emerging ESDI was indicative of stresses building up within the alliance.

Some in Washington expected that NATO would be further "globalized." The Clinton administration saw the mission of defusing the threat posed by weapons of mass destruction as an integral part of NATO's mandate into the twenty-first century. For this purpose, it proposed the establishment of a Center for Weapons of Mass Destruction as a clearinghouse for intelligence-sharing among the NATO allies, in order to arrive at more unified threat assessments. In addition, Washington pushed for greater collaboration to deter weapons of mass destruction and to defend allied populations and territory against them. The US position reflected the American call for extending NATO's mission to defend common allied interests in Europe and elsewhere.

The US vision triggered considerable concern among Europeans that the new mission, which would play up the vastly superior US military capability, might reduce Europe to a junior partner in the pursuit of American interests in places such as the Middle East. At the core of the disagreement were two divergent views held by the United States and its European allies of what the security-projecting missions should be and how far beyond allied borders such missions ought to be sanctioned. The Europeans continued to take a regional position, in keeping with their primary foreign policy interests, while the US emphasized a more global role for NATO as a tool for the security of the developed Western democracies.

Placing a clear limitation on the American vision of the new NATO, the Europeans and Canadians insisted that if NATO were to act out of area in cases that were not specifically self-defense, it could do so only under a mandate from the United Nations Security Council. Compromise between the American and European positions was likely to water down the mission statement to a level of generality that would allow for divergent interpretations in the future. The issue became further complicated by a move by the coalition government of the German Social-Democrat and Green parties (with considerable support from non-nuclear allies) to reopen the debate on the role of nuclear weapons in NATO. During the December 1998 meeting of NATO foreign ministers, the new German foreign minister, Joschka Fischer, challenged NATO to reduce its dependence on nuclear deterrence, offering a "no first use" policy option.

The discussion among NATO governments over the alliance mission would soon be overtaken by the Kosovo crisis, which deepened in the winter of 1998-99. From the start, the allied response would serve as a potent reminder of how far NATO had already traveled from its original mission of collective defense against the Soviet threat. NATO's warnings to Serbia, especially the statement on January 28, 1999, that is was ready to use force to end human rights violations in Kosovo,[1] could have already been viewed as a de facto expansion of NATO's mandate to include the new mission of "extending freedom, human rights, civility, and the rule of law in Europe."[2] At the time, however, the Americans and the Europeans chose to interpret the initial NATO decision to threaten the use of force in Kosovo in different ways. While US envoy Richard Holbrooke called Kosovo a "precedent," the Germans and the French still insisted that it was "merely a special case."[3]

NATO's Fiftieth Anniversary Summit, held in late April of 1999 in Washington, D.C., had originally been planned as a gala celebration. However, it was overshadowed by the allied military operation in Kosovo, then already underway. The members adopted a revised Strategic Concept, with wording that included "common values of democracy, human rights, and the rule of law." The document articulated NATO's broad commitment to the security of the "Euro-Atlantic area," stating that "the Alliance not only ensures the defense of its members but contributes to peace and stability in this region."[4] Among others, the new Strategic Concept endorsed the efforts to build the European Security and Defence Identity (ESDI) within NATO, as a follow-up to the decisions taken in Brussels in 1994 and Berlin in 1996.

The Washington summit endorsed two Partnership for Peace documents intended to strengthen the program and the Defense Capabilities Initiative (DCI) that would increase interoperability in NATO for power projection missions. The allies affirmed their commitment to the Mediterranean Dialogue initiative with Egypt, Israel, Jordan, Mauritania, Morocco, and Tunisia, and launched the Weapons of Mass Destruction (WMD) initiative to include the creation of a WMD center at NATO headquarters in Brussels. Finally, NATO adopted the Membership Action Plan that, while keeping the enlargement option open, deferred future decisions on enlargement until the year 2002.

Most important, however, was the statement on Kosovo, in which the allies reiterated their determination to step up the air campaign against Serbia.[5] At the Washington summit NATO was eager to show that, having staked its credibility in the Balkans, it would see the military operation to a successful conclusion, regardless of the misgivings that some among the members had about the events leading up to the crisis.

The 1999 Kosovo Campaign

The military action against Serbia between March and June 1999 will have a profound impact on the direction of NATO's evolution. The long-term legacy of the campaign is yet to be fully appreciated. Still, the seventy-eight days of NATO's aerial bombing halted the Milošević regime's increasingly brutal efforts to keep the province under Belgrade's control. The operation succeeded without the need to commit NATO's ground troops, although it appears that a mounting threat of NATO ground action finally led to the Serb agreement to NATO's terms.

The bombing campaign tested allied unity and showed that, despite disagreements over tactics, NATO members were able to commit to a common military action and to see it through. The decision to use force in Kosovo reflected the American view–shared by some of its allies—that military power ought to be used to defend common democratic values. Though the campaign succeeded, the argument between those in the alliance who maintained that NATO should not have acted in Kosovo without a UN sanction, and those who felt NATO could do it without appealing to international institutions has yet to be resolved. Likewise, NATO continues to seek common ground for those members who were eager to codify the action as a way of the future for NATO and those who do not wish to do something like Kosovo again.

Overall, in the wake of the war in Kosovo the American perspective on NATO's future mission has gained momentum. For better or worse, NATO has assumed primary responsibility for the Balkans, notwithstanding Russia's limited participation in KFOR. Debates over the efficacy of the strategy employed in Kosovo will continue; nevertheless, NATO has demonstrated that it can launch out-of-area operations without a UN mandate and sustain allied consensus in the process. Still, as NATO troops assigned to KFOR deployed in Kosovo, the key question for the alliance was whether the operation would be an exception or a precedent-setting event for the future.

The 1999 air campaign against Serbia has also reignited a debate over the need for Europe better to coordinate its foreign policy and to develop its own forces for similar future contingencies, so that it would not have to rely again on American power. However, during the early discussions after Kosovo it was uncertain whether the Europeans would in fact be willing to commit the resources necessary to make such forces a reality.

Not sufficiently noticed amidst the Kosovo campaign was the far-reaching new role taken on by NATO. In effect, NATO has guaranteed the borders of almost every state of Europe (excluding the former Soviet Union), since during the campaign NATO pledged to uphold the borders of non-member states in the Balkans, with the exception of Serbia. The Romanian and Bulgarian decision to close their airspace to Russian transport aircraft in the wake of the Brussels-Moscow confrontation over the nature of Russian participation in KFOR, made the two countries act as if they were associate members of NATO. Today Romania and Bulgaria, as well as other states in the region who supported NATO during the air campaign, expect their actions to be rewarded with eventual membership. These expectations may prove to be too high; how the alliance will deal with them, however, will be an extremely delicate issue in the years to come.

The Kosovo operation also meant that the initial test of Poland, Hungary, and the Czech Republic as NATO allies came much sooner and in a different form than many had expected. As of this writing, all three new members have or will contribute troops to KFOR, though their actions during the campaign had varied greatly and the three received widely divergent marks in their first test of allied solidarity. Poland passed the test with flying colors, Hungary received only a satisfactory grade, and the Czech Republic had problems passing at all and needed "extensive tutoring" from Brussels and Washington even to make it.

Poland proved to be among the most pro-US allies within NATO, with public opinion polls showing consistent support for the bombing campaign. Moreover, among all NATO countries, the Poles exhibited higher support levels for ground force action against the Serbs than most other NATO members. A small Polish contingent was deployed to Albania during the air campaign, and a Polish airborne infantry battalion has joined KFOR in the US sector after the air war.

Hungarian support for NATO's mission was adequate, though it was tinged with seemingly excessive timidity and concern for safety of its own territory. Hungary allowed US aircraft to use two of its airbases, and the experience demonstrated the viability and NATO compatibility of its air traffic control and air sovereignty systems. After the air campaign, as requested by Brussels, Hungary denied the Russian permission to fly through its air space during the stand-off over Russian participation in KFOR. Also, a Hungarian combat service support unit has been assigned to support KFOR's activities. But during the campaign Budapest argued strenuously against NATO using Hungary as a staging area for any ground combat operation against Serbia. And, in an action that raised some eyebrows among other NATO members, the Hungarian government used the issue of Kosovo to pursue its own regional agenda, arguing the case for greater rights to ethnic Hungarians in the Vojvodina region of Serbia and in Romania.

Czech behavior during the bombing campaign was probably the biggest disappointment to NATO, with the Czech Republic ranking just behind Greece in terms of its open dissatisfaction and disapproval of NATO's action. Czech President Václav Havel again emerged as a lonely pro-NATO voice amidst condemnations of the action by the majority of the Czech political elite and the public. This distancing at the political level was moderated somewhat by the actual deeds of the Czechs, with a Czech field hospital deploying to support the operation, and then a reconnaissance company joining KFOR in the British sector. The Czech troop contribution may grow further if the Czech government deploys a battalion-size force, authorized by the parliament. Still, Czech behavior during the Kosovo air campaign demonstrated the continued low appreciation of contemporary security issues in Europe, among both the elite and the general public. This political problem could reappear in the future, even if the Czech military made an appropriate contribution at the military level, for it is tied to longstanding patterns in Czech history.

The Regional Dynamic

Today NATO finds itself more than ever before enmeshed in the system of overlapping Euro-Atlantic security organizations, which, in addition to the EU and the Western European Union, includes the Partnership for Peace program, the Euro-Atlantic Partnership Council, and the Organization for Cooperation and Security in Europe. Though NATO and the European Union remain central to the emerging security architecture, the other organizations provide a network of interlocking institutions that blur the distinction between NATO members and nonmembers, including the successor states to the former Soviet Union. The 1999 enlargement of NATO changes the institutional dynamic outside the core of the Euro-Atlantic security system.

Historically, NATO has always been closely linked to Europe's integration by providing a security framework for the evolving economic and political union. The 1999 NATO enlargement can contribute to the widening of European integration by providing a security framework for the future economic integration of Poland, Hungary, and the Czech Republic into Europe. Considering the mixed signals that emanated from Bonn and Paris in early 1999 regarding an early EU enlargement decision, for Warsaw, Budapest, and Prague to become EU members may prove much more difficult than had been expected. Still, prospects for extending the EU into central Europe sometime in the early twenty-first century are arguably better than they would have been otherwise, because the 1999 NATO enlargement has brought Poland, Hungary, and the Czech Republic into a security structure shared by the key members of the European Union. In the years to come, the three states' shared aspiration to join the EU will have a direct impact on the internal NATO and the internal Washington dynamic.

Although most of the discussion of NATO enlargement has focused on political and military institutions, one has to appreciate the potential effect of the 1999 enlargement in the context of central European history.

Throughout the twentieth century, the region was the site of some of the world's bitterest national antagonisms, as well as a prize in the imperial contest between Russia and Germany. From this historical perspective, NATO enlargement has the potential for beginning the process of a lasting reconciliation among the central Europeans. Hungary's aspirations to join NATO have already helped to defuse tensions in its relations with Romania, and in the Czech case they moderated Czech-Slovak relations.

The regional axis most affected by the post-1999 NATO framework is the Polish-German relationship. For the Poles and the Germans, the enlargement has offered a secure framework and an oversight mechanism for what can become the "second great European reconciliation"— a historic shift in Polish-German relations parallel to the Franco-German reconciliation after World War II. In light of the dramatic disparity in the economic and military potentials of Germany and Poland, it is doubtful that the bitter legacy of the Second World War would be effectively overcome outside a larger, multinational framework such as the network of relations present within NATO. Notwithstanding the short-term policy objectives and the often contradictory policy rationales that guided the NATO enlargement process, 1999 closed the chapter on Polish-German hostility.

The impact of the 1999 enlargement on NATO-Russia relations is more problematic. Though Russia is no longer a power on a par with the former Soviet Union, it remains the most unpredictable security variable in Europe. The NATO-Russia Founding Act, agreed upon during the March 1997 summit between Presidents Clinton and Yeltsin, was the price NATO paid for Moscow's grudging acquiescence in the enlargement decision. The creation of the Permanent Joint Council that brought Russia into the allied deliberative process was intended to defuse the danger that enlargement might trigger a renewed round of Russian hostility and pressure on the region. However, if the Russian presence in NATO paralyzes the allies' ability to reach consensus, it may prove to have been too high a price to pay. And even if the institutional mechanism works effectively, Russia is unlikely to reconcile itself easily to future NATO enlargement—a process Russian elites across the political spectrum see as a visible sign of the country's diminished power and influence. Even if

Russia ultimately accepts the idea of its former central European clients belonging to NATO, it is highly unlikely that it will welcome an "engagement policy" reaching directly into the former Soviet republics (especially the Baltics and Ukraine). If NATO's policy of remaining open to further enlargement is to remain credible, then the United States and its allies must accept its negative impact on NATO-Russia relations and weigh their collective interests accordingly.

If the worst predictions about renewed Russian hostility toward the West were to come true, Russia would still be in no position to confront NATO in Europe with a conventional military option in the foreseeable future. The decline in Russia's economic and military potential has reached such levels that its status as a developed country is in doubt, and trends continue to point further downward. In 1998, Russian infant mortality outpaced births, and the population fell by more than 600,000 to 146.6 million.[5] Chaos reigned in the Russian administration, while the Russian military all but decomposed. The threat that the Russian army might launch a large-scale military operation into central Europe will remain purely hypothetical for years to come, even if the current political turmoil in Moscow were to give rise yet again to assertive imperialism. In short, it is possible that Moscow will be unable to recover its former position as a global power, and although Russia will remain an important regional player in Europe, the era of Russian imperial drive may be over. The more urgent short-term security threat stems not from renewed Russian geopolitical assertiveness but from the danger of Russia's accelerated decomposition.

If NATO perseveres in its commitment to a special relationship with Russia, it remains to be seen whether the alliance can play a role in limiting the security threats that might be generated by continued postcommunist turmoil in Russia, or whether further enlargement will in fact fall hostage to Russian objections. Still, engagement offers Moscow the option of participating in a larger context of European security. Free of direct threat from the east, the new members of NATO should be able eventually to initiate a process of reconciliation with Russia and improved relations with other neighboring states based on genuine partnership. It remains to be seen, however, whether post-Yeltsin Russia will share this view of NATO and choose engagement as the preferred option. Depending on the level of Russia's concern over the Islamic states along its periphery and, especially, over China, antagonism toward the West need not be a given. And finally, one must allow for the possibility that enlargement may be impeded not only by Russia but also by allied concerns over diluting the alliance and, ultimately, duplicating the OSCE.

On the geostrategic level, NATO's enlargement was selected by the Clinton administration as the preferred formula for coming to terms with the consequences of the breakdown of the Soviet empire and the end of the Cold War. It is expected that by moving east, NATO will stabilize the periphery of unified Germany and contribute to the consolidation of democratic transition in the region. For the three new entrants, NATO membership will go a long way to dispel concerns about a future threat from a resurgent Russia or pressure from a unified and dominant Germany. Its impact on the alliance itself and on NATO's relations with Russia remains uncertain. Because NATO's enlargement and its evolution in the direction of collective security are taking place simultaneously, the success or failure of the integration of Poland, Hungary, and the Czech Republic will go a long way toward testing the founding principles of the "new" NATO.

In conclusion, the 1999 NATO enlargement is most significant in the context of changes taking place within the alliance. There is no question that the Russian dimension is important and that Russia remains a player in European politics. It is certainly crucial for NATO to continue a good working relationship with the Russian government and the Russian military. Russia remains an important partner for NATO both in terms of the Partnership for Peace program and further joint peace operations. In the coming years, however, it will be more meaningful to focus on the political rather than the security dimension of the NATO-Russia relationship. In the near future, of greater importance to NATO will be the continued debate over relations with Ukraine and over whether the Baltic states' aspirations to join the alliance should override Moscow's objections. Likewise, the future of NATO enlargement along the southern axis will have to be addressed, especially in the aftermath of the war in Kosovo.

The queue for future NATO membership is already long. In addition to the Baltic states (of which Lithuania is a possible NATO entrant in the next decade), the front-runners include Slovenia and Slovakia. Slovenia is probably the most plausible candidate for early accession because of its relatively affluent society and its emerging small but effective armed forces. Following the ouster of Vladimír Mečiar from power, Slovakia's prospects for NATO membership improved considerably, because the country geographically links Poland, Hungary, and the Czech Republic. Romania's candidacy for membership has had strong support from the southern NATO members, but its continued economic problems constitute a serious obstacle to membership. Prospects for Bulgaria's membership are uncertain for similar reasons.

The above considerations notwithstanding, NATO's approach to future enlargement is bound to be affected by the outcome of the 1999 Kosovo operation. Although the Membership Action Plan (MAP), announced by NATO during the April 1999 Fiftieth Anniversary Summit in Washington, D.C., reaffirmed that "the door to NATO membership under Article 10 of the North Atlantic Treaty remains open," it also cautioned that participation in the MAP "does not imply any timeframe ... nor any guarantee of eventual membership."[6] With NATO now firmly committed to the Balkans and the allies looking at the substantial costs of postwar reconstruction, enthusiasm for another round of enlargement any time soon has been dampened. Likewise, if and when the next round of enlargement takes place it will probably focus on the states in the Balkans. NATO's troop deployments in the region point that way. In mid-1999, in addition to the unfolding KFOR deployment of 57,000 in Kosovo (where the allies would provide the majority of the troops), NATO already had 30,000 troops in Bosnia, 10,000 troops in Macedonia, and 7,500 troops in Albania.[7]

In addition to the southern axis of enlargement, one should also consider Europe's former "neutrals"—Sweden, Finland, and Austria. They all belong to the EU and have been increasingly drawn to NATO. In the coming years, depending on the direction their internal debates take, any or all of them may choose to apply for NATO membership. All three are affluent democracies with ample resources to become meaningful contributors. They have already taken steps toward greater compatibility with NATO, and it is unlikely that if they applied to join they would meet much resistance.

In the coming years, if NATO's evolution continues in the direction of further enlargement as just outlined, Poland, Hungary, and the Czech Republic will have the potential to become assets for the alliance in dealing with prospective new members. Much depends, however, on the way the 1999 entrants themselves handle enlargement. If they are successfully integrated, then enlargement will be given a boost; if they lag in integration, their failure will have negative repercussions throughout central and eastern Europe. In the final analysis, the success or failure of the 1999 enlargement will be judged by the military and political contributions made by Poland, Hungary, and the Czech Republic to NATO's mission, as well as by the direction the evolution of NATO as a whole will take. In this regard, the defining factor will be the long-term impact of the Kosovo campaign and NATO's commitment to the Balkans. Considering the potential cost to the allies of stabilizing southeastern Europe, the region may define the limits on NATO's future sphere of action, including enlargement, for several years. The next decade will show whether the new allies are going to be equal partners or second-class citizens, and whether the NATO they have joined will still meet their own national security objectives.

Notes

1. Elaine Sciolino and Ethan Bronner, "Crisis in the Balkans: The Road to War," *New York Times*, 18 April 1999.

2. Roger Cohen, "NATO Shatters Old Limits in the Name of Preventing Evil," *New York Times*, 18 October, 1998.

3. Steven Erlanger, "US to NATO: Widen Purpose to Fight Terror," *New York Times*, 7 December 1998.

4. *The Alliance Strategic Concept* (Brussels: Press Release NAC-S 99-65), 24 April 1999.

5. "Special Washington Summit Issue," (Brussels: NATO Update http://www. nato.int/docu/update/1999/u990421e.htm), 21-27 April, 1999.

6. *Membership Action Plan*, (Brussels: NATO Press Communique NAC-S 99-66, 24 April 1999).

7. William Drozdiak, "NATO Looks to the Balkans for Growth: Baltic States Fear They May Get Overlooked in Expansion," *Washington Post*, 7 July 1999.

CONTRIBUTORS

ZOLTAN BARANY is an associate professor of government at the University of Texas at Austin. He has written extensively on eastern European politics and ethnic issues. His publications on civil-military relations include *Soldiers and Politics in Eastern Europe, 1945–1991*, as well as articles in scholarly journals such as *Armed Forces and Society, Comparative Politics, Journal of Democracy, Journal of Political and Military Sociology, Journal of Strategic Studies,* and *Political Studies* and in numerous edited volumes.

DALE R. HERSPRING is professor and head of the Department of Political Science at Kansas State University. He is the author or editor of eight books and more than sixty articles. His most recent published work includes *Russian Civil-Military Relations* and *Requiem for an Army: The Demise of the East German Military.*

SEAN KAY is an assistant professor of politics and government at Ohio Wesleyan University. He has worked as a specialist on US foreign policy and international relations at the Institute for National Strategic Studies in the US Department of Defense, where he served as an advisor to the US Department of State on NATO enlargement ratification. He is the author of numerous book chapters, journal articles, and editorials in major newspapers dealing with NATO and European security. Most recently, he wrote *NATO and the Future of European Security.*

ANDREW A. MICHTA is the Mertie Willigar Buckman Professor of International Studies at Rhodes College and a visiting scholar at the Hoover Institution at Stanford University. He is the author or co-editor of six books and a number of book chapters and articles on central and eastern European politics. His books on central European security issues include *Red Eagle: The Army in Polish Politics, 1944–1988; East Central Europe after the Warsaw Pact: Security Dilemmas in the 1990s;* and *The Soldier Citizen: The Politics of the Polish Army after Communism.*

THOMAS S. SZAYNA is a national security analyst in RAND's International Studies Group and associate director of the Strategy, Doctrine, and Resources Program in RAND's Arroyo Center. His research concentrates on global conflict issues in the post–Cold War era, peacekeeping and interventions in intrastate strife, military reform in the former communist states, and European security. In addition to numerous journal articles, his recent RAND writings include *Intervention in Intrastate Conflict: Implications for the Army in the Post–Cold War Era* and *East European Military Reform after the Cold War.*

INDEX